Reminiscences of

Rear Admiral John F. Davidson

U.S. Navy (Retired)

U.S. Naval Institute

Annapolis, Maryland

1986

Preface

Rear Admiral John Davidson's special fondness for submarines and the Naval Academy shine through in this account of his life and naval service. He tells of becoming a midshipman at the Academy mainly because his brother was too old to accept an appointment when available. In addition to being graduated from the Academy in 1929, Davidson later served as chairman of the Department of English, History and Government in the 1950s, then returned to serve as Superintendent from 1960 to 1961. He clearly relished the top job at his alma mater and here provides a great number of stories which will doubtless be of value to those studying the history of the institution.

Service in submarines was also a highlight of Davidson's career, starting with an S-boat in the 1930s and leading later to command of the Mackerel and the Blackfish. He commanded the latter in both the Atlantic and Pacific. One of his junior officers was Ensign Eugene Wilkinson, later to be the first skipper of the nuclear-powered USS Nautilus. After the war, Davidson commanded Submarine Division 62, Submarine Squadron Two, and the tender Orion.

During his time ashore, Davidson served in officer detailing in the Bureau of Navigation and Bureau of Naval Personnel. He provides some fascinating insights into the business of assigning officers to various duties. He was also in the plans and policy business in OpNav and had overseas tours in Canada and Turkey. The admiral has a delightful capacity as a storyteller, which makes this an enjoyable volume to read, whether he is describing the aftermath of an earthquake in Long Beach in 1933 or telling of a speech by President John Kennedy at the Naval Academy in 1961.

Befitting his experience as a chairman of the Academy department teaching English, Admiral Davidson has gone through the transcript and supplied a number of corrections to smooth the transition from oral speech to the printed page. Susan Sweeney of the Naval Institute oral history staff has done an excellent job of indexing the volume, and Deborah Reid of the Institute has supplied her customary fine touch in the transcribing and smooth typing.

                                        Paul Stillwell
                                        Director of Oral History
                                        U.S. Naval Institute
                                        December 1986

REAR ADMIRAL JOHN F. DAVIDSON
UNITED STATES NAVY (RETIRED)

John Frederick Davidson was born in Olean, New York, on 3 May 1908, son of Perry A. and Annie Smith Davidson. He attended Warren High School, Warren, Pennsylvania, and entered the U.S. Naval Academy, Annapolis, Maryland, as a midshipman from Pennsylvania, on June 17, 1925. Graduated and commissioned ensign on 6 June 1929, he subsequently advanced to the rank of rear admiral to date from 1 August 1956.

After graduation from the Naval Academy in June 1929, he served until September 1930 as a junior officer in the engineering department of the USS Utah (BB-31). Transferred to the USS Arizona (BB-39), he had communication and gunnery duties during the period ending in April 1933. He was a student at the Submarine School, New London, Connecticut, from July to December 1933, and in January 1934 joined the USS Cachalot (SS-170) as communications officer. When detached in April 1936 he was ordered to the Bureau of Navigation (later the Bureau of Naval Personnel), Navy Department, Washington, D.C., for a tour of duty in the detail section of the Officer Personnel Division.

From September 1938 until March 1939 he served as executive officer and navigator of the USS S-45 (SS-156), a submarine of the Atlantic Fleet, and from April 1939 until October 1940 commanded the USS S-44 (SS-155), also operating with the Atlantic Fleet. He then assumed command of the USS Mackerel (SS-204) and remained in command of that submarine, another unit of the Atlantic Fleet, after the outbreak of World War II, until June 1942. From July of that year until March 1944 he was commanding officer of the USS Blackfish (SS-221) and was awarded the Legion of Merit with Combat "V," and the Silver Star Medal for heroic service in that command. The citations follow in part:

Legion of Merit: "...[he] conducted an important reconnaissance of a strange and poorly charted coast, acted as a navigational beacon for orientation of United States amphibious forces involved in the landing operations, and torpedoed, probably sinking, a 5000-ton enemy blockade runner. Under his capable leadership during subsequent war patrols, the BLACKFISH aided in maintaining a blockade of enemy shipping lanes and, on one occasion, attacked two enemy anti-submarine vessels, sinking one of them and successfully evading severe depth-charge attacks despite minor damage sustained. By his inspiring devotion to duty, Captain Davidson aided materially to the successful landings in North Africa..."

Silver Star Medal: "For conspicuous gallantry and intrepidity as Commanding Officer of a United States Submarine during the Sixth and Seventh War Patrols of that vessel against enemy Japanese forces in alien waters. Undeterred by extremely severe hostile countermeasures and the presence of numerous anti-submarine vessels, Commander Davidson maintained constant contact with the enemy ships for extended periods of time and, skillfully maneuvering his craft into advantageous striking position at every opportunity, pressed home a series of vigorous torpedo attacks which resulted in the sinking or damaging of an important amount of Japanese shipping..."

During the period April to December 1944, he served as training officer on the staff of Commander Submarine Training Command, Pacific, at Pearl Harbor, Hawaii, and during the remaining months of the war and until May 1947, was again assigned to officer detail in the Bureau of Naval Personnel, Navy Department. Again ordered to sea, he successively commanded Submarine Division 62, the submarine tender Orion (AS-18), and Submarine Squadron Two, for a year each. In August 1950 he reported to the Canadian National Defense College, Kingston, Ontario, as a student, and completed the course in August 1951.

In September 1951 he returned to the Naval Academy where, until May 1954, he served as head of the Department of English, History and Government. He assumed command of the USS Albany (CA-123) in May 1954, and after 16 months in that command reported in September 1955 to the Office of the Chief of Naval Operations, Navy Department. There he served as Assistant Director, Politico-Military Policy Division until January 1957, and as Director of that division for the ten months following.

He was Commander Cruiser Division Five from December 1957 until October 1958, when he was assigned as Chief of the Navy Group, Joint U.S. Military Mission for Aid to Turkey, with headquarters in Ankara. On 22 June 1960, he assumed duty as Superintendent of the U.S. Naval Academy and Commandant of the Severn River Command, Annapolis, Maryland, and in September 1962 reported as Commander Training Command Pacific Fleet. He served as such until relieved of active duty pending his retirement, effective 1 April 1964.

Besides the Silver Star Medal and the Legion of Merit with Combat "V," Rear Admiral Davidson has the American Defense Service Medal with Bronze "A"; the American Campaign Medal; European-African-Middle Eastern Campaign Medal with stars; Asiatic-Pacific Campaign Medal with two stars; World War II Victory Medal; and the National Defense Service Medal.

Authorization

The U.S. Naval Institute is hereby authorized to make available to individuals, libraries and other repositories of its choosing the transcripts of five oral history interviews concerning the life and career of the undersigned. The interviews were recorded on 23 August, 28 August, 4 September, 11 September, and 2 October 1985 in collaboration with Paul Stillwell for the U.S. Naval Institute.

The undersigned does hereby release and assign to the U.S. Naval Institute all right, title, restrictions, and interest in the interviews. The copyright in both the oral and transcribed versions shall be the sole property of the U.S. Naval Institute. The tape recordings of the interviews are and will remain the property of the U.S. Naval Institute.

Signed and sealed this 27th day of August 1986.

John F. Davidson
Rear Admiral, U.S. Navy (Retired)

Interview Number 1 with Rear Admiral John F. Davidson,
U.S. Navy (Retired)

Place: Admiral Davidson's home, Annapolis, Maryland

Date: Friday, 23 August 1985

Subject: Biography

Interviewer: Paul Stillwell

Q: Admiral, I'm happy we finally have a chance to get together. You're one of the few living ex-superintendents of the Naval Academy that we haven't yet included in this series.

The normal practice is to start at the beginning and go back to one's earliest memories. What are your memories of your parents, please?

Admiral Davidson: I don't know how much of this is memory, or how much was told to me after I was old enough to remember, but I was born in Olean, New York, on the third of May 1908. My father at that time was a private secretary to a Mr. Franchot, whose daughter was the mother of Franchot Tone of the movies. That's one of the memories I have. In any event, he had previously worked in the chemical laboratory of the--I believe it was the Vacuum Oil Company. He decided that he wanted to get into business for himself; so in 1912, when I was four years old, he moved the whole family--and there were six children by that time--to Warren, Pennsylvania, where he bought a half-interest in

Davidson #1 - 2

what was then a dry goods store. That grew into a full-size department store eventually. I arrived in Warren, Pennsylvania, when I was four years of age, and I went through all my schooling there through high school. In 1925, I entered the Naval Academy.

Q: Had your father had some business background other than just being a secretary up to that point?

Admiral Davidson: No, he didn't have any business background that I know of. My father, as a matter of fact, didn't have the benefit of education beyond the eighth grade, and at one time he worked in the telegraph office of a railroad near Erie, Pennsylvania. He had to go to work, I guess, because the family needed help in those days. How he got to Olean, New York, I'm not sure. That's where he met my mother, and that's where they were married, where they had all of their children.

Q: What are your recollections of your mother?

Admiral Davidson: She was the peacemaker, maybe. With six children, her life had to be somewhat demanding, I imagine. My father was the disciplinarian, and my mother was the one who smoothed it over with us. My memory of her in those days, in my youth, is pretty faint. I do recall--this is jumping around a little bit--but I remember going home to see her after I made flag rank. She was a widow, and we sat around for about a week in front of the fireplace and talked of old times. I learned that she knew that I smoked cigarettes from the time I was 14 on. I didn't realize that she knew it.

Q: What are your memories of Warren? What sort of a town was it?

Admiral Davidson: Warren was a town of between 13,000 and 14,000 people. I'm told that at one time it was the wealthiest per capita town in the United States. Later, some town in Massachusetts passed it. But the money in Warren was made originally in lumber and then subsequently in oil. When I was a boy growing up, there were five rather large oil refineries there in Warren. One of them, in which my next younger brother worked all his life, made about 90% of Quaker State motor oil. It was sold under all kinds of names. It was sold out of its own gas stations as a certain kind of oil, but it was the same thing that went into the can that was sold as Quaker State.

Q: It could be that your father knew about this per capita wealth through his oil connections.

Admiral Davidson: It might be. His business was very successful. He managed to put--the two oldest children were girls; they both were sent to college for four years. My older brother went to the University of Michigan, where he was helping put himself through school, but with some help from my father. My next younger brother went to the University of Pennsylvania on a basketball scholarship and finished the Wharton School there. The youngest boy had a varied educational career. He went to VMI for one year and disliked it very much, but he wouldn't give up, because he didn't want people to say he was a quitter.* He wouldn't go back for a second year, however. From there he went to Allegheny College in Meadville, Pennsylvania. He did not finish college but went to work for the Talon Fastening Company. They sent him to Philadelphia. They made zippers. He's the only member of the family that is now deceased. I have a sister who is 84, one 82, a brother who's 80, and I come along at 77. My other brother is 76.

Q: Did your mother have more education than your father?

Admiral Davidson: Yes, but she didn't go to college, to my knowledge. I suppose in the late 1800s that wasn't unusual.

Q: Did they provide help and encouragement for the children getting it because they hadn't? Do you think they had a greater

---

*VMI--Virginia Military Institute at Lexington, Virginia.

appreciation?

Admiral Davidson: I would assume so, although it just was never questioned that we were going to school and were going to go to college. I might tell at this point, because it ties in with my older brother, how I happened to go to the Naval Academy. My older brother was about to start his junior year at the University of Michigan. He had started in chemical engineering, but for some reason or other decided that that was not what he wanted to do, so he went into a civil engineering course. In the summer after his sophomore year, he had a job working for the state of Pennsylvania on the roads. He was on a survey crew and worked with the Department of Highways. It was during that summer that he somehow met a congressman and asked the congressman for an appointment to West Point. The congressman said he had no appointments for West Point, but he could give him a second alternate to the Naval Academy. He said he'd like that. He went back to Michigan for his junior year. He came home at Thanksgiving time to say that he had just been notified that he was already too old to enter the Naval Academy and asked me if I would like the appointment. I first said, "Where's the Naval Academy and what do they teach?"

He said, "Well, you go in the Navy."

My mother wasn't very happy about that, because her idea of the Navy was the sailor who came ashore and had too much to drink and found himself a floozy. In any event, I then met the congressman and asked for the appointment. My brother had a principal appointment, but when I asked for the appointment, the congressman said, "Well, it wouldn't be fair to my first and second alternates to move you up just because your brother dropped out. So I'll give you the second alternate and I'll move the other two up one."

In order to qualify, I needed to beef up my high school curriculum, because I had been taking a classical course preparing to be a lawyer. I thought I'd go to the University of Michigan also and become a lawyer. So I went over to the high school and arranged at Thanksgiving time to make up everything I had missed that year in chemistry and physics. I intended to drop Virgil in Latin, because I thought six subjects would be too difficult, especially when I was working in a gas station evenings. But the Latin teacher, God bless her soul, talked me out of it. So I made up the two subjects, and I continued with my Virgil.

Then in the spring I took what they called the substantiating examinations for entrance to the Naval Academy. These examinations were in math and English only, and they were just simply supposed to prove that you had taken both of them in high school. In any event, those examinations were taken at the post office. The postmaster would forward those to the proper place for grading, and then you would hear how you made out. When the time got very close and it got to be the first of June and I hadn't heard anything, I was pretty concerned. One night while at dinner, the phone rang, and it was the secretary to the congressman. She wanted to know why I hadn't taken the exams. Of course, I said I did. She got busy then and traced and found that the postmaster had sent them to Washington when he was supposed to have sent them to the Naval Academy for grading. Then she was able to get them, send them down to the Naval Academy, where they were graded. I was called within 48 hours and told that the boy with the principal appointment had failed and that the number two appointment didn't show up, and I automatically made the grade. So there I was about to go to the Naval Academy. They told me I had to be there on the 17th of June, and high school graduation wasn't until the 22nd of June, so I arranged to have my diploma mailed to me, because all of the work was finished. So that's how I happened to come down here on the 17th of June, 1925.

Q: How well had your high school and junior high and so forth prepared you for the Naval Academy?

Admiral Davidson: I think quite well. I didn't know how to study when I came here. That was one problem that I had. Part of that stemmed from the fact that in my high school, if you made 90 or above, you didn't take any examinations. There were daily

Davidson #1 - 8

marks and that's all. The only time I ever took an exam in high school was when I had to take a Latin exam that last year, after that fine friend of mine, Jessica Bates, made me keep on taking Virgil when I didn't want to. I made 88 or something like that, and I had to take the final exam. But this was one of my great difficulties plebe year. I didn't know how to take an examination. I sort of froze on them. I remember in a Spanish examination one time, when I'd already had the same year of Spanish, I got a 2.5 because I failed to turn the question sheet over and realize there were two more questions.

Q: Had you been in any sports when you were in high school?

Admiral Davidson: No, and for a pretty good reason. I had a lot of problems with my knees. I don't think they actually dislocated, but they came close to it. Under doctor's orders, I didn't do anything in contact sports. I tried to do a little running, but we didn't really have a track team there.

When I came to the Naval Academy, I decided that I would try to go out for everything. During plebe summer, I think I tried to do a little cross country running. Then when the fall came, I decided that I'd go out for football. I was 6'0" and I weighed 117 pounds, and I went out for football. The coach of the plebe football team that year was a lieutenant commander medical officer on duty at the hospital. One of my classmates was Whitey

Lloyd.* Whitey Lloyd later became a Marine general. Whitey Lloyd was about 6'4", weighed about 220 pounds, and he had won all of the track honors at someplace in New Jersey--low hurdles, high hurdles, etc.** He was a running back. I attempted to tackle him one time with my whole 117 pounds, whereupon the coach came over and said, "Would you turn in your suit after practice?" I asked him why. He said, "Because I don't want you over in the hospital where I would be putting you back together again." So that was the end of my effort to show that I could play football.

Thereafter at the Naval Academy, I confined my athletics to track, where I managed to make the training table. I didn't even make a letter. I got my numeral one year, I guess, and I ran the low hurdles. The rest of my activity--I was a catcher for the sixth company baseball team. Why, I don't know, because I couldn't throw to second base to save my neck.

Q: Did you have any problem passing the physical entrance exam?

Admiral Davidson: Yes, to this extent. I took the physical exam here at the Naval Academy, and they told me I was too much underweight. So I went out to Carvel Hall for three days and

---
*Midshipman Russell Lloyd, USN, class of 1930, later brigadier general, USMC. Lloyd began with the class of 1929 but was turned back a year prior to graduation.
**The 1930 edition of the Lucky Bag indicated Lloyd's home town as Chatham, New Jersey.

drank milk, ate bananas, and all the food I could possibly get, and came back.* They reexamined me and said okay, they'd take a chance. I had never really gained any weight. I don't believe I weighed over 122 when I graduated, maybe 125.

While I'm on the subject of weight, when I went up for lieutenant, I guess, the Bureau of Medicine and Surgery noted with concern that I didn't weigh but about 128 or 126, and each year I would get a letter saying, "You will take immediate steps to gain weight." Those steps resulted in the habit of eating and drinking everything I could, and then when I started to gain, I couldn't stop. I was finally passed for the promotion to lieutenant on the basis of a committee of doctors at the old department down on Constitution Avenue. There was a very fine old captain by the name of Captain Clifford there, and he suggested to the group who were examining me that they measure my bones.** They came up with no wrist, no ankle, and besides, at much more weight, I wouldn't be able to carry it anyway. So they passed me.

Q: Do you think the smoking had any factor in that inability to put on weight?

Admiral Davidson: It probably did have some, but I don't know.
_____
*Carvel Hall was a hotel across King George Street from the Naval Academy.
**Captain Addison B. Clifford, MC, USN.

I didn't think of that.

Q: Wasn't smoking against the rules at the time at the Academy?

Admiral Davidson: My memory is that we were not allowed to smoke before breakfast, and you were not allowed to smoke anyplace but in your room. Of course, I used to smoke every morning before breakfast until a very, very amusing incident happened. I had on a regular midshipman's bathrobe one morning, when there was a knock on the door and the duty officer entered. I had a cigarette in my hand, and I slipped it up in my sleeve a little, thinking he had just come to see that we were all turned out. Well, it turned out he was the company officer of our next opponent in company baseball, so he decided to stop and have a chat. While we were chatting, the smoke began coming out of my bathrobe under my chin. I had to drop the cigarette on the floor and step on it. He continued. He didn't bat an eyelash. Finally, he left. When I thought he was really gone, I suddenly heard a knock again, and he opened the door and he said, "Mr. Davidson, you'd better stop smoking before breakfast. Someday somebody will catch you." And he left. Out of due respect for him, I never smoked before breakfast again when he had the duty.

Q: Do you remember who that was?

Davidson #1 - 12

Admiral Davidson: I believe it was Lieutenant Challenger.*

Q: I understand there was a duty officer from those years called Red Magruder.** What do you recall about him?

Admiral Davidson: The only thing I really remember about him didn't actually happen to me, but it was told all through the company. He walked into a first classman's room with his white gloves on, walked all around the room, used the white gloves to see if there was any dust, and finally put the man in charge of the room on report for dust on a box. The box contained four or five bottles of whiskey. That's the story that was always told about him.

Another story that was told about him--I don't know if it's printable or not. We had what we called midshipman in charge of the deck, the MC. They were usually right at the top of the ladder from one deck up to the next deck. One time when Red Magruder was making his rounds, the MC on one of the decks up above was called by one from down below, who said, "Better watch out. Here comes that redheaded son of a bitch." Magruder heard it. He went to the boy and said, "I don't want to ever hear you call me redheaded again."

That's one of many old stories about Red Magruder. That and

---
*Lieutenant Harold L. Challenger, USN.
**Lieutenant Commander Cary W. Magruder, USN.

Davidson #1 - 13

how he had a one-track mind. If he had his mind on dust, it didn't make any difference what it was on. You might have had a girl in the room. If she didn't have any dust on her, fine, it was all right.

Q: What do you recall about that plebe summer, the indoctrination from civilian life?

Admiral Davidson: Like most of us, I guess, I wondered if I'd made a terrible mistake. Of course, we didn't have many upper class around. We were brought up mostly by the duty officers. I remember that we had a drillmaster who was a lieutenant, very Prussian, whom we called "Belly Up, Chin In," because he came along to you, and he hit you here, and then when you went down that way, he hit you again.

Plebe summer wasn't a tough one. I think the toughest part that I ran into was the first cruise I went on. We were in coal-burning battleships in those days, and I was in the Utah shoveling coal down there in that fireroom and being seasick at the same time. I wondered at the time if I'd made a terrible mistake, and how I would get out of this mess. But strangely enough, pride overcame my discomfort, because I didn't have the guts to go home and say I couldn't take it. That's the only reason I stayed, I think. I just didn't have the guts to go home.

Davidson #1 - 14

Q: Where did that cruise go?

Admiral Davidson: That was an East Coast cruise. We visited Newport, New York, of course Guantanamo Bay, and perhaps Charleston, South Carolina. An East Coast cruise. I can't remember any other ports we put in to.

Q: You lived essentially like enlisted men rather than officers, didn't you?

Admiral Davidson: Yes, in hammocks, in sleeping compartments.

Q: Tell me about sleeping in a hammock.

Admiral Davidson: Well, actually, in a ship that's rolling, that has any motion at all, it's far better than a bunk, because at least you feel steady there. You stay there; you don't feel the roll of the ship. We did terrible things to people sleeping in hammocks. Pretty nearly always somebody had his arm over the side, and we used to get a cup of warm water and hold his hand in it. Very soon he'd wet the bed. You're recalling some terrible things to me that I had forgotten all about.

Q: How was the life of a sailor in those days? Was it a hard life?

Davidson #1 - 15

Admiral Davidson: I don't think so. Gee whiz, after I was graduated, I went to the Utah as an officer, and there were enlisted men on there who had been on 11 years. They seemed to be perfectly happy, perfectly content. Of course, they paid a seaman a great big sum of $21 a month, and he got his food.

Q: How capable were they, would you say?

Admiral Davidson: We ensigns learned from them. The Naval Academy was just the beginning of our education. We learned from the petty officers and chief petty officers. Without them, we wouldn't have been much help to the ship. No question about it, we learned from them. I think as the years went by, they got smarter and smarter and smarter, particularly in the field of any kind of engineering and electrical systems, and so on. They knew more than we did. The only thing that deteriorated as the years went by were their manners. The manners of all youth always seemed to go downhill. During the Thirties they were just abominable.

Q: Did you get over your initial discomfort that caused you to think you might want to leave?

Admiral Davidson: Yes, because that was the last coal-burning cruise, and I was never subjected to that again. But you know,

Davidson #1 - 16

for somebody who weighed about 122 or 123 pounds to get at the end of a coal shovel down in a hot fireroom was some experience. We had great big buckets. You measured the coal that we burned in buckets, and the buckets were like big GI cans, really. They slid those across the floor plates to where the firemen were and dumped them in front of the fire boxes; and the firemen threw the coal into the fire box. I think sometimes I must have put as much of my dinner into that bucket as I put coal. I was so darn sick and just exhausted.

Q: I hear that the Welsh coal was a real character-builder because it was so powdery.

Admiral Davidson: Yes. When we coaled ship, what a mess. We were covered with coal dust from head to foot. Everybody but the captain was down there shoveling coal when we coaled ship. Even the executive officer was down there.

We were entertained in Newport at a beautiful party at The Breakers.* Wasn't that the Vanderbilt home?

Q: Yes.

Admiral Davidson: I saw classmates there with their ears so

---

*The Breakers, an ornate mansion in Newport, Rhode Island, was Cornelius Vanderbilt's "summer cottage."

Davidson #1 - 17

full of coal dust they needed a bath.

Q: What do you remember about your other cruise?

Admiral Davidson: That was my youngster cruise. My second class cruise I was in the Nevada. We went to the West Coast, down through the canal and out to stop at Long Beach and San Francisco, and then back to Guantanamo. We always ended up at Guantanamo for target practice. That cruise was far more comfortable. The Nevada was a larger ship than the Utah, a little bit more comfortable living, and by that time, I was a second classman, which made quite a bit of difference, too.

Q: Were you involved in the gunnery in that ship?

Admiral Davidson: I don't remember what I did until I was an ensign. When I was an ensign, I was in the Arizona, and I was a turret officer. I can't remember on the midshipman cruises what I did about gunnery.

Q: Was there much exposure to aviation before you were graduated from the Academy?

Admiral Davidson: Very little, very little. I believe the first time I ever even had a ride in an airplane was when I was an ensign. I went to preliminary flight training in Norfolk at the naval air station there. Currently retired Vice Admiral P.D. Stroop took me up for the first time and did his best to see if he could get me airsick.* He was pretty good at that.

Q: Did you have three cruises altogether? Was there one other one?

Admiral Davidson: Yes. You made one after plebe year, and after youngster year, and after second class year. The last was another East Coaster, as I recall. I had one West Coast and two East Coast. This was '26, '27, and '28. For some reason, we couldn't go to Europe. We all were very, very disappointed to think we had gone all the way through the Naval Academy without a European cruise.

When I was graduated in '29, I was ordered to the Utah, which was going to make a midshipmen's cruise and was going to Europe, and I was tickled to death. Then they decided that they'd rather not have any brand-new ensigns on the trip, so I was sent to the New York for the summer months to wait until the Utah came back.

Q: What a disappointment.

---
*Lieutenant (junior grade) Paul D. Stroop, USN. Stroop's oral history is in the Naval Institute collection.

Davidson #1 - 19

Admiral Davidson: Yes. I went later. The following year, I was an ensign on the Utah, and we did go to Europe.

Q: Did people take advantage of the trip to Cuba to get away from the Prohibition that was then in force in the States?

Admiral Davidson: Yes, indeed. Yes, indeed. Have you been told any stories about how we used to bring it back?

Q: I'd be interested in yours.

Admiral Davidson: In the old Utah the junior officers' mess was up forward and had a storeroom below the deck of the mess, and there were portholes. I think we went into the navy yard and the first lieutenant arranged to have a larger than normal porthole installed, almost at the waterline. One night the bumboats came out and delivered all the booze through that porthole, and it was stored in the junior officers' mess storeroom. Everybody was in on it, I understood, except the skipper. The commander had his order in and everybody else had their orders in.*

---

*The commander referred to here was the ship's executive officer.

Subsequent to that loading, we began to have some trouble with what they called blisters on the side of the ship.* We had one that was starting to peel, and we were ordered back to the Norfolk Navy Yard to be repaired. We had to come north at about ten knots or less to be sure we didn't do more damage. On the way north, suddenly there were a great many intoxicated sailors on board. We couldn't find out how they were getting it. We finally did find out. Some of our Filipino stewards, who had access to that storeroom, were selling it. We were in a terrible position, because we couldn't very well put them on report for selling our illegal hooch. We did a terrible thing. I don't think I was a ringleader in it, but I knew about it. We took up a collection of watches and other valuables from various junior officers' rooms and put them in these Filipino stewards' lockers, and then staged an inspection and got them all for theft, which they were guilty of to begin with, but we had something legal. Most of them were discharged and sent back to the Philippines. There were three or four involved.

Yes, we did bring it back, and we had a big scare. I had the deck one night in the Norfolk Navy Yard, when the junior supply officer, whose name was Al Randolph, called me from home and said that he had just been tipped off that the customs people were

---
*Blisters were metal bulges built onto the sides of warships to protect them from damage by mines, bombs, and torpedoes. Usually the blisters were added a number of years after initial construction in an effort to modernize older ships.

going to make an inspection the next morning, and we'd better get the booze off the ship.* So we started a telephone campaign and we were able to get almost every officer to come in that night, and it was off by 1:00 or 2:00 in the morning. We got all the booze off the ship before we had the inspection the next day.

Q: What did you smuggle it out in?

Admiral Davidson: Mostly in suitcases which were taken off in automobiles.

Q: How was the social life for midshipmen on those cruises?

Admiral Davidson: It seems to me that there was always a dance of some kind, but they weren't so popular with the midshipmen. Sometimes you had to draft. If some very lovely lady in San Francisco decided to give a party, usually the officers in charge of the midshipmen would have to designate a certain number to go, and you had to go.

Q: Why the reluctance?

---

*Lieutenant (junior grade) Alfred P. Randolph, SC, USN. Randolph was attached to the Naval Supply Depot, Hampton Roads. He was a friend of several of the Utah's junior officers and so provided the warning to Davidson.

Davidson #1 - 22

Admiral Davidson: I don't know. They had more fun on their own, I guess.

Q: Was there a glamour associated with being in the Naval Academy at that time?

Admiral Davidson: Oh, yes. Oh, yes. Brass buttons could get you a lot of places. I don't know whether they still do or not, but they did in those days.

Q: What do you remember about the academic side of the Academy?

Admiral Davidson: I struggled a little bit, because I didn't know how to study the first year. Then everything seemed to fall into place until I got to something like thermodynamics and I began to have a little struggle. I wasn't too sharp in electricity. But I had no problems at all with the humanities. They were my easiest subjects. Of course, we all took exactly the same things, except we had two languages. You could either be a Frenchman or a Spaniard, but everything else was just exactly the same.

Q: How useful do you think the education method used then

was--the rote learning and man the boards and so forth?*

Admiral Davidson: I think I'd have to say it was adequate. If you had even an approximate photographic memory so that you could read the lesson, you'd probably remember enough to pass all right. I don't think we understood a lot of things that we learned.

Jumping away from your question, later, when I was head of the English, History and Government Department, I thought that people like Ned Potter, who was in my department, and some others, developed really useful approaches.** For instance, in history, they would divide a class into two groups, one supporting Halsey when he did so and so, and one saying he did wrong, and then they would debate it. We didn't worry about what day it happened or how many rowboats there were. The main thing was we remembered all about that battle by the time the debate was over with. I thought that was far more interesting and a far more effective way to teach in that particular field of history. Now, you can't quite do that in some subjects. Mathematics was always my stumbling block. Probably 75% of my trouble was that I

---
*The classroom routine at the Naval Academy during that period called for midshipmen to receive slips of paper with questions pertaining to the day's lesson. They would then answer the questions on the blackboard, and the instructor would grade their written answers. There were few classroom lectures.
**E.B. Potter, long-time former professor of history at the U.S. Naval Academy, has written a number of books, including biographies of Fleet Admiral Chester W. Nimitz, USN, and Fleet Admiral William F. Halsey, Jr., USN.

was slow. They would have a mathematics exam with ten problems, and I never would get more than seven of them done by the time the time was up, which gave me a maximum of 2.8. That's about what I was getting.

Q: It sounds as if the approach you described with Professor Potter was challenging the students to think.

Admiral Davidson: Right. That's exactly what was going on. I don't know how you do that in Spanish. I can see how you'd do it in many of the English courses and the history courses. I don't know how you'd do it in chemistry. You either know it or you don't know it.

Q: Which professors or instructors do you particularly remember?

Admiral Davidson: I always will remember the Spanish professor, Señor Fernandez.* He was--if my memory is not faulty, and a lot of other people in the foreign language department could verify this--my memory of Señor Fernandez was that he was aboard one of the Spanish ships as a steward at the Battle of Santiago and was taken captive. The captives were brought here to Annapolis.

---

*Instructor Arturo Fernandez.

Davidson #1 - 25

They even brought the Reina Mercedes eventually.* When the prisoners were all released, somehow or other he got himself a job in the foreign language department, and he eventually became the number one professor of Spanish here. I remember him because he used to call me Debijohn, Señor Debijohn.

Q: I would think he could make a Spanish class interesting with that kind of background.

Admiral Davidson: He did. I enjoyed him thoroughly.

Q: Another one I heard that was very good at that was Slipstick Willie.**

Admiral Davidson: Oh, yes, Slipstick Willie.

Q: What do you recall about him?

Admiral Davidson: Not very much during the time that I took electricity, but I remember him at a time when I was head of department. There were demands being made for more time for the

---
　　*The Reina Mercedes was a former Spanish ship captured during the Spanish-American War of 1898 and taken to Annapolis as a station ship. Midshipmen were assigned to live on board the ship for periods of time as punishment to various offenses.
　　**Instructor Earle W. Thomson was in the electrical engineering and physics department, called "juice" class.

electrical engineering department because of all the advances and all of the new discoveries and inventions and so on. They wanted more and more time. The only place to get it was from the humanities. Admiral Turner Joy was the Superintendent, and at the curriculum committee meeting, Slipstick Willie presented the case for the electrical engineering department, and a very, very strong case for their getting more time.* I was a captain and head of a department. Admiral Joy turned to me and said, "Captain Davidson, do you have a reply to Professor Thomson?"

I said, "Well, I think the only reply I can make is this. I have now been an officer for about 25 years, and as far as I know, I have never been required to remove a vacuum tube from any piece of equipment and put in a new one, to say nothing of knowing what went on in the vacuum tube."

Turner Joy said, "Touche."

Q: You mentioned the Reina Mercedes. Did you ever get sent to the ship yourself?

Admiral Davidson: That's a long story. Yes, I definitely was sent there. This is what happened. My first class year, my class was very small. There was just one first classman on each table in the mess hall. Every month we had examinations. We

---
*Vice Admiral C. Turner Joy, USN, was Superintendent of the Naval Academy from August 1952 to August 1954.

had daily marks for a month and then took an exam. Then we shifted sections in accordance with where we stood. We had gone down to lunch during exam week, and a classmate of mine by the name of Pete Carver was two tables away.* He had suggested at formation that maybe we ought to sit together and discuss the forthcoming examinations. So when we arrived at the mess hall, I went down and sat at his table instead of my own. During the course of the lunch that day, a second classman, who had originally been in our class but had been turned back a year, by the name of Nick Lidstone, decided to have the plebes do a reciprocating engine.**

Each plebe represented a cylinder, and if there were eight of them, they had eight cylinders, and they had to fire in order, like, "One! Two!" Firing involved bouncing up from your chairs and the duty officer was Morton Deyo, who observed it.*** He didn't come over, but he sent the five-striper--now it's a six-striper, but then it was a five-striper--Charlie Trescott, in my class, over to see what was going on. I didn't know anything about this.

Q: Since you were at the other table.

---

*Midshipman Lamar P. Carver, USN.
**Midshipman Nicholas A. Lidstone, USN.
***Lieutenant Commander Morton L. Deyo, USN, later rear admiral.

Davidson #1 - 28

Admiral Davidson: At 4:00 o'clock that afternoon, Morton Deyo at the main office sent for me and said, "I've been waiting to see your report on Midshipman Lidstone."

I said, "For what?"

He said, "For hazing." I didn't know anything about it. He said, "You have seen fit to neglect your duty, but I can't neglect mine." I got 40 demerits and a week on the ship. This was early fall of first class year. At that point, I had had one demerit plebe year and none in youngster and second class years. Suddenly I got 40 at a time when they counted.

My battalion officer was a commander by the name of Battle.* He decided to do battle for me. He went to see the executive officer of Bancroft Hall, who was Thaddeus Thomson, known to the midshipmen as "that bastard Thomson," and recommended that I not be given this class A offense, that I could be given an improper performance of duty, which was class B.** He pointed out that a classmate of mine who was a four-striper, fourth battalion commander, had had something very similar happen at his table, and he had been given a warning. So Battle did battle, but he lost. Thad Thomson decided that I had to go to the ship. So I went to the Reina Mercedes. The concession was that they wouldn't reduce me in rank. I was a chief petty officer, something like that, so I could still keep my chevron. That made

---
*Lieutenant Commander Charlton E. Battle, Jr., USN.
**Commander Thaddeus A. Thomson, USN.

me senior on the ship, and that was the reason I was in charge down there.

The first thing that happened involved a young Marine junior by the name of McDougal, a plebe in the class of '32; his father was a Marine officer.* He was on the ship when I got there, and he got me in trouble. McDougal had been there for 100 days for everything under the sun. His most recent one--he had taken off all his clothes and dived off the Reina Mercedes at night and taken a swim and got caught. The next thing was the one that involved me. They found a lot of canned goods missing from the Reina Mercedes commissary, and they were found in a vacant locker, and he turned out to be the culprit. He had taken them and hidden them away. He was reported again, but I was also reported for improper performance of duty, which added 40 more demerits. So there were 80, and we were allowed 125, I believe it was. They didn't extend my time on the ship, but about a day or two later, we'd all been to class, and, as was the custom in those days, after class the ship's squad assembled out in front of Bancroft Hall by Tecumseh. The senior midshipman marched the ship's squad back to the Reina Mercedes. We were marching along that day. That day at noon formation, an order had been read out that a second classman had been caught beating a plebe's ass with a broom, and the second classman was given so many demerits and

---
*Midshipman David S. McDougal, USN, was eventually graduated in the class of 1933.

Davidson #1 - 30

ordered to the ship, and the plebe was given so many demerits for allowing himself to be beaten. The order said, "All fourth classmen will cultivate a spirit of revulsion toward maltreatment." Well, on our way marching back to the ship, Pat Humphrey, in my class, who was down there for some minor thing, decided to have this plebe "revulse."* So he kept saying to him, "Mister, revulse." So the plebe went through every type of antic there was, as unmilitary as it could be, and in spite of my saying, "Knock it off," they didn't.

When we arrived at the ship, Bull Halsey, who was the commanding officer of the Reina--later Admiral Halsey--called me over and said, "What in hell was going on in that formation?"** So I told him. He put me on report for improper performance of duty, and I got another 40. So in about ten days time, I had 120 of my allowed total of 125, and I was graduated with 121. But I was in danger of being kicked out for going over the top of demerits, and I myself hadn't done anything very wrong.

Q: The situation kept compounding because if you hadn't been there in the first place, those things wouldn't have happened.

Admiral Davidson: Anyway, my roomates were very good. We

---
*Midshipman Pat L. Humphrey, USN, class of 1929.
**Captain William F. Halsey, Jr., USN, was commanding officer of the USS Reina Mercedes from 1927 to 1930.

Davidson #1 - 31

shifted the in-charge-of-room plate. When it was my turn, I didn't take it. They put it up, so if there was anything wrong with the room, why, they took the blame, and I got by the rest of the year without any. But I did stand the main office watch for the Army-Navy game. We didn't play Army my first class year. I think we played Dartmouth in place of Army that year.

Q: Do you remember anything else about Halsey from your time in the ship?

Admiral Davidson: No. That's the only time I ever had any contact with him, except I really thought he was a pretty wonderful guy. I don't think it was his fault. He was just carrying out some sort of duty.

Q: When you got to be Superintendent, was it ever brought up that you'd had all these demerits?

Admiral Davidson: No, no. But for some reason I am reminded of a story which I think Ned Potter may have related at one time or another in one of his books on Nimitz. When I was Superintendent, Admiral Nimitz wrote to me and said he had had a letter from a first classman who was trying to do a term paper; that his term paper was on the subject of interesting anecdotes about the Naval Academy. He had written to a lot of people to ask for anecdotes, and one letter had been written to Admiral Nimitz. Admiral Nimitz had written an anecdote, and then decided to send it to me as Superintendent, because, he said, "It might be that you and the commandant would prefer not to have this published, because it might undermine discipline."

I read it and replied that we thought it was so wonderful we'd like to see it published. It seems that back in 1905, when they were building Bancroft Hall, Nimitz lived on the fourth deck, above where the main office is now, and there were still a lot of granite blocks down at the end of the building. It had become a custom on Saturday nights for all to go up on the roof and have a beer party. Then, as they finished a bottle of beer, they'd throw it over and it would land on the granite down there, and the duty officer would call out, "Where are those beer bottles coming from?" This particular week they had to shake a round to see who would buy the beer, and Nimitz, the company commander, lost.* On Wednesday, which was a day that they allowed the first class to go to town, particularly to start ordering their graduation uniforms and so on and so forth, Nimitz took his suitcase and went out to a tailor on Maryland Avenue. When he went in the tailor shop, there was nobody in evidence, and finally he walked back to the back of the tailor shop, where the tailor did a lot of his work. Here was the tailor fitting a

---

*"Shaking a round" refers to the old children's game of rock, paper, and scissors, made with hand signals.

suit, a civilian suit, on a gentleman. The tailor looked up and said, "Ah, Midshipman Nimitz. What can I do for you?"

Nimitz said, "I wonder if you could get this suitcase filled with beer and I'll pick it up later? Here's the money."

The tailor said, "Sure."

So Nimitz came back later, got the beer, they had their party on Saturday night. On Monday morning, Nimitz was in charge of the section going to "juice" class and marched his section over to "juice," and went in the door of the classroom, stood at attention, and said, "I report my section."* The instructor was the gentleman that the tailor had been measuring for the suit. He was a lieutenant commander. Admiral Nimitz said in his letter to me, "You know, I was so indebted to him. I waited for three or four weeks to hear the bad news. I was so indebted to him, I always wanted to meet him and thank him for his kindness in not doing anything about it. He was later killed, and I never got to tell him."

Q: Probably the three or four weeks that he spent in suspense was a worse punishment than if something had happened.

Admiral Davidson: Right. Absolutely.

Q: How was the social life in Annapolis--the hops and so forth?
---
*"Juice" class--electrical engineering.

Admiral Davidson: Nobody believes me today, but I was sort of a red mike.* I didn't drag. Once or twice I dragged blind to help out somebody, and I usually felt that I got stuck, so I wasn't very enthusiastic about it. But the hops were very well-attended. In those days, we just went down there in Dahlgren Hall and danced around in circles, you know, and people went out and tagged.

Q: Why the hesitation on your part?

Admiral Davidson: I don't know. I probably didn't have any money, among other things. My father was a great believer--the Naval Academy wrote a letter and said, "We want all midshipmen to be equal, so please do not send your son any money. We already give him an allowance, $3 a month as a plebe and $5 as a youngster, and $8 second class, and $12 first class," out of which you had to buy your cigarettes.

Q: Your father was very scrupulous about that.

Admiral Davidson: He thought as long as they asked him not to send it, he didn't want to violate it.

---

*Red mike--a midshipman who dated infrequently or not at all.

Q: What do you remember about the Superintendent, Admiral Nulton?*

Admiral Davidson: He was the Superintendent when I entered the Academy. Mostly I remember that Mrs. Nulton seemed to rule the roost. That's what we all thought. She was the boss. Admiral S.S. Robison was Superintendent when I was graduated.**

Q: C.P. Snyder was the commandant.***

Admiral Davidson: That's right.

Q: What do you recall about him?

Admiral Davidson: Not much. The one I remember was his predecessor, Sinclair Gannon, I remember better.****

Q: What do you recall about him?

Admiral Davidson: He had a beautiful daughter. He used to get us all together in Smoke Hall and gave us a lot of hell about our

---
*Rear Admiral Louis M. Nulton, USN, was Superintendent of the Naval Academy from February 1925 to June 1928.
**Rear Admiral Samuel S. Robison, USN, was Superintendent from June 1928 to May 1931.
***Captain Charles P. Snyder, USN, later a four-star admiral.
****Captain Sinclair Gannon, USN.

conduct in the yard and so on and so forth. We all stood in awe of him a little bit. Snyder, I just don't seem to remember much about him. Thad Thomson was the one we all remembered. Boy, he was a so and so.

Q: Was there a great spirit of competition fostered among the midshipmen--the idea that this is where you're going to stand for the rest of your career, so you'd better do well?

Admiral Davidson: Yes, yes. You know, actually, Paul, I think probably in some midshipmen, yes. In others, it didn't seem like it.

Q: How did you react?

Admiral Davidson: I wanted to stand well enough so that I would get promoted as rapidly as possible, and in that connection, it might be of interest to hear what happened to me. First class year, when I had all this happen to me, I was assigned a minus 1.5 in conduct. I don't know how you get a minus 1.5, but I did. They had a formula which affected your "grease mark," your aptitude for the service mark. First class year, it was weighted higher than anything else. So consequently, when June arrived, the end of the year, and I saw my class standing, I stood about 140 in a class of about 240. As I sat and studied this, I wondered, even with that minus 1.5, how my "grease mark" could be that low. So I sat down to work it out and study it, and this is what I found out. I was in the hospital one month that year. While you're in the hospital, they don't assign you an aptitude mark. So there were seven marks added up, including this very low one. I didn't get minus 1.5 in "grease"; I got it in conduct, but that affected the "grease." I ended up with seven marks, which was divided by eight, as though I had eight marks. So I trotted down to see Commander Battle, and he took me up to see Commander Thomson. That's the one time Thomson reacted well to me, anyway. He called Washington, called BuNav, and held up diplomas and commissions until they could redo it, and I was graduated 84 in my class instead of 140.* So it was a real important item, just that one little error.

Of course, old Thad Thomson stood me up there at the beginning of first class year and said, "You'll never be a naval officer. You haven't got what it takes. I predict that you'll never make it." I often wanted to see him after I made flag rank, because he didn't make that.

Q: It doesn't exactly seem like the way to inspire a midshipman.

Admiral Davidson: No. I wasn't very happy with him. One of the

---
*BuNav, the Bureau of Navigation in Washington, D.C., was responsible for personnel administration.

things that happened was this--on first cruise, we got to Boston, I was taken sick, mainly some sort of a tummy problem. They took me off the cruise and put me in the naval hospital in Boston, where I lost a lot of weight. I got way down. Then, when I was well enough to travel, the ship had gone to Guantanamo, so they sent me back here to the Naval Academy to wait for the return of the cruise before going on September leave. As far as I know, I was the only upper classman here. The rest of them were away on a cruise and the plebes had just come in.

It was my understanding--I didn't think I was doing anything wrong at all--it was my understanding that as long as I performed whatever duties I was given to do, that in the evening I could go out in town if I wanted to. So I was accustomed to walking right out the Maryland Avenue gate. The "Jimmy legs" would say hello.* I wore civilian clothes, I did everything. Well, he discovered that. He didn't give me any demerits, but he really clamped down on me, and I wasn't allowed to go anywhere after that.

Then the day that the ships came in and all the battleships were anchored out there, leave was beginning on these ships, and I had my reservations and a berth in a train to go home from Baltimore that night. About 10:00 o'clock in the morning, old Thad Thomson sent for me and said, "You are a qualified skipper

---

*Jimmy legs--Naval Academy civilian policemen.

of the sloops," the larger yachts we had. We had one called the Robert Center and one was the Argo. He said, "You have qualified as skipper of those, and all of the commissioned officers who are qualified are tied up today, and a group of plebes and their parents want to go out and sail around the battleships. So you'll have to take them out," which meant I was going to miss my train. I tried to explain to him. Oh, he really took off. That's when he told me I'd never be a naval officer. So I had to go, and I did miss my train. I never was very happy with Thad Thomson about that. What a guy!

Q: Which classmates of yours were you closest to as a midshipman?

Admiral Davidson: I guess I was closest to Rags Parish.* He was a company commander my first class year, and his roommates, one of them was Dicky Ballinger, and one of them was George Ashford, and the other one was one of the Dinty Moores, there were two Dinty Moores--C.J. Moore.** They were all about 5'4". Rags Parish was captain of the All-American lacrosse team. George Ashford was a candidate for Olympic wrestling. Dicky Ballinger was, as Spike Webb used to say, "the best boxer I ever

---
*Midshipman Elliott W. Parish, Jr., USN.
**Midshipman Richard R. Ballinger, USN; Midshipman George W. Ashford, USN; Midshipman Clarence J. Moore, USN.

Davidson #1 - 40

trained."* I don't know what they had in common with me, because I didn't have any of the talents that they had. I also was very close to my roommates, Ben Coe and Don Bush.**

Q: Others I know from that class are Roy Benson and Kemp Tolley. How close were you to them?***

Admiral Davidson: I've been very close to Roy since, but I didn't know Roy very well when we were midshipmen. Roy was the leader of the NA-10, the band. And Kemp Tolley, of course, I've known him well since, but I didn't know him at that time that well. I knew who they were. See, we entered with about 440 and we graduated about 240. I think you knew something about practically everybody.

Q: Were you involved in any extracurricular activities, like working on the Log?

Admiral Davidson: No. First class year was the only year we were allowed to play golf, and I played golf over at the old

---

*Hamilton W. "Spike" Webb was involved in Naval Academy athletics from 1919 to 1954, including more than 20 years as varsity boxing coach.
**Midshipman Benjamin Coe, USN; Midshipman Donald P. Bush, USN.
***Midshipman Roy S. Benson, USN, later rear admiral; Midshipman Kemp Tolley, USN, later rear admiral. Both are subjects of Naval Institute oral histories.

course, where Perry Circle is now. We had a nine-hole course.*
I played golf and I played in the finals with a classmate by the
name of Hank Twohy, who beat me on the first extra hole.**

Q: Do you have any recollections about the marching and drilling?

Admiral Davidson: Only one very vivid incident. First class year, as whatever I was, chief petty officer, in the sixth company, Rags Parish was company commander. George Ashford was subcommander, and I was on the staff with Pete Carver, who was the color bearer.*** My parents came down for the first time, and we had a dress parade, passing in review. I was on the company staff, carrying a sword, and when they said, "Eyes right," I came down and jabbed George Ashford in the heel, knocking my sword out of my hand and causing him to stumble, right in front of my mother and father. That's the only thing I remember about my marching. We did recover the sword, and George recovered his balance.

Parades were a little bit different in those days. For instance, the manual of arms was done to music and by memory.

---
*Perry Circle, beyond the Naval Academy's gate 8, is a housing complex for Navymen and their families.
**Midshipman Henry B. Twohy, USN.
***Midshipman George W. Ashford, USN; Midshipman Lamar Peyton Carver, USN.

Davidson #1 - 42

There were no orders given for right shoulder, left shoulder. The whole drill was music, which certainly speeded it up a lot.

Q: What value do you see in that as a training tool for midshipmen?

Admiral Davidson: I still think it's very important. I think it adds to their military bearing, military presence, everything. I just really think it's important to do it. And it's a discipline; that's another thing. It's a discipline they all need.

Q: How much did you see of hazing?

Admiral Davidson: My plebe year we saw a lot of it. But my later years, I never saw any of it when I was head of the department or Superintendent. Of course, there was a lot of hazing when I was a plebe. We used to be told to call the decks, and we'd lean over and say, "Ground deck," and knock on the floor, and say, "Ground deck," and somebody with a broom would swing it and knock you flat on your face, and you'd get up. Then first deck, second deck, third deck, fourth deck. Actually, I don't think that ever hurt me. The one that hurt me was a first classman who used to give your skin a pinch and tell you to say when it hurt. That was about as sadistic as anything I could think of. There was plenty of it. It was certainly illegal as could be. It was supposed to be an offense for which you could be discharged.

Q: But who's going to report on a senior?

Admiral Davidson: Of course, that's another thing. I don't know whether they do it anymore or not. I'm not up on this sort of thing. You never reported a classmate. That was cause for being put in Coventry, practically.* You just didn't report a classmate.

Q: How much emphasis was there on the honor code when you were a midshipman?

Admiral Davidson: None. As a midshipman, we didn't have one. This was started about 1950 or '51 by Admiral Hill.** Out here we had pretty good debates about whether we should adopt the same thing West Point had or not. We decided we couldn't quite go along with the West Point form of honor code. I think the problem sometimes has been that seniors put a junior on the spot. Let me give you an example. It does a lot of damage to the honor system. One of the things I had to deal with occurred when a

---
*"Coventry" meant that no one would speak to a given midshipman, acting as if he had ceased to be part of the group.
**Vice Admiral Harry W. Hill, USN, Superintendent of the Naval Academy from August 1950 to August 1952.

midshipman, marching back to class one day, fell out of ranks before he got to Bancroft Hall and ran ahead in order to be first in line for barbershop. The duty officer, who was a lieutenant, saw him. So he walked into the barbershop and he said to the boy, "Did you fall out of ranks early?"

And the boy said, "No, sir." So he was put on report for lying, for which he could be discharged, and went through the class honor system, the academic board and everything else. It ended up in the Secretary of the Navy's office, and he disapproved it.

Well, as it so happened, the midshipman was one of our best tackles, and the brigade said if this had been John Doe, he would have been kicked out, but because he was a good football player, somebody got to the Secretary and said, "Let's hold on to him." It did a lot of harm to the honor concept as it existed. So one of the things I tried to do was indoctrinate all officers and the senior midshipmen. If you see somebody do something that's a violation of the regulations, you go up to him and say, "You're on report for what you did." You don't say, "Did you do it?" The reason for this is if you talk to--I'm not too much for talking to psychologists--but almost all children are born with this defense. If you say, "Did you do that?", a normal child's defense is, "No, I didn't do that." And a lot of them get over it by the time they're ten. Some don't get over it by the time they're 30. And therefore, you've got to just call the shot as you see it, and not give them a chance of really doing something terrible like telling a lie. It's sort of an automatic defense.

They tell me this boy went right up to the main office after he got out of the barber chair and told the duty officer, "Yes, I did fall out. I didn't mean to say that." He still put him on report.

Q: When did that incident occur, when you were Superintendent?

Admiral Davidson: Yes, as I remember.

Q: It seems like a pretty mild thing to kick somebody out of school for.

Admiral Davidson: For lying?

Q: But he went back afterward.

Admiral Davidson: Yes. But you know, lying is lying. It's sort of like the little girl that's only a little bit pregnant.

Q: Was there anything comparable to an honor code, if not a name like that, during your time as midshipman, a military code of ethics?

Admiral Davidson: Not to my knowledge. We were always taught, "We do not lie, steal, or cheat." But there was no honor system where, if you were found to have done it, maybe it would just be between you and the commandant of midshipmen. No, we didn't have an honor code, or what now we call an honor concept. I think we came out with a pretty good system, actually. I never could see how the West Point system could work, because it calls for you, if you break a regulation, to go in and report yourself.

Q: Or if you see somebody else.

Admiral Davidson: Or if you see somebody else do it. But we had a very, very strong code here that you never reported a classmate. I remember telling the section I was marching to class one time after I had all these demerits, I said, "You know, if you misbehave in ranks and get caught, that's the same as trying to put me on report, because I'm in charge. If the duty officer comes up and says anything, I'm going to say you're already on report, classmate or no classmate, because the reverse would be true. You'd be putting me on report."

Q: What were your duties as the chief petty officer?

Admiral Davidson: Just to muster the company at formation and make a report to the battalion office.

Q: What do you recall about your graduation ceremony?

Admiral Davidson: It was in Dahlgren Hall. I can't for the life of me remember who the speaker was.

Q: It might have been SecNav. Was that Charles Francis Adams at that point?*

Admiral Davidson: I think so. I can't remember for sure. My own graduation was so overshadowed by the ones I went to later when I was head of department and Superintendent. We all threw our hats, the same thing there. I can't be sure who made the commencement address.

Q: You talk about throwing the hats, which is still done all these years later. What do you see as the value of tradition at the Naval Academy?

Admiral Davidson: I hardly know how to answer that. It helps develop a loyalty to the service, to the Naval Academy, and to your brother officers, and so on. I suspect that tradition often serves a purpose of urging on somebody to do something almost beyond his capability, because it's expected of him. Pride.

---
*Charles Francis Adams, Secretary of the Navy (SecNav) from March 1929 to March 1933, was the 1929 Naval Academy graduation speaker.

Davidson #1 - 48

He's too proud not to follow the tradition, as long as the traditions are good.

Q: One of your predecessors, Admiral Holloway, said that one of the things that the Naval Academy was supposed to do was instill the customs and traditions of the service.*

Admiral Davidson: Right. I agree with that.

Q: How much choice did you have on your first duty station, then, after you had been graduated?

Admiral Davidson: When I was graduated, we all had to go to major ships for two years. Major ships were considered to be the battleships and cruisers, and at that point, I think we just had the Saratoga and Lexington as the major carriers. We could not go to aviation, could not go to submarines, and we could not go to destroyers until after two years. So principally, your choice was which fleet you wanted to get to, I guess. I wanted to go to the Atlantic Fleet, and I put in for the Utah, because some of the rest of us put in for the Utah. Rags Parish put in for the Utah as did another classmate, Friskie Carmichael.** We all

---
*Rear Admiral James L. Holloway, Jr., USN, was Superintendent of the Naval Academy from January 1947 to April 1950.
**Ensign George K. Carmichael, USN.

ended up together on the Utah.

Q: What do you remember of your first experiences on board?

Admiral Davidson: As I say, I went to the New York that summer, and we visited the city of New York, where I spent all the money I had saved. I had nothing left to pay for my uniforms. Then on the Utah--I went to her in the fall--and I think it was then that we went to Guantanamo for our gunnery practice. That's when we brought back the liquor. I was in the Utah--I'd have to look at my orders for what year it was--but the Utah eventually was decommissioned, and almost as a group, we were lifted and sent to the Arizona, which was then being modernized in the navy yard there in Norfolk, and we all just moved over there. The Arizona went to the West Coast and was based in Long Beach.

Q: What are some of the recollections you have in the Utah about your development as an officer?

Admiral Davidson: My first assignment on board the Utah was in the black gang.* I was the junior division officer in the boiler division. An officer in the class of '27, two years ahead of me, was the boiler division officer. He was a very rough diamond.

---
*Black gang--the engineering crew.

He weighed about 300 pounds, an extremely rough diamond. I learned to stand the engineering watch as officer of the watch. I didn't have any opportunity to stand underway watches on the bridge, but I stood lots of deck watches in port. It wasn't until I reached the Arizona that I had much time under way and any possibility of any shiphandling.

Q: What was the junior officers' mess like in Utah?

Admiral Davidson: It was a group of people out of the classes of '29, '28, and '27, all of us ensigns. In those days you had to stay an ensign three years. Quite a variety, quite a variety. I'm trying to recall who all was there in addition to Rags and "Friskie"--Taylor Keith.* One very, very amusing class of '27 boy by the name of Tolson, Dave Tolson, had two voices.** He would answer the phone on board the ship in a very deep voice, "Tolson speaking."

Some of us would reply, "Go on--we know you."

And then he'd giggle and he'd get back to his real high-pitched voice. It's one of the amusing things that I remember.

Q: Where did the ship go while you were on board? What type of

---

*Ensign Robert Taylor S. Keith, USN. As a captain, he was Commandant of Midshipmen from 1954 to 1956.
**Ensign David W. Tolson, USN.

operations?

Admiral Davidson: We went to Europe on the midshipmen's cruise. I think we went first to France, and from there to Germany, and then to Scotland. I suppose, by that time we had to go back to Guantanamo for gunnery practice. We had been to Guantanamo before the midshipmen's cruise. When I first went to the Utah, right after the midshipmen's cruise in '29, we went down to Guantanamo that fall. The next year we went to Northern Europe.

Q: Were there any fleet exercises while you were on board?

Admiral Davidson: Not to the best of my memory. I don't think we ever did. Later, when I was in the Arizona, I think we had some, but they don't stand out in my memory.

Q: The Utah by then had been converted to oil, so she was probably pretty easy.

Admiral Davidson: Oh, yes. We didn't have a coal-burning problem. I think my youngster cruise, which was in the summer of '26, was the last coal-burning cruise.

Q: What do you remember about engineering watches?

Davidson #1 - 52

Admiral Davidson: Long, deadly hot, just sort of tiring.

Q: Are there any of the ship's more senior officers that you especially remember?

Admiral Davidson: The captain of the Utah when I arrived was Captain Train. I think it was Russell Train.*

Q: Were there any special recollections you had of that brief period in the New York?

Admiral Davidson: I think Roy Benson was in the New York, and Jimmy James, too.** I'm trying to remember the name of the skipper, who was very, very dapper.*** When he went ashore, he was decked out like a million dollars. We had an admiral aboard that ship, too.**** It was a flagship.

Q: Anything more on the Utah before you went to the Arizona?

Admiral Davidson: Not in particular. I thought it was a very happy ship. I enjoyed the Utah, and my only disappointment was

---
*Captain Charles R. Train, USN.
**Ensign Ralph K. James, USN, later rear admiral and subject of a Naval Institute oral history.
***Captain Edward S. Jackson, USN, was commanding officer.
****Rear Admiral Harley H. Christy, USN, Commander Battleship Division Three.

that when all of us were picked up and moved over to the Arizona, that they left me in the same boiler division, but only temporarily. In the Arizona I began to get into the gunnery game a little bit.

Q: The Utah was demilitarized at that point, wasn't she?

Admiral Davidson: Yes. She went out of commission.

Q: She became a target ship.

Admiral Davidson: She became a target ship, and they finally sank her out in Pearl Harbor, didn't they?*

Q: Right.

Admiral Davidson: As they did the Arizona, where we all went. Sank her, too. The Arizona--I do remember two or three very outstanding characters. One was the captain. The original captain's name was C.S. Freeman, who later became Commander Submarine Force and he'd never been in a submarine in his life.**

---

*The Utah was demilitarized in 1930 under provisions of the Washington Treaty. The ship remained in commission as an auxiliary miscellaneous (AG-16) and became a mobile target vessel. The Utah was sunk at Pearl Harbor, when it was believed the ship was mistaken for an aircraft carrier by the Japanese.
**Captain Charles S. Freeman, USN, later vice admiral.

He was known as somewhat of a sundowner, but his executive officer was such a so and so that it made the captain seem like a pretty nice fellow.* The executive officer was the same one I've told you about from my Naval Academy days, Thaddeus A. Thomson. He was about as ornery a person as you could imagine. I'll give you one or two examples. I had been aboard the ship in the navy yard less than a week, and I had asked the first class boatswain's mate--when I first went there, I wasn't assigned to engineering; I was assigned to a deck division, the first division. I had asked the first class boatswain's mate of the first division to take me on a tour of my division and point out everything I ought to know about it. We were up in the forward crew's head, as far forward as you could get, when Commander Thomson arrived. The ship was in overhaul, you see. He said to me, "Why haven't those tiles been laid?" First time I'd ever been in there.

Well, I'm afraid I'd forgotten my plebe training, and I said, "I don't know, exactly, but I'll find out."

He took off. He just blew me in front of enlisted men and everybody. He told me that he remembered me of old, and he was sure I was never going to be worthwhile as a naval officer.

---

*A "sundowner" is an extremely strict officer; the term derived from a commanding officer's requirement that all officers had to be back aboard ship by sundown.

Davidson #1 - 55

Q: This confirmed it.

Admiral Davidson: This confirmed it. That one I could pass off, but later I had the deck one afternoon when we received a group of about 200 enlisted men that came from other battleships to fill out the crew. I was the officer of the deck that afternoon. So when I wrote up the deck log, I took carbon copies of the orders for these groups and put the copies in the deck log. Well, about 6:30 that evening, I had been relieved and I was going ashore, and a Marine orderly caught me at the gangway and said, "Commander Thomson would like to see you."

So I dashed down to the cabin and stuck my head in. He looked up and he said, "Get the hell out of here!"

So I got the hell out of there. I hadn't gone 20 steps, and the Marine said, "Commander would like to see you." So I got the news finally. I was in civilian clothes. He wouldn't talk to me in civilian clothes. I had to be in uniform. So I finally got in uniform and went back down there. Meanwhile, I was going to be very late for a dinner engagement.

He got out the log. He said, "Do you know the regulations about preparing the deck log?"

I said, "Yes, sir."

He said, "You realize as well as I do that every name, serial number, and rate must be printed in the handwriting of the officer of the deck. I want you to do it before you go ashore."

There were over 200, and if you ever saw enlisted men's serial numbers, they're about that long, you know. There was the possibility of all kinds of errors.

I went down to my room, and I sat there until 2:00 in the morning doing 200 names. It had to be printed; you couldn't write it. Well, that was typical of Thaddeus Thomson, and I never got to the point where I liked him at all. As a matter of fact, I understand that he had command of a cruiser later and almost had a mutiny, he was so unpopular.* Yet he was a handsome devil.

One of the stories we used to tell about him was he was not only very handsome, he had a lovely wife, and they lived in Norfolk when the ship was in Hampton Roads. The stories the ensigns told was that we went to call on him--this was during Prohibition, of course--and he offered us a drink, and every time you'd get your drink down near the bottom, he'd insist on filling it up again. Finally, after he'd given you three or four, he would take you to the front door, and then we always said he dashed around to the back door, came out and met you out at the gate, and put you on report for being drunk. That's what we thought of him.

---

*As a captain, Thomson was the first commanding officer of the heavy cruiser Wichita (CA-45) when she went into commission on 16 February 1939. One of the ensigns in the ship's wardroom at the time was Paul R. Schratz; his oral history describes Thomson in much the same vein that Admiral Davidson's does.

Davidson #1 - 57

Q: What did you think of that old custom of calling on the seniors?

Admiral Davidson: I think it was wonderful in the days when the Navy was not so unwieldy, but nowadays, with people living so far apart, I think it would be impossible to expect it. But it was a very nice idea. We all called, and they always returned. I think probably as long as the Navy was small enough it was good. When I first went to Washington for duty in the Bureau of Navigation, which is BuPers now, there were a total of 11,000 officers, including supply, chaplains, doctors, and line officers.* We had almost that many in the submarine force by the end of the war, I guess.

I thought that was very nice. The ladies put on hats and white gloves. The men got dressed up properly. The call was supposed to be about 20 minutes, so you couldn't get in too much trouble.

Q: What values and benefits came from those calls?

Admiral Davidson: I think a certain amount of recognition for the younger officers by the captain. On a big ship like a battleship or cruiser, carriers, the young officer could serve

---

*BuPers was the Bureau of Naval Personnel.

three years and the captain not know who he was, really not know who he was. But I think when they'd all call, he at least might be intrigued enough to want to know him better. My captain always invited me to go play golf with him. Maybe he might not have if I hadn't ever gone around to call.

Q: Was that an option? I thought calling was something you had to do.

Admiral Davidson: Yes. I don't think there was any regulation that required it, but it was tradition in the Navy. It was very customary to do it, and we all did it.

Q: You were going to tell me about Captain Kerrick before you got off on Thomson.*

Admiral Davidson: Captain Charlie Kerrick was one of the most wonderful gentlemen I ever met, but maybe he was too gentlemanly to be very forceful. Then again, there was another one, Captain Baughman, he was a commander then. I was his aide, aide to the exec.** Commander Baughman was a real fine gentleman. I think Freeman was probably a real seaman, but he was straitlaced. Oh, gee, he was straitlaced. I don't think he believed in playing

---

*Captain Charles S. Kerrick, USN.
**Commander Cortlandt C. Baughman, USN.

cards, dancing, or anything. But Kerrick was just a real nice person to know, and as far as I was concerned, the ship was much happier when we had Kerrick than it was when we had Freeman, and certainly it was better when we had Baughman than when we had Thomson.

Q: What did your duties involve as aide to the exec?

Admiral Davidson: You sat in the executive officer's office and you sorted out all the mast cases, just principally like being a secretary. Everything came across your desk, and you decided which had to go to the exec and what didn't have to go to the exec.

I have to tell you a rather amusing story about Commander Baughman. We received a letter one time from a woman in Long Beach. She said that her 14-year-old daughter had had sexual relations with ten members of the Arizona crew, all in the boiler division or engineering division. She said in her letter, "I am not writing to cause any trouble for those men at all, but I think you should know, the ship should know, that my daughter has syphilis."

So old Commander Baughman said, "Let's get them all up at mast." We had them all in the exec's office. He said to the first man, "Did you ever have sexual intercourse with this girl?"

The man said, "Did I ever have what?" He didn't even know

what it was.

"Well, did you ever . . .?"

"Yes, sir."

"How much did you pay her?"

"Two dollars."

Number two, "Two dollars."

Number three, "Two dollars."

It got up to about number nine, and he said, "How much did you pay her?"

"Nothing. I didn't pay her nothing."

He came to number ten, and he said, "How much did you pay?"

He said, "Four dollars." That brought down the house.

We made them all go down to sick bay and be examined. They were never charged with anything.

Q: Were there a lot of mast cases when you were in that role?

Admiral Davidson: Oh, yes. On a ship that size, you've got a mast every day.

Q: You mentioned you were in one of those deck divisions. What were your duties there?

Admiral Davidson: I was the turret officer. In the first place, I was in the first division as the junior division officer, and then, before I became a lieutenant (junior grade), while I was still an ensign, Captain Freeman sent for me one day, and he said, "I want you to take over turret two from Lieutenant de Rivera, who has orders and is leaving."* Well, this was a big boost for me, you know, to be a turret officer as an ensign, because it had been a full senior lieutenant's job. So I took it over. Of course, the turret officer is the division officer. He does all the administrative work of a division officer, plus his part of the ship for maintenance and cleanliness, for everything--plus the fact that he sits up there behind the big guns and directs the firing, the loading, and so on, of the turret crew. It's quite a big job, because your turret goes all the way down to the bottom of the ship where you have the handling rooms, powder rooms, and all that.

Anyhow, about three or four days after I had taken over, the captain sent for me, and he said, "The commander tells me you have not moved into the wardroom." The JO mess was ensigns only, and then after that you went to the wardroom.**

I said, "I'm just an ensign still."

He said, "You're a division officer now. You're supposed to be eating in the wardroom." So I went back and reported to the commander that I was a new member of the wardroom mess. About this time, one of my classmates, who was an aviator and senior to

---
*Lieutenant Horace L. de Rivera, USN.
**JO--junior officer.

me by about three numbers, decided to take exception to this. He thought he should be the first one to go to the wardroom, and he wasn't, because he wasn't a division officer; he was an assistant.

So they used to give me a hard time. Every time I walked into the JO mess, they'd say, "No wardroom officers allowed. Get out of here." All that sort of stuff, you know. Finally, when he was finally promoted to j.g., and all the rest of them, they all moved into the wardroom. The mess boys had gotten accustomed to seating me at a certain place in accordance with my seniority, and so they had me sitting ahead of Roy Jackson.* He took off. He called the mess boy over and said, "I want you to know that Lieutenant (j.g.) Davidson is junior to me, and I'll sit here, and he can sit down there." Funny things come back to your mind when you start talking.

Anyway, I was in that ship until 1933, and always in that job in the turret. Then the gunnery officer, Lieutenant Commander Burrough, was a former submarine officer.** And I had been very disappointed about not getting into aviation, but they had failed me on my physical exams every year, and finally I had to give up by 1933. I was told by a flight surgeon once, "You know, if the Bureau of Medicine and Surgery turns you down once, no flight

---
*Lieutenant (junior grade) Roy Jackson, USN.
**Lieutenant Commander Edmund W. Burrough, USN.

surgeon is going to pass you until you can correct the problem, and you can't correct the problem because it's a history of a certain . . ." I had spinal meningitis as a child.

The gunnery officer said, "Why don't you go into submarines?" He was my guiding light from then on. I put in for submarines. They passed me physically, and that's when I went into submarines in '33.

Q: Can you describe what it was like being in a 14-inch turret when you were firing?

Admiral Davidson: Noisy, noisy. Otherwise, you had earphones on. You just watched the machine-like work of the men for loading.

Q: Are there any incidents you recall in relation with exercises?

Admiral Davidson: No. We didn't ever have a hangfire.* Maybe once in a while a misfire, but never a hangfire. We never had any real danger. I don't know that we ever hit too many targets. We didn't shine in any way. We weren't the best in the fleet.

---

*Hangfire--a delay or failure of the explosive charge in the gun; if the round cannot be fired, it must be removed, creating the danger of exploding in the turret.

Davidson #1 - 64

Q: Did you stand deck watches?

Admiral Davidson: Oh, yes, I stood officer of the deck watches. For some reason or other, when I was an ensign and became a turret officer, all my deck watches were midwatches, 12:00 to 4:00 in the afternoon and the midwatch at night--I guess because I was the junior one.

Q: Was there a fair amount of formation steaming in that time?

Admiral Davidson: Yes, pretty much.

Q: What were the useful qualities for an OOD in that?*

Admiral Davidson: Good eyesight and alertness, I guess, depth perception, although I believe if you had a good person punching your stadimeter, why, you were going to know your distance all the time anyway.

Q: How much training did you get in tactics as a watch officer?

Admiral Davidson: I don't think any great amount. I don't really know that battleship tactics were a great thing, except

---

*OOD--officer of the deck, in charge of conning the ship.

you didn't want somebody to cross your T, and that's the way old Admiral Pluvy Kempff made himself pretty famous, I guess, because he managed to cross the T of somebody else out there in the fleet problem and became quite well-known.* You know the story about Kempff, do you?

Q: I've heard of him.

Admiral Davidson: He's the one whose father was an admiral. When he was coming up for admiral, he went to see each member of the selection board. He didn't expect to be selected for admiral, but he knew that all the members of the selection board were friends of his father's. So he went to each one individually and said, "It would just kill my father if I didn't get at least one vote." According to the way he told the story, "As far as I know, I'm the only person who was ever unanimously selected."

Q: What else do you remember about him?

Admiral Davidson: He smoked incessantly, wearing his bridge

---

*Rear Admiral Clarence S. Kempff, USN. Crossing the T--a naval surface warfare tactic in which one battle line crosses an opposing battle line at a right angle. The fleet doing the crossing can employ all guns in a broadside. The other fleet, by contrast, is limited to using only the forward guns of each ship.

coat, and the ashes went down and he rubbed them in til they looked green. That's what I remember about Kempff.

Q: Was he the flag officer in the Arizona?

Admiral Davidson: No. He wasn't. I knew him later. He was commandant of the shipyard in Portsmouth, New Hampshire, when I was putting a submarine in commission, and I had to go call on him. That's when I saw him doing all that brushing the ashes. That's when he told me the story about his selection. When I came away from that meeting in his office, my captain asked me when I got back, "Did he tell you about his promotion?"
    I said, "Yes."
    He said, "He tells everybody."

Q: Who was the admiral in the Arizona?

Admiral Davidson: We didn't have an admiral aboard. The admiral was in the Pennsylvania, which was a sister ship of the Arizona. We didn't actually have an admiral on board.

Q: Pennsylvania had the fleet flag.

Admiral Davidson: Yes. There were various division flags, but we weren't one of them. I think we were in the same division with the <u>Pennsylvania</u>, so it was a fleet flag and we probably didn't have to have a division flag aboard.

Q: What liberty ports did you hit while you were in that ship?

Admiral Davidson: Just the West Coast. We went up to overhaul in Bremerton, overhauled in Bremerton, visited San Francisco, of course, and Long Beach. We went out on a fleet problem and anchored in Lahaina Roads.* We were quarantined there. I don't know if we had a case of smallpox or polio or something. They decided that we should be quarantined, and our mail all had to be fumigated when it left the ship.

Q: Did you get into Pearl Harbor at all?

Admiral Davidson: No. We were the ship that didn't get into Pearl Harbor because of our quarantine. By the time we came out of quarantine, we were steaming back to the West Coast. That's my memory. Somebody may be able to shoot a hole in some of my memories, but that's the way I recall it.

Q: Pearl Harbor was not all that well-developed by that time, was it?

---
*Lahaina Roads is off Maui in the Hawaiian Islands.

Davidson #1 - 68

Admiral Davidson: No.

Q: What do you recall about Long Beach and San Pedro as a home port area?

Admiral Davidson: Inside the breakwater, we had a beautiful anchorage there. We ran good boat schedules, and we had, of course, water taxis that you could always use. As far as liberty was concerned, San Pedro liberty wasn't worth going to, but you could always go up to Los Angeles. I think Long Beach was considered a little bit better for liberty. I had a classmate that said he knew Ginger Rogers, who came from his home town, and he bet he could take us all up to Hollywood to meet her, but we didn't meet her.* She had sort of outgrown him.

Q: What sort of things did bachelor officers do on their off days?

Admiral Davidson: We had a house, four of us, I guess. Four of us had a house out in an area known as Naples, the Long Beach area. We made beer, and we were able to buy government distillery brandy, and we had parties. We always felt that on Friday night and Saturday night you had to drink enough to make

---
*Ginger Rogers, the movie star of the 1930s and 1940s.

up for the fact that you didn't drink Sunday night, Monday night, Tuesday night, Wednesday night, and Thursday night. We had to do it all in a couple of nights.

Q: Why was it so concentrated?

Admiral Davidson: We went to sea during the week. You couldn't drink all week long, so you had to get it all in on the weekends.

Q: Was this after Prohibition had been rescinded, or was this illegal?

Admiral Davidson: It was still illegal. I'm surprised I didn't lose my car one time, because I think it was Taylor Keith that didn't have a car. A government distillery was up near Pasadena someplace. He said, "How about my taking your car to go up and get us two five-gallon jugs of that brandy?" So I let him take it. When he got back, he had been worried the whole way back. He said, "I'm sure that was a cop following me the whole way." If it had been caught, I'd have lost my car.

Q: What business did the government have making brandy during Prohibition?

Admiral Davidson: I suppose for medicinal purposes. They

weren't supposed to sell it, but Taylor had a friend up there who sold it. You know, in this country all these things seem illegal as hell, but there are places around the world where that's the only way they make a living.

Q: I wonder how foreigners during that era looked on America for that.

Admiral Davidson: I don't know. I can remember, for instance, after that, I went to submarine school. We certainly made our liquor up there. We used to go to the drug store and buy bourbon drops of some sort and drop them in alcohol and water, and they'd taste like a bourbon. Scotch was very hard to duplicate. Gin we could make. If you had juniper berries, you could make gin. Beer was fairly easy, although I never believed in tying up the bathtub to that extent.

Q: Were you in Long Beach during the big earthquake?*

Admiral Davidson: Oh, yes. Thank you for reminding me. That was quite an experience. I had just been married, and we had moved into an apartment in Long Beach. We were sitting in the

---

*The earthquake on 10 March 1933 at Long Beach was one of a series in the Southern California area; 58 people were killed in Long Beach.

Davidson #1 - 71

apartment in Long Beach about 5:00 o'clock, and George Ashford had come up. He was an aviator by then. He had come up from Coronado, and there were one or two of us, and my new wife, and all of a sudden, everything began to shake. We had a kitchen full of beautiful china that was given by my wife's parents. It all came off the shelves and crashed when it hit the floor. We looked out the windows, and across the street was an apartment house, and it looked like somebody had taken a knife and cut right down through it, and you were looking into every room. You could see people in the bathroom, and having dinner, and all this sort of stuff. The bricks had landed on top of the cars in the streets, a lot of rubble. The only person with presence of mind was my wife, who said, "Turn off all the gas," which we did, to be sure there were no gas leaks.

Anyway, we were then invited to move aboard ship. We took the wives and children. That <u>Arizona</u> was a madhouse for a week. We had all the wives and all the children on board that ship.

Q: Where did they live?

Admiral Davidson: They moved officers out of their rooms into bunk rooms, and made the rooms available to the wives and children. I think the funniest incident I remember--I mentioned a man by the name of de Rivera, whom I relieved as a turret officer. De was in the shower with his little tiny baby in his arms down in the lower wardroom country when I went in to take a shower. He handed this baby covered with soap to me, and said, "Hold on to it while I get washed off." I remember that very distinctly. That little monkey was so slippery, I was afraid I was going to drop him right down the drain, but we made out.

But anyway, Captain Kerrick decided that we should entertain all of the wives and children. He even arranged to catapult a plane one day for everybody to watch. The bridge games in the wardroom just had the wardroom snowed under all day long, but we got away with it. I was not permitted, because I was married, to go ashore on shore patrol. They sent all the bachelors, and they came back with fantastic stories about having to direct traffic, do this and that.

Q: There was fire fighting, too.

Admiral Davidson: Oh, yes. It was quite a week. All the ships were loaded with dependents, and they said it served a great purpose.

Q: Did the enlisted men bring their families on board?

Admiral Davidson: Yes. You can't imagine what a madhouse it was. It was so foreign to us. We had cots all over the place.

Davidson #1 - 73

Q: Sort of like a big adventure to the families.

Admiral Davidson: Yes. I had forgotten all about the earthquake. That happened in March of '33.

Q: You haven't mentioned the courtship and meeting your wife and so forth. How did that come about?

Admiral Davidson: Most of my friends had become aviators, and I had been turned down, as I told you. I used to go down to Coronado once in a while. I went down there one time, and George Ashford, who was a very close friend of mine from the Naval Academy, had a date with a girl whose father was the executive officer of a cruiser in Long Beach. She was down there for the weekend, and I met her. On subsequent trips down there, I saw her quite often, and so one fine weekend, with George along as a witness and with Sue Rule, who was an old friend of my wife's, as a witness, we went down to Mexico and got married. We went back to Long Beach and we didn't tell anybody.

The following week, I was out on a ship at sea when her father had orders to become commandant at Guantanamo. He informed Helen that he was going to be leaving in a certain length of time, so she decided to send me an MSG from Trona

Davidson #1 - 74

Field, or wherever it was.* So the MSG came through and told me of the plans, and I decided to send one back. I sent one back saying, "Don't go with your parents. I'll find us someplace to live." Something like that. She wasn't home when it got there, and her mother read it. So when I came in, all hell had broken loose, and the parents didn't approve of our getting married in Mexico. They decided that we had to have a proper wedding, and we had a proper wedding.

Q: What was the reason for not telling them initially?

Admiral Davidson: We thought we had been sort of reckless and maybe they wouldn't approve. Her dad was a pretty strong-minded guy out of the class of '09.** That's the way we got married, and then we got orders to submarine school to go that summer, and we went to New London. That brings back the earthquake and my getting married.

Q: What do you recall about that period in New London?

Admiral Davidson: We went to New London, and we found a place to live. I went to submarine school. She drove me to school every

---
*MSG stands for message, but usually meant to be an informal or personal communication.
**The bride's father was Commander Edward C. Raguet, USN, who was executive officer of the USS Louisville (CA-28).

morning. We had a neighbor who didn't have a car, and she drove him, too. Every time he found fault with her, I reminded him that he depended upon her. He eventually got kicked out of the Navy for being dependent on people.

Submarine school was a good experience. We were in R-boats in those days, and they taught us to dive the boat, charge the batteries, and to know a little bit about the torpedoes.* As far as the shooting of torpedoes, that was almost like a man trying to shoot ducks--you lead them a little bit and then shoot. In the R-boats, we didn't have any equipment like the torpedo data computers. The thing that appealed to me about the submarine course was the chance for early command, to be your own boss, almost your own boss. You always had somebody bossing you. I always thought that I was not a very good executive officer. I was a far better skipper.

Q: Why do you say that?

Admiral Davidson: I believe I had the good fortune to be able to judge the people that worked for me and to let the ones that I judged to be really competent do it all. Later in life I had a skipper who stopped by and asked my chief of staff if I was the same Admiral Davidson who used to let everybody do all his work

---
*Twenty-seven R-boats were commissioned in the U.S. Navy in 1918 and 1919 and represented World War I submarine technology.

Davidson #1 - 76

for him. I agree, I was. I seemed to be lucky at judging people.

I just finished writing a letter today and mailed it to John Hattendorf, the Ernest J. King professor at the Naval War College.* He wrote and asked me to try to give him some insight into the thinking of Admiral Richard Colbert on the subject of multilateral cooperation.**

I've just replied to him today, told him I was afraid I couldn't be very much help on what he wants, my memory of Dick Colbert's ideas of multilateral cooperation. I don't know what Dick thought. So I wrote and told him, "I'm afraid I'm not much help, because Dick Colbert was a young commander, and he was my executive officer in Albany, and my memory of him is that he was an exceptionally capable administrator, a wonderful shipmate, and so on, but as to his ideas or the beginning of his ideas on multilateral cooperation, I don't believe I was ever really exposed to his thinking.

However, I do remember," said I, "that when I was OP-61, which was politico-military policy, I requested that he be assigned as my deputy.*** This may be some indication that I had

---
*John Hattendorf holds the Ernest J. King Chair of Maritime History at the U.S. Naval War College, Newport, Rhode Island.
**Vice Admiral Richard G. Colbert, USN, was president of the Naval War College from 1968 to 1971.
***The Office of the Chief of Naval Operations in Washington is called OpNav and offices and individuals are identified by an OP number.

a great deal of confidence in his capability in the field of politico-military policy which might border on multilateral cooperation, if that's any help at all. The only thing was that they turned me down. They didn't let me have him."

I didn't go into the reasons either with him, but I'll tell you. The Vice Chief of Naval Operations said no, because Dick Colbert was married to an English girl.* That's the reason he gave me. I was never given an adequate reason. I suspect it was really because he wanted an aviator in the job.

Q: I talked to Admiral Rice, who also had the <u>Albany</u> when Colbert was there, and he spoke very highly of him also.**

Admiral Davidson: Oh, yes, yes. Dick was my exec for the whole time. I relieved Rice in the <u>Albany</u>, and Dick was my exec for the whole time. There's no question about it; he was just a real good officer. I had every confidence in him. I felt that I didn't have to be there. I didn't have to be there. And as a result, I let him do it, too. That's another thing. Admiral Holloway used to say--not the young one, but he's dead now, the father--used to say, "The secret of success is to pick the right guy and then let him do it."***

---
*The VCNO was Admiral Donald B. Duncan, USN.
**Vice Admiral Robert H. Rice, USN(Ret.)
***Admiral James L. Holloway, Jr., USN. His son, Admiral James L. Holloway III, USN, was Chief of Naval Operations from 1974 to 1978.

Davidson #1 - 78

Q: Repose in him special trust and confidence.

Admiral Davidson: Yes. But you've got to pick the right one. Some people don't seem to have much talent along that line. I think, if I had to brag about myself, I would brag a little bit on being a judge of people. I suppose a lot of that came from all my experiences in BuPers.

Q: Talking about submarine school, you had some notable classmates there such as John McCain, Mush Morton, and Jimmy Dempsey.*

Admiral Davidson: Yes.

Q: What do you recall about them from that period?

Admiral Davidson: Jack McCain. I think if I had to describe Jack, it would be to say that he's about as enthusiastic a person as I ever saw in my life. I don't think he ever quite tried to think something all the way through before he acted, if that makes any sense.

Q: Sort of impetuous, then?

---
*Ensign John S. McCain, Jr., USN, later admiral; Ensign Dudley W. Morton, USN, later lost in submarine Wahoo, 11 October 1943; Ensign James C. Dempsey, USN, later rear admiral.

Admiral Davidson: Yes, very impetuous, but I was always fond of Jack. With all due respect to his memory, I think all of us were surprised as hell when he made flag rank. Then when he went on to four stars, we were flabbergasted. He developed that speech. He had a speech that he gave over and over and over again about sea power, and he had it down to where I don't think he had to look at a note. He could just spiel it off, rapid fire, and he had a certain amount of real good humor in this. Then his wife made a great contribution in that she spent half her life in the gallery of the Congress getting acquainted with all the congressmen. She was one of the most beautiful gals you ever saw when they were married. She and her sister were just gorgeous.*

Q: I hear he had two wives.

Admiral Davidson: Oh, he always told that story. That's Jack. I knew his children when they were little tots. My last wife used to pick them up to take them to school in New London sometimes. She said she never saw so many runny noses in her life. Young John has turned out very well, a congressman.**

---
*Mrs. Roberta McCain was extremely close to her identical twin sister, Rowena. Admiral McCain often escorted both of them to various events and social gatherings, hence his story of having "two wives."

**John S. McCain III, member of Congress, was elected to the House of Representatives from the 1st District of Arizona in 1982 and again in 1984. In 1986 he was elected to the U.S. Senate. He retired from the Navy as a captain in 1981. He was a prisoner of war in North Vietnam from 1967 to 1973 during part of which time his father was Commander in chief Pacific.

Pinky--and I can't tell you what Pinky's real name was--but Pinky was very difficult for me when I was Superintendent and he was plebe.* He looked like butter wouldn't melt in his mouth. Oh, boy. I can see him marching into chapel just like he was never going to do anything wrong in his whole life, and yet by the first of April of plebe year, he was about to be kicked out for too many demerits. Charlie Minter and I decided to save him. Charlie was the commandant.** Charlie called him in. We agreed that the last report that had come in, we would not process, because it would put him over the top, if he would swear and promise to behave until June. Well, Charlie had him in and had an hour's talk with him in the commandant's office. He pleaded. Oh, by gosh. "My grandfather was an admiral, my father was an admiral. My brother is a very successful officer. I want to be here."

That afternoon at 5:00 o'clock, Charlie called me and said, "Admiral, you won't believe it. Pinky has just been put on report by an English professor for taking off his shoes in class. He said he can think better in his bare feet."

So I tried to call Jack McCain, and he was in the Med, and I called Roberta, whom I knew real well. "Roberta, I hate to do this, but we've got to kick old Pinky out." He not only had the

---
*Midshipman Joseph Pinckney McCain, USN.
**Captain Charles S. Minter, Jr., USN, later became Superintendent of the Naval Academy, and later vice admiral. His is the subject of a U.S. Naval Institute oral history.

other report that put him over the top; now he'd got another on top of that. So I don't think Pinky wanted to be here, because he went from here out to San Diego and organized one of those groups of demonstrators against Vietnam or against Korea or against something. That's too bad. Well, that was Jack McCain.

Jimmy Dempsey is gone now, too, isn't he?

Q: Yes.

Admiral Davidson: He's gone. Mushmouth Morton--he and Red Coe were a great pair.*

Q: Was Morton as fearless, reckless, or whatever term you want to use, when you knew him, as he became in the Wahoo?

Admiral Davidson: Sort of, I think. Sort of. Not as reckless and not as daring as Sam Dealey. Did you ever hear of Sam Dealey?**

Q: Oh, sure. I've heard him linked with Morton. They were two of a kind.

---
*Commander James W. Coe, USN, commanding officer of the USS Cisco (SS-290), sunk by Japanese in September 1943.
**Commander Samuel D. Dealey, USN, commanding officer of the USS Harder (SS-257), sunk during his sixth combat patrol in August 1944. During his five patrols in the Harder, he sank 16 ships for 54,000 tons, including four destroyers and two frigates. He was awarded the Medal of Honor posthumously.

Admiral Davidson: Yes. Right. Sam Dealey was in the same class. Frank Lynch was Sam Dealey's exec, and then later was the skipper of one of my division boats, and I rode him down around the Horn, and he told me about the patrols with Sam.* He said after some of these attacks, Sam would go down and be sitting in his little cabin down there, crying his eyes out, and say, "Frank, never let me do that again. That's stupid. I'm risking the life of every man on board." And about that time, the officer of the deck would say he had sighted something else, and then he'd do it all over again. He's the one who developed the business of putting up the periscope so an attacking ship could see it, and when the attacking ship steered for it, he'd fire right down his throat. Frank said the depth charges sometimes went off right over the top of them as the ship blew up.

Q: I heard Morton was much the same way in that he had some officers in his wardroom--Dick O'Kane was one of them--that would sort of hold him back when he got these really wild ideas, and then they all left, and there was nobody who would stand up to him.**

---
*Commander Frank C. Lynch, Jr., USN.
**Commander Richard H. O'Kane, USN, was the leading submarine skipper of World War II, credited with sinking 24 ships for more than 93,000 tons. He was one of eight survivors of the USS Tang (SS-306) sunk in October 1944. He was awarded the Medal of Honor and retired from the Navy as a rear admiral in 1957.

Davidson #1 - 83

Admiral Davidson: Yes. You know, there's an officer here in town, Gene Fluckey.* Have you ever had to interview him?

Q: I'd like to. I've met him.

Admiral Davidson: Gene apparently didn't know fear of any kind. He went into harbors and did things that really, there's no reason he came out, except he had to be capable, in addition to taking all these chances. But Gene Fluckey is quite a skipper, has the Congressional Medal and everything else. How he lived through it, nobody's quite figured out yet. As a matter of fact, I had a little something to do with his being detached, because he wanted to go out on another patrol, and I was the detail officer by then, and I talked Admiral Lockwood into either denying him, or talking him out of it.** I said, "We need Gene Fluckey in the Navy. I don't like to see him going out taking one more chance, because we're probably going to lose him. He's getting so he doesn't believe anything can stop him."

Q: That's what Slade Cutter told me, that after you get about your fourth or fifth patrol, then you think you're invincible,

---

*Rear Admiral Eugene B. Fluckey, USN. As commanding officer of the Barb (SS-220) from April 1944 to August 1945, Fluckey was credited with sinking over 95,000 tons of Japanese shipping, the most for any skipper in the Pacific.
**Vice Admiral Charles A. Lockwood, Jr., USN, Commander Submarines Pacific Fleet.

and that's when you take too many chances.*

Admiral Davidson: That's when you get in trouble.

Q: How did Morton get that name Mushmouth?

Admiral Davidson: I guess that's the way he talked. I don't know. I can't remember now.

Q: What do you remember about the instruction, the teaching itself at submarine school?

Admiral Davidson: All of our instructors were young submarine officers. I guess the courses were pretty well laid out for them to follow. I think we learned pretty much what you could possibly learn, with the exception that you didn't get too much experience. Experience had to come from actually getting out there and doing it. Of course, it was all peacetime when I went to submarine school, and we were very cautious about our diving procedure and everything else. We didn't try to see how fast we could get down. That all came along the first year of the war, when we realized we had to dive in a hurry. We had to take a few

---

*Captain Slade D. Cutter, USN (Ret.). As commanding officer of USS Seahorse (SS-304), Cutter was credited with sinking 19 ships for 72,000 tons. He is the subject of a Naval Institute oral history.

chances on that.

Red Coe was one of the funny ones in that group. There was Mushmouth Morton and Red Coe.

Q: What do you recall about Coe? He was later lost during the war.

Admiral Davidson: Yes. Red Coe is one I remember real well. I had known Red Coe as a midshipman, because his sister and my sister had known each other in college, so when he arrived at the Naval Academy and I was an upper classman, I knew of him. Anyway, when we went to submarine school, I remember we were in "juice" class one morning.* The first class of the morning started at 8:00 o'clock, and Red was absent. He wandered in about 8:30 or 20 minutes to 9:00, and the instructor was a lieutenant. I believe what he said was something along this line, "Well, Mr. Coe, what excuse do you have today?"

And Red said, "You know that road coming out here along the river, coming out to the submarine base from the big bridge? You know that curve there that has a great big tree on the right? I was coming around that curve just as carefully as I could, when suddenly that tree moved out and just knocked the hell out of my car."

---
*"Juice"--electricity.

Q: What did the instructor say?

Admiral Davidson: "Take your seat."

Q: Were the instructors a competent lot?

Admiral Davidson: Yes, I thought so. I thought so.

Q: We've talked about the competition at the Naval Academy. Would you say there was more or less of it at submarine school?

Admiral Davidson: I don't recall. There was some competition based on the fact that I believe in those days you were assigned in accordance with your class standing. If you stood first, you got your first choice of where you went.

Q: And some people were trying to avoid the Asiatic Fleet.

Admiral Davidson: Yes. Some people wanted the Asiatic Fleet. For instance, my last wife's first husband deliberately wanted to go there. He was in submarine school following me, and he went to China. He was lost later in Tullibee.*

---

*Lieutenant Commander Charles F. Brindupke, USN, commanding officer of the USS Tullibee (SS-284), lost in March 1944.

Q: What do you recall about your escape training?

Admiral Davidson: Very good, very good. It never bothered me very much. I didn't worry about it at all. I thought it was pretty effective.

Q: Did you use the Momsen lung or deep breathing?*

Admiral Davidson: We used Momsen lungs. I never practiced the deep breathing business. I used Momsen's lung even before I found out that he didn't invent it.

Q: Oh, really? I didn't know that.

Admiral Davidson: Well, he got the credit for it, but I think somebody else really came up with the idea. He may have developed it.

Q: Well, it will ever after be known by his name.

Admiral Davidson: Right. Swede Momsen was the godfather to my

---

*Lieutenant Charles B. Momsen, USN, demonstrated to the Navy in 1928 an oxygen rebreathing device he had developed for escaping from submerged submarines. The device later was not considered effective by all submariners. See Clay Blair, Jr., Silent Victory (Philadelphia: J.B. Lippincott Company, 1975), pages 65, 768.

stepdaughter, and I used to know Swede quite well, but he's gone now, too.

Q: What do you remember about Momsen's personality?

Admiral Davidson: Not much, really. I liked him all right. I never worked for him directly that I can remember. He was around Pearl Harbor there during the war when I came back in. I don't remember.

Q: What do you remember about the approach practices in those R-boats?

Admiral Davidson: They were pretty primitive. We learned a lot in the attack teachers, I think.* I don't know that we learned too much, actually, in the boats. You're getting me now where I'm fuzzy about a lot of things.

Q: Was there much training in doctrine and how you would use the ships in wartime?

Admiral Davidson: Not at the submarine school, because at that time we didn't have the capability of doing what we called

---

*Attack teachers were full-scale mock-up trainers in which to practice approaches to targets.

Davidson #1 - 89

end-around, which we developed during the war. When you spotted a convoy, you surfaced and ran around and got ahead of it and dove up there and tried to knock them off as they came through. Those were the tactics that were really developed during the war. I don't remember ever having any of that. Well, we didn't have boats capable of running around. When we had the old S-boats and the R-boats, we were limited to ten knots, and we couldn't run around anything with that.

Q: I've heard people talk about the great spirit that submariners had for the submarine force. Did you begin to pick that up?

Admiral Davidson: I was very proud to be a submariner, and I never wanted to be a sub-mariner.

Q: What was the appeal?

Admiral Davidson: Among other things, early command. Among other things, the quality of the crews and the officers. The captain of a submarine had what I considered a very useful--I don't know whether you'd call it a weapon--but you could declare anybody psychologically unsuited, and he'd be immediately detached from the ship. Now, I thought this was a great thing to have in your hand, because people didn't want to be detached.

They wanted to succeed as submariners, and, among other things, they didn't want to lose the extra pay, which is always an incentive.*

Q: Did you consider that the R-boats and S-boats of that era were hazardous?

Admiral Davidson: Not at the time. I didn't really think so at the time.

Q: They didn't look primitive, except in retrospect.

Admiral Davidson: Yes. When I left the S-boat, I had command of the S-44, and when I left that, I went up to the Electric Boat Company and commissioned the Mackerel. The Mackerel was almost the spitting image of one of the fleet boats, but it was only the tonnage of an S-boat. It was a very small submarine. It didn't have any legs. We couldn't go very far, so it could not have operated properly in World War II on those long patrols, but it was a good coastal submarine.

Q: What do you remember about the crowded living conditions in the R-boats and S-boats?

---

*Submarine officers and crew members received additional hazardous duty pay.

Admiral Davidson: R-boats, nothing, because we never lived aboard. We just went to school and went home. But S-boats, I made some cruises through the Caribbean and down Panama Bay, and so forth. I didn't think we were so crowded. We didn't have very many people. We had four officers, including the captain, four officers and something like 30-some men, maybe. I think the discomfort was in the hot climates and the hot temperature of the ocean. We didn't have air-conditioning. We had numerous electrical casualties from moisture. That was the great benefit of air-conditioning. We eliminated 90% of our electrical casualties that came from moisture, plus we provided enough water to wash clothes. It took it right out of the air.

Q: There were distinctive odors in the submarines.

Admiral Davidson: Yes. There were diesel odors always from way back, you know. Our wives used to say in Coronado that when we came ashore in a boat to the ferry landing in Coronado and started walking down Orange Avenue, they said they could tell when we got within three blocks of the house. They could smell us.

Q: Admiral Benson, in his oral history, told about a time when he was in the Pentagon and had to escort somebody down to visit a submarine. When he got home that night, his wife said, "You were in a submarine today, weren't you?"*

What do you remember about the instruction ashore, the subjects you covered, and so forth, at submarine school?

Admiral Davidson: What did we study? We studied storage batteries, torpedoes, and diesel engines. That's about all, I guess. Maybe some course in auxiliaries, pumps, and things like that. It must have been adequate, and it couldn't have been too difficult, because I finished. I never was a nuts and bolts man. I leaned much more heavily on the humanities.

---

*Rear Admiral Roy S. Benson, USN, is the subject of a two-volume Naval Institute oral history.

Interview Number 2 with Rear Admiral John F. Davidson,
U.S. Navy (Retired)

Place: Admiral Davidson's home, Annapolis, Maryland

Date: Wednesday, 28 August 1985

Subject: Biography

Interviewer: Paul Stillwell

Admiral Davidson: In 1933 I finished submarine school, and in accordance with the system then in use, I must have stood fairly well, because I was able to request and get assigned to the USS Cachalot, which was building in the navy yard in Portsmouth, New Hampshire. There were two submarines being built at the same time and were sisters, the Cachalot in Portsmouth and Cuttlefish at the Electric Boat Company.

I reported to the Cachalot in January of 1934. The ship was building. I don't think we left Portsmouth until probably the fall of 1934. We had made a shakedown cruise in the meantime and gone back for post-shakedown overhaul. Then we proceeded to San Diego, which was to become the home port for the Cachalot. We were assigned to Submarine Division 12, which consisted of sort of an unusual mix of boats. There were two very large ones, the Nautilus and the Narwhal, and then there were three only a bit smaller called the Barracuda, the Bass, and Bonita, and then we had the Dolphin and the Cachalot and the Cuttlefish, all of us in one division. I think the thing that I remember most about it was that we went on a fleet problem, and the new commander of the submarine force was none other than the same C.S. Freeman who had been my skipper in the Arizona, and, to the best of my knowledge, he had never had any submarine duty in his life. But he insisted that when we were traveling from point to point, not really operating on a problem, that we cruise in formation.

It was almost an impossible thing to do, because the submarine diesel engines had what was known as critical speeds. For instance, in the Cachalot, we could run our engines for five knots, for ten knots, and for 15 knots, but we couldn't run in between those speeds, or you'd shake the engines to pieces--they vibrated so badly. So here we were crossing to Pearl and on out to Midway all the time steaming along, trying to keep position on each other, and no two boats could go the same speed, so we were jockeying all the time.

One of the coincidences that I remember, I thought one time I was about to see the end of the world. I really thought I had seen it. I was the officer of the deck. We at this time were alone at sea somewhere near Midway--flat calm, absolutely beautiful day. I was the officer of the deck, and we were steaming along at about ten knots on the engines, and I was sitting on the bridge rail, which was customary. For some reason or other, I don't know whether I dozed off, but anyway, I suddenly looked up, and as I had last remembered the sun was dead ahead; and I suddenly looked up and the sun was way back here on the quarter. I thought the world was coming to an end. The world is really coming to an end, because here the sun has moved from there to around here in about ten minutes. I was about to call the captain and report this to him, when I looked over the stern and we were going in a circle. We had been on the automatic pilot and something had happened to it. It had tripped out, and we were going in a circle with about ten degrees right rudder, and I hadn't realized it at all. That's one of my memories about cruising in the Cachalot.

The rest of my time in the Cachalot was very much a normal young submariner's cruise. I was the communications officer, the commissary officer, and because I was the JO, I soon discovered that I was the charging officer. We had to charge batteries when in port, usually every third day, and there were only three watch officers. So they arranged to always have the batteries charged on my watch. One of the reasons I remember--I was a heavy smoker, and you weren't allowed to smoke during the battery charges, so I had to give up smoking every third day. Otherwise, the cruise was pretty normal.

I had a wonderful skipper. His name was Merrill Comstock.[*] When I say wonderful, he was wonderful, because he let his officers do their job. A great example: Max Stormes was the first lieutenant, and one day while bringing the boat alongside

---

[*] Lieutenant Commander Merrill Comstock, USN.

the tender in San Diego Bay, the skipper and I were standing on what was called the cigarette deck.* Max was coming in alongside. In those days we had rails around the deck of the submarine, and we had a jackstaff up there permanently established. Max came in a little fast, and about that time Dutch Buerkle, who was the engineer officer, stuck his head up out of the engine room hatch and yelled up to the skipper, "Ask Max if he knows he's still going ahead two-thirds."**

And the skipper picked up what we called a deck wrench and threw it back towards Dutch and said, "You tend to the engines. Max is running the ship."

So what happened was that Max surged forward too far, and when he backed full, he busted the jackstaff under the tender's anchor. He ripped off the jackstaff and about 30 feet of railing alongside, but he finally settled his boat alongside. The skipper never said boo. He just stood there and observed this with his arms crossed, and shortly thereafter he went ashore.

The next day at lunch, he was sitting there and nobody was saying anything, just having lunch, and all of a sudden the skipper said, "Max, you're the first lieutenant. You tore the boat apart yesterday, damn it, get it fixed." And that's all that was ever said. I'm sure it didn't affect the fitness report or anything.

---

*Lieutenant Max C. Stormes, USN.
**Lieutenant (junior grade) Elmer C. Buerkle, USN.

As far as I was concerned, I learned a great deal from Merrill Comstock, because he knew how to be a commanding officer. A lot of people thought he was pretty stern. He had a cast in one eye--incidentally, C.S. Freeman had a cast in one eye, too--and they looked pretty stern at times. But Merrill had a way of doing things that appealed to me.

For instance, one Saturday morning we were having an inspection while in port, and he started in the forward torpedo room. Gov Hobby was the exec, and Max and Dutch and I were all accompanying the captain through the boat.[*] We went through the forward torpedo room and then into the forward battery room, which was also where the officers' staterooms were and where the officers' head was, and so on and so forth, and the officers' pantry. He was almost through that second compartment and said, "Gov, I'd like to have you call my boat. I'm going to go ashore. And incidentally, will you please let me know when the boat is ready for inspection?" Period. That's all he said. We were all just ashamed of ourselves. How could we let this guy down completely? I promise you there was never another time when that submarine wasn't just spic and span. He was so different from a lot of skippers that we could observe there in the division who would rave and rant and raise hell and call people names, and so on and so forth, but Merrill never did. He was just calm.

---

[*]Lieutenant William M. Hobby, Jr., USN.

Q: You felt like you had let him down if you hadn't done what was supposed to be done.

Admiral Davidson: Right. That's the surest way never to let it happen again. As an aside, many years later when I was working for Arleigh Burke, I'd left my number two in politico-military policy in charge while I was off on a speaking tour.* When I came back, Arleigh Burke sent for me, and he said, "Get rid of Red Stroh. Get rid of him."**

I said, "Admiral, why?"

He said, "He gave me the worst advice for a meeting of the Joint Chiefs of Staff I ever had, and he just isn't qualified to be in that job as your deputy."

I said, "Admiral, I didn't choose him, but at the same time, I think he's doing a very fine job. How did he let you down?"

He said, "Well, he told me so and so, so and so, and so and so."

I said, "Well, Admiral Burke, that's what I told him to tell you."

He looked at me for a minute. Incidentally, this was 7:00 o'clock in the evening. He looked at me for a minute and said, "Damn it, Johnny, you know what's wrong with you?"

---
*Admiral Arleigh A. Burke, USN, Chief of Naval Operations from August 1955 to August 1961 and subject of several volumes of U.S. Naval Institute oral history.
**Captain Robert J. Stroh, USN, later vice admiral.

I said, "There's a lot of things, Admiral, but you tell me." I was a two-star admiral at this time.

He said, "Once a week you should lose your temper and just eat somebody's ass out whether he needs it or not."

And I said, "Well, Admiral, I've always felt there were two ways to run railroads--that way and my way, which is to somehow handle it so that the culprit feels so guilty that he'll never let it happen again. And you don't have to bawl him out to get that; you just make him feel bad." Well, that's an aside.

Q: I wonder if you could describe what went into that period in the shipyard when you were getting the Cachalot ready to go.

Admiral Davidson: She was being built in Portsmouth, New Hampshire, at the navy yard, and I reported to her early in January in 1934. Several things stand out in my mind. I remember one three-week period when the warmest day was 22 below zero. We always had automobile trouble and so forth. I also remember we were to try to flood the dry dock and go to sea for some trials, and I remember being sent down into the dry dock while it was still empty to see if I could observe the operation of the flood valves, called kingstons, which were operated hydraulically from within the ship. Everything was so cold and the hydraulic fluid was so cold that we couldn't get the valves to open and close as they should. We finally were successful.

I can remember going to sea on trials and standing one-hour watches on the bridge because of the cold, except for the skipper, Merrill Comstock, who stayed up there as much as four hours once, and both cheeks cracked from frost.

The other thing I remember about the *Cachalot* is that it was the rollingest ship that was ever built. We had a team from the then-Bureau of Engineering, later Bureau of Ships, who came up to see if we could find out why the *Cachalot* had what they called a snap role, which is a very quick period--probably half of what it should have been. It came out that it had something to do with the metacentric height that had been built into this, and there was a young engineering officer by the name of Armand Morgan, I believe, who used to say, "Oh, he's a low metacentric height enougher."* I remember there were great debates about it, and I wasn't sure what was wrong, but I did know it was a very uncomfortable ship to ride in any kind of a sea. It wasn't too bad if you headed into it, but if you were in a trough, it was a very uncomfortable ship. Probably the only time I can remember that I was seasick was the first time we went out in *Cachalot*. I was really seasick.

---

*Lieutenant Armand M. Morgan, Construction Corps, USN, later rear admiral. Metacenter is the point of intersection of a vertical line through the center of buoyancy of a floating body. When this point is below the center of gravity, the body becomes unstable.

Davidson #2 - 101

Q: How would you describe that class as a transition between the S-boats and the later fleet boats?

Admiral Davidson: It had the same general silhouette as a fleet boat, but it was far smaller, of course, and it probably didn't have but a small percentage of the legs, the cruising capacity as the larger boats had.* I suspect it was a fairly decent interim. It was far better than the old Barracuda class. They were great big, clumsy, hard-to-handle boats.

Q: How were they in terms of habitability and living comfort?

Admiral Davidson: As I recall it, the Cachalot wasn't bad at all. I don't think we had air-conditioning in those days. It wasn't until I got into the Blackfish, I believe, that we had air-conditioning. Except for that rolling, I think it was pretty habitable.

Q: You haven't described too much about your training program, what you went through to get your dolphins.

Admiral Davidson: Ah! I don't remember what I went through,

---

*The Cachalot was designed with the intended theoretical endurance of 75 days and 10,000 miles, but this range was never achieved. Range actually was less than 9,000 miles. A cruising range of more than 12,000 miles was necessary for patrols from Pearl Harbor to reach Japanese waters and return.

Davidson #2 - 102

except what I saw in my records here today. I jotted down when they recommended me. My captain recommended me as having demonstrated, in my time on board, that I was ready for qualification in submarines, and I was given some sort of an examination by a qualification board which came on board. I was required to do everything--take the boat away from the tender, take it out to the operating area, be officer of the deck when it came back, tie it up. I was the diving officer when we were out there. The only thing I don't remember, I don't think I had to shoot any torpedoes or anything, but I was the diving officer. They recommended me as qualified in submarines. That was approved by that board, and it was a whole year later that the commanding officer then recommended that in the year that I had been a qualified officer, that I demonstrated to his satisfaction that I was ready for qualification for command. Then I was designated, I believe by the bureau, as qualified. That was April of 1935. I was recommended for qualification for command in March of '36, and was qualified for command in April of '36. In May of '36 I went to the Bureau of Navigation for duty. So I had just finished being qualified.

Q: You said last time that you weren't particularly a nuts and bolts man, so I guess you had overcome that to whatever degree was necessary.

Admiral Davidson: I managed to learn how to charge the batteries, anyway. Qualification for command under Merrill Comstock was, I felt, relatively easy because he gave you an opportunity. He let you handle the ship, he didn't interfere, and all he did was observe. Then if he approved, why--one of the things that Merrill Comstock did for me, for instance, which he actually was criticized for doing--Lockwood was the division commander, I believe, and we were all tied up to the tender in San Diego, and the tender was to go to the navy yard.* So the division commander issued an operation order which called for the boats to get under way one at a time from alongside the tender, stand out to channel, lie to, and when the tender disappeared down the channel, then the largest boat, the Nautilus, was to come in and tie up to the tender's buoy, and then the rest of us were to come in one at a time and tie up to her. It was a complete operation order, called for everything to get under way at 7:00 a.m., this, that, and the other thing.

The night before, Merrill Comstock said, "Who's got the duty tomorrow?"

I said, "I have, sir."

He said, "Well, I want you to be prompt, and I don't want you to delay anything. I want you to get under way on time, I want you to stand out to channel, I want you to be back sharply

---

*Commander Charles A. Lockwood, Jr., USN, Commander Submarine Division 13, 1935-1937.

alongside when they call you, and I'll be aboard later in the morning." Just like that.

So Gov Hobby, who was the exec, learned that.* He said, "I'll not come aboard until after you're back alongside the buoy." So Max and Dutch said the same thing, so here I was.** I was at that point not qualified for command. I was just qualified. Period.

I can hear Lockwood to this day calling down with a megaphone from the deck of the tender. "Has your skipper come aboard yet?"

"No, sir." I didn't tell him he was not coming. "No, sir."

So he said, "What are you supposed to do?"

I said, "Well, my orders are not to delay things, to get under way on time."

"All right." So when the time came, off we went.

Afterwards, I understood that Lockwood sort of scolded Merrill Comstock about this. But Comstock said to him, "Have you any complaint about the performance of the ship?"

"No, it was very well done, maybe better than a couple of the others," which helped me.

Q: And does wonders for your confidence.

---
*Lieutenant William M. Hobby, Jr., USN.
**Lieutenant Max C. Stormes, USN, was the first lieutenant and gunnery officer. Lieutenant (junior grade) Elmer C. "Dutch" Buerkle, USN, was engineer officer.

Davidson #2 - 105

Admiral Davidson: Yes, it sure does. I felt he trusted me. Not only that, I thought I worked harder at it than some of the skippers who came back and it was routine with them.

Q: It's like the point we were making before. You made a special effort not to let him down in that situation.

Admiral Davidson: Right.

Q: What do you recall about that long journey from Portsmouth around to the West Coast?

Admiral Davidson: Nothing out of the ordinary, with the exception of some incidents of our stewards. We had two Filipino stewards in the wardroom. The captain told them that they couldn't go ashore in Panama unless they got their hair cut. I don't know how familiar you are with the submarine with its conning tower and it had what we called a conning tower hatch which went up, and a conning tower door which went aft, and then there was a little sort of sheltered space just aft of the conning tower door and underneath the bridge deck. So while cruising on the surface down through the Caribbean, these two boys who had orders to get their hair cut decided to cut each other's hair. They left the conning tower door open and the hatch down through the control room, and went up there and shaved each other's head just bald. But the trouble was that the engines were sucking the air in through the door, down the hatch, back through the control room, through the galley, through the enlisted living compartment. We had black hair all over the place.

The next morning these two boys came in to serve breakfast and were wearing their white hats. The captain said to one, "Take off your hat." He took it off. Bald-headed. Needless to say, they didn't try to go ashore. They were so ashamed of themselves, they didn't try to go ashore in Panama. We stopped in Panama for two or three days just for recreation and liberty.

The finale of that trip was--I had the deck--it was probably about 3:00 o'clock in the morning, just off San Diego. We were arriving in San Diego that day. There was a terrific "thump" you couldn't believe. Shortly thereafter, the quartermaster reported to me that the pitometer log was not registering. The pitometer log was a shaft that could be lowered down through the hull of the ship and registered the speed we were making through the water. So we withdrew it and went on into port.

About two days after we got there, a whale washed up on the beach near the Coronado Hotel, and the assumption is that we hit that whale. And when we finally went into marine railway, the pitometer log had been bent right up almost against the skin of the ship. So that was the finale of that trip. We think we hit a whale.

Davidson #2 - 107

Q: You mentioned the engines that could only go in increments of five knots. Were those the old HORs?*

Admiral Davidson: Those were HORs, but the Cachalot had a very unusual setup. When they designed the Cachalot, the HORs available were eight cylinders, and they decided to attempt to beef them up a little bit by adding a cylinder, so they built nine-cylinder engines. Someplace along the line, I think they forgot to take into account that there would be some imbalance and they would have critical speeds. I'm not enough of an engineer to know what happened when they put the ninth one on there, but we did have critical speeds and they couldn't be run in those speeds. Fortunately, we could run usual speeds of five, ten. One-third was five knots, two-thirds was ten, and standard speed was 15.

Q: In general, how reliable were they, other than that?

Admiral Davidson: Pretty good. They were way ahead of the S-boats in that we could back down on them. In the S-boats, you had to stop your engines, throw out the engine clutches, and then back down on the motors, which is what we used for propulsion

---
*Cachelot had M.A.N. engines (Maschinenfabrik-Augsburg-Nurnberg) of German design, but built by the New York Navy Yard. H.O.R. (Hooven-Owens-Rentschler) was the U.S. licensee for M.A.N., later built a superior diesel submarine engine based on M.A.N. designs.

submerged. But in the Cachalot, we could back down by shifting the cam shaft or something. I don't know just how it did work, but we could back down on it. They were fairly reliable. I don't think we had too much trouble with them.

Q: Do you have any other recollections of Lockwood?

Admiral Davidson: He was a division commander when I first knew him, and when I last knew him, he was Commander Submarines Pacific Fleet, of course.

Q: What from that time in the division do you recall about him?

Admiral Davidson: We didn't see much of him. I don't recall he ever rode the boat. If he did, I didn't know about it and don't remember.

Q: How would you describe the mission of the submarine force in those years?

Admiral Davidson: I don't know, Paul. Probably more scouting than anything else. We weren't a very effective attack ship. They used to say about the Cachalot that it really wasn't a submarine; it was a small ship capable of short periods of submersion. We certainly didn't have any great armament. We

Davidson #2 - 109

were probably more fitted for scouting than we were for anything else. I think the old S-boats were quite effective for harbor protection and close inshore work. It wasn't until we had the fleet boats that we had any legs at all. We carried sufficient torpedoes. One of the great problems of the submarine force in the early days was the torpedoes. We had hopeless torpedoes.

Q: This was certainly the problem for you in the Blackfish.

Admiral Davidson: Yes.

Q: What do you remember about the Cachalot's operations in the Pacific once you got out to your home port?

Admiral Davidson: We operated in and out of San Diego, firing our torpedo practices. What did we use for targets? I guess they towed ships as targets. We fired our torpedo practices out there with practice torpedoes, which had to be recovered. What did they use the Cachalot for? They used the Cachalot to go out and lie on the bottom for some test that I've already forgotten. I know we were out there for days lying on bottom. We made fleet problems. We went all the way to Midway.

Q: From San Diego?

Davidson #2 - 110

Admiral Davidson: From San Diego.

Q: You had a pretty decent voyage, then.

Admiral Davidson: Yes. We went to Pearl first.

Q: I see.

Admiral Davidson: We went to Pearl and then to Midway and back to Pearl, back to San Diego. The <u>Cachalot</u> had legs enough to do that.

Q: Do you recall any operations against the surface ships in those fleet problems?

Admiral Davidson: At least we were supposed to, I think, get in there and make an attack here and there. I don't recall anything very exciting, so I don't remember if we were ever able to get in or not.

Q: What do you recall of Pearl during that time? That was pretty exclusively submariners' province, wasn't it?

Admiral Davidson: Yes. Of course, most of the boats there at that time were S-boats. The big boats were in San Diego, and the

S-boats were in Pearl Harbor.

Q: Any more on Cachalot?

Admiral Davidson: I learned a hell of a lot from Merrill Comstock, and I ended up the tour in the Cachalot with sort of a reward, in a way, and I found it out this way. I was about to put in for postgraduate school, and I thought what I wanted was postgraduate school in ordnance. It seemed in those days that people who were ordnance PGs always went to the top. Engineering PGs were sort of end-of-the-road. I wasn't sure that I had the mathematic background and so on to be successful in it. All of a sudden a letter came from the detail office in Washington to our skipper, saying, "What would you say to John Davidson as the assistant to the submarine detail officer in the Bureau of Navigation?"

And Merrill blew me up to the sky, and then convinced me that that's what I ought to do. I said, "What about PG school?"

He said, "The best PG you can get is the Bureau of Navigation. If you get it in personnel, that's the best postgraduate work you can do." This was 1936, when I normally would have gone to postgraduate school. I ended up going back to the Bureau of Navigation as the assistant submarine detail officer and with additional duty as the detail officer for all ensigns and jaygees. My boss had two hats--submarine detail and detail officer for all ensigns and junior lieutenants. He split the job in the office and gave me all the ensigns and jaygees to handle, and he handled the submarine desk. That was perhaps as fascinating a job as I ever had, because in those days we were on Constitution Avenue in the old Main Navy Building along with BuShips and BuAer and all of those.* I had an opportunity to observe how the Navy was run. Adolphus Andrews was the chief of the bureau.** Chester Nimitz was a captain and he was the assistant chief, and my boss turned out to be, if anything, even more influential than Comstock had been. My boss was Swede Hazlett.*** He turned out to be one from whom I could learn every day something. He was just a fantastic person. Then I had enough contact with Admiral Nimitz when he was captain to learn a lot from him, too.

Of interest, perhaps, to people nowadays would be how we handled the personnel situation in those days. We had no computers. We had no way of keeping lists. It was plain everyday pen and ink drudgery--really pencil, because you had to erase a lot. We had what we called a slate book, and in that slate book I had to print each year first name, middle initial, last name, rank, and serial number of every ensign and every junior lieutenant in the Navy. That was one column. Duty

---
*BuShips--Bureau of Ships; BuAer--Bureau of Aeronautics.
**Rear Admiral Adolphus Andrews, USN.
***Commander Edward E. Hazlett, Jr., USN.

assignment was the next column. I don't remember all the columns, but there were columns all the way across in a big ledger. After you had made up that whole thing, then you had a column "to be ordered to"--the next duty assignment. Also we had what we called a data card. Each year you had to submit a data card and put all of the various items in there, your marital status, your three requests for next duty, and all such things. Have you heard of these things?

Q: Preference cards.

Admiral Davidson: Preference cards. We just called them data cards at the time. In any event, it was plain drudgery to do all that, and I always printed it so it could be read. All ensigns were either in battleships or cruisers or carriers as junior officers. Some of the jaygees by that time had gotten into destroyers and so on. But if you had in mind transferring anybody, each year I would write a letter to the captain of the Arizona and the captain of the Oklahoma and the captain of the California and say, "It is planned to send Ensign So-and-so to submarine school. It is planned to send So-and-so to flight training." And you gave them a slate of what you planned to do. It was all in a personal letter. That's when I first learned to dictate letters. At first I used to write them out longhand and let the secretary copy them, but I found out that was too time-consuming, so I learned to dictate those letters. But it was very personal. You wrote a letter to every commanding officer and you corresponded with the individual officers a great many, many times, and a lot of very unusual things came up as a result of doing that. But you soon felt that you knew and recognized the name of every young officer in the Navy, because you'd printed his name so many times, where he wanted to go, whether he was married.

Of interest, perhaps, to somebody would be something like this. A letter from a senator came in--I think that he was from Pennsylvania, I've forgotten, it doesn't make any difference--saying that the parents of a young ensign were very, very disturbed because he was on a destroyer on the West Coast and he very much wanted to be on one on the East Coast. I looked up in my book and found the boy had requested to continue duty on the West Coast. He was very happy. So Swede Hazlett, my boss, said, "Why don't you write him a letter and get a personal opinion."

I wrote a letter to this young man. He wrote back. By that time I think I had made lieutenant. He said, "Dear Lieutenant Davidson, The last thing in the world I want is to come east. What the trouble is, I'm engaged to marry a girl out here in Long Beach, and my parents don't want me to marry her, because they've got a girl back there in Johnstown, Pennsylvania, they think I should marry. So they asked the senator to intervene and get me ordered east." So we informed the senator very politely that we had a letter from the boy himself that gave us his reason that he was very much in love and intended to get married out there, and that he would not like to be sent back. The senator understood. That was one of the many types of little things that came up.

Captain Nimitz had a letter from a senator once requesting something, which he sent down to me to prepare a reply for his signature. I was pretty much green in the job, and the day after it went up for his signature, he appeared in the office and sat on the corner of my boss's desk, and said to me, "John, I have this letter you prepared for my signature. Before I sign it, I wonder if you've ever heard the story about the difference between a lady and a diplomat."

I said, "No, sir."

He said, "Well, if a lady says 'no,' she means 'maybe.' When she says 'maybe,' she means 'yes.' If she says 'yes', she ain't no lady. With a diplomat, if he says 'yes,' he means 'maybe.' If he says 'maybe,' he means 'no.' If he says 'no,' he ain't no diplomat."

So while I was digesting that, then he turned to me and he said, "Do you think you could rephrase that letter?" Because what I think I had said was no in the letter to the senator, and he didn't feel we should be that undiplomatic. He was a wonderful guy.

Q: What else do you recall about him?

Admiral Davidson: A lot of just little things. I lived in an apartment on Columbia Road, right where it joins Connecticut Avenue, and California Street. I used to come out of my apartment and walk across to the intersection of these streets and pick up a bus to go down to the Main Navy.

One morning when I was still a young jaygee, I guess, Admiral Nimitz was getting off the bus right there. He said to me, "Come and walk with me. You need the exercise." So I walked all the way down to Main Navy Building, which was a "pretty fur piece," and it became a habit every morning. He lived out in Chevy Chase. He took the bus in that far and then walked the rest of the way to get his exercise, and I walked with him. I don't remember what we talked about, but it was a privilege to walk with a man like that. I didn't realize he was going to be commander in chief some day, but he was a captain, assistant chief of the bureau. I walked with him every morning, but in the afternoon I didn't, because we didn't always leave anywhere near the same time. He was accustomed to walking back up that hill almost to that same point and then catching the bus home.

One very hot summer morning I decided, "It's too hot to walk, because by the time I get there, I'll be soaking wet." We wore civilian clothes in those days before the war, of course. I decided I wouldn't walk. He got off the bus just about the time I was going to get on it. He said, "What are you going to do?"

I said, "Well, I thought I'd ride this morning, Captain. It's so hot, if I walk I'll be soaking wet by the time I get there." We didn't have air-conditioning, of course, in the Navy Department.

He said, "If you are not soaking wet when you get there, how long after you're in your office will it take you to get soaking wet?"

And I said, "About 20 minutes."

He said, "What's 20 minutes?" So I walked with him. That's another little memory I have of Admiral Nimitz.

Q: Was he fond of telling these stories that he is so famous for during the walk?

Admiral Davidson: Great. Great. I don't know whether this is a good place to put in another story about Admiral Nimitz and his aide, who was Gene Fluckey.* Have you ever interviewed him?

Q: No. I'd like to.

Admiral Davidson: He's here in town, you know. He would be just full of stories. At the risk of stealing one of his thunders, let me tell you a little story that Admiral Nimitz told himself

---

*Commander Eugene B. Fluckey, USN.

at a dinner in his honor, and I can't remember--the Statler Hotel, perhaps, in Washington, my wife and I were there--at a time when Gene Fluckey was his aide. Perhaps he was telling the story long after this, but he told that story of something that happened when Gene Fluckey was his aide and he was CNO. It seems that he had to go to Richmond, Virginia, to make a speech one day. Mrs. Nimitz was to accompany him, and they had a beautiful, big sedan. The seats were covered with white seat covers and all that sort of thing. Gene Fluckey hopped in the front seat with the driver, and the Nimitzes were in the back seat, and they went to Richmond.

On the way home, they were ahead of schedule, and Gene said, "Admiral, we go practically past my home here in Arlington [or Alexandria]. Could I interest you in stopping and having a glass of iced tea and saying hello to my wife and my little girl?"

Admiral Nimitz said, "We'd be glad to." So according to Admiral Nimitz, who was telling the story, he went in and it was rather warm, they sat down, and they had their iced tea. Marjorie wasn't home, and neither was the daughter at that point. The daughter was a little girl. All of a sudden, the daughter came in, and she had almost every child in the neighborhood with her. She had at least three or four. It sounded like there were a dozen, but at least three or four children with her. They were all introduced to Admiral and Mrs. Nimitz. Then Gene thought it was time to shoo them out. He shooed them out, and they left via the kitchen. Within about five minutes, Admiral Nimitz said, "Gene, what's the water doing coming under the door?" Here was water flowing from the kitchen into the living room under the door.

He ran out there, and what the children had done, they had stopped up the kitchen sink with a stopper, and they were sailing a boat in it, but they had gone off and left the water running. It overflowed, and the whole kitchen was about yea deep. According to Gene, Admiral Nimitz took off his coat and rolled up his sleeves and helped Gene clean up the water.

Well, then it came time to leave, and they walked out the front door. The driver jumped out and opened the back door of the car for Admiral and Mrs. Nimitz to get in. Gene had two long-haired dogs, little but long-haired. The neighbors had just fertilized their yards with something that smelled very much like manure, and the dogs had been over there rolling in it, and they jumped in the car first. Anyway, it ended up that the Nimitzes had to get in the front seat with the driver, and Gene stayed home. They had to get in the front seat with the driver, who took them back to their quarters.

I was at that time the senior submarine detail officer, and Gene called me in the morning and said, "Have you got a good job for me someplace at sea?" He said, "I'll tell you all about it sometime. I wouldn't be surprised if Admiral Nimitz would ask for a new aide today." That's the story that Admiral Nimitz himself passed on.

    Let's see. Where were we?

Q: We were talking about him as the assistant to Adolphus Andrews. What do you remember about Andrews?

Admiral Davidson: Sort of a tough, tough, difficult person to really know at all. I don't think I knew him. I remember only two or three little incidents. One incident was that with the graduating classes--and I can be wrong of what years, but I believe '30, '31, '32--no, not '32, because my last wife was married to a boy in '32 and they were married right after graduation--but some place along the line, they made a decision that when you were graduated, you would serve under a revocable commission. I think it was for two years. At the end of two years, you would take an examination, and the results of that examination would count a certain percentage toward your standing and rank, and your fitness reports would count the other percentage. Among other things, it said while serving under a revocable commission, the following reasons may--it didn't say will--but said may be considered cause for revoking your commission. One of those was marriage. In other words, they were telling boys that they couldn't get married the first two years. Actually, by law they could not forbid them getting married. The only thing the Navy could do is say, "If you do get married, we probably won't want you." If you're under revocable commission, there's no problem. You can just be let go.

The first thing that came up while I was the assistant submarine detail officer, and when I was the detail officer for all ensigns and jaygees, the first thing that came up was a young lady called the Superintendent of the Naval Academy and said, "Will you make my husband come back to me?"

And the Superintendent said, "Your husband is who?"

"Well, he graduated last June, and we were married, and he's gone off to sea and he doesn't even answer my letters."

So the Superintendent dutifully reported this to the bureau. So we checked with the boy and found he admitted, yes, he was married. So Adolphus Andrews had to make the decision, and he decided we should revoke his commission. Well, that was sort of sad, but that upset the applecart somehow. I don't know the things that went on in between, but one fine morning Adolphus Andrews called down to our office and said, "I had a telephone call at 2:00 a.m. from the Baltimore Sun. The informant said that he had definite information that at least 100 ensigns serving under revocable commissions were married, and what were we going to do about it." So Adolphus Andrews turned the job over to me to find out.

Well, after a long talk with Swede Hazlett, my boss, and also Captain Nimitz, we decided the thing to do was take that data card and see what we could find on the data card, because there was a paragraph in there, "marital status." In going through that, we found 18 or 19 who had left it blank. So they hadn't falsified anything; they just hadn't filled it in. So we made the decision to send that data card back via the young officer's commanding officer. This was a little controversial. We thought maybe we should send it to the boy. But we talked about such things as we don't want to put him in the position where if he's married, he'll say no and get in worse trouble. So we sent it via the commanding officer and asked the commanding officer to find out what the answer should be.

Well, I think of those, we got back about--maybe we sent more than 18 or 19, because it seems to me we had to dismiss 18 out of two or three classes that were involved, because they were ensigns three years. In any event, we had to dismiss those boys. It was sort of a difficult thing. Adolphus Andrews, I don't think, had any choice, because the paper was going to hound him. We solved it all. The only thing that ever came out of that, I'm not going to mention his name here--well, no, I guess he's dead now, but anyway, one of our very, very fine ex-football players was in that group, and his card came back listing himself as single. Not long thereafter, the Navy football coach from here, or he had been coach at one time, I don't think he still was, he was in the office talking to the boss, and he said he had heard about this business and he said, "So-and-so and his wife live right across the street from me."

And Swede Hazlett said, "So-and-so and his wife?"

He said, "I said So-and-so and his girlfriend." So we were pretty sure that maybe he falsified it. We never followed up on it. We just felt that it was going to involve way too much to get a scandal like that going.

Q: I'm wondering what was the reason for not allowing marriage. What was the rationale for that?

Admiral Davidson: The only thing I can think of is we were paid so little and it would be very difficult to support a wife. Also I think there was going to be a lot of separation. I don't remember why they picked it. Of course, they couldn't forbid it. As I say, they could say, "We don't want you if you do get married," but by law you can't forbid a person from marriage. I don't know why we had the revocable commission. You see, going back a little bit, when the class of '28 and the class of '29 were graduated, we were just a handful. 1928 had about 180, we had about 240 in '29, and then all of a sudden we had big classes again--700, 800, 900. It was Depression time, absolute Depression time, you know, from '30 to '33 or so.

Q: A good many in the class of '33 didn't get commissioned.

Admiral Davidson: Half of '33 were not commissioned. Eventually all were permitted to come back, pretty much, those who wanted to. They were split. We had '33 A, B, and C. C were the group that came in and became very much behind their time, because '33B were commissioned just before '34, so they really didn't lose anything. '33C not only didn't come in just before '35, they came in after '35. So they became the top of '36, really. They were about three years behind.

I can't answer that question as to why, but those are my memories of the way it happened in those days.

Q: Another figure that came in there at BuNav was Sunshine Murray.* Do you recall him?

Admiral Davidson: Ah! Sunshine Murray relieved Swede Hazlett during my tenure. I do want to say a little bit about Swede Hazlett first. Swede Hazlett was the class of 1915, and he was a submarine officer. He had grown up from boyhood with Dwight Eisenhower in a little town out in Kansas.** As I recall Swede's account of this, and I've since heard other people try to give a slight variation of it, they went through high school together. They were boyhood friends, and they stuck together through thick and thin. Swede received an appointment to the Naval Academy,

---

*Commander Stuart S. Murray, USN, later admiral, is the subject of a two-volume U.S. Naval Institute oral history.
**Dwight D. Eisenhower, promoted to General of the Army in 1944, was later the 34th President of the United States, serving from January 1953 to January 1961.

and Ike received an appointment to both the Naval Academy and to West Point. My memory of Swede's account to me is that he and Ike arrived in Annapolis together and looked the place over, and Swede stayed. Ike said, "Well, I think I'll go up to West Point and look it over and compare." He ended up taking the appointment to West Point in the same class, the class of '15. Swede had told me about this, and many years later, when I was on duty here at the Naval Academy as head of department, Ike was elected President. Swede, by this time, had had to retire while he was my boss, because he had a very, very severe heart attack. The aorta blew up and he had to retire.*

When Ike was elected President, he was on this trip before being sworn in, and he wrote a personal letter to Swede, who at that time was retired and living down in Chapel Hill, North Carolina, where, after he had retired from the Navy, he had taught for a while. He wrote to Swede and asked him if he would recommend somebody to be a naval aide, and Swede then wrote to me and said, "I have written to Ike and recommended you. I don't know anything about what he's going to do about it, but I recommended you, and you'd better talk to Admiral Turner Joy, the Superintendent, your boss, and alert him that it's quite possible you might be jerked out of there in the middle of the year."**

---
*Commander Hazlett was retired from active duty in January 1939. In June 1943, he was promoted on the retired list to the rank of captain.
**Vice Admiral C. Turner Joy, USN, Superintendent of the Naval Academy from 1952 to 1954.

So I went to see Turner Joy, and he said, "BuPers has promised me they wouldn't do these things, but if the President of the United States asks for somebody, he's going to get him."*

So we sat on pins and needles, wondering what was going to happen. Well, finally, Swede got a reply, which was written by Ike longhand, which I had to return to Swede because he wanted it for his archives. I didn't even make a picture copy of it. It was a most amusing letter. It said, "Dear Swede, I have no doubt that Captain Davidson would be a very, very, very fine aide. However, I am not looking for military advice; I'm going to get that from the Joint Chiefs of Staff. What I'm looking for is somebody to light cigarettes and hold coats. I don't think I want a captain or a colonel. I want somebody for just that purpose--to light cigarettes and hold coats, and I'll get my advice from the Joint Chiefs of Staff. Furthermore, it's been my experience that big gnats beget little gnats ad infinitum." I remember that paragraph.

So later, when he came down to visit Turner Joy and play golf with him, I had an opportunity to talk to President Eisenhower about all of that sort of business. In fact, the interesting

---
*BuPers--Bureau of Naval Personnel.

thing was, the President took Ned Beach.* So I don't know whether Ned thought he was being picked to hold coats and light cigarettes or not.

Q: Any more on Hazlett?

Admiral Davidson: Hazlett lived on for quite a while. Then he died of a combination of his heart and cancer, I believe.** But he was just a tremendous influence on my career. He had the ability to persuade people to do things they didn't want to do. He always told me that the sign of a very good detail officer was one who could issue a set of orders to an officer to a job he didn't want and have the officer come and thank you from the bottom of his heart.

One of the cute stories I remember about him was in the detail business. He was trying to fill a job in Guantanamo Bay. The head of the detail office had asked for a captain for some job down in Guantanamo Bay, and nobody seemed to want it. It was not one of the jobs that was sought after, and it was not one of the stepping-stones to flag rank. So he wrote and offered two or three different captains other, even worse, assignments. They

---

*Commander Edward L. Beach, USN, submariner, the author of Submarine! (New York: Henry Holt & Company, 1952) and the novel Run Silent, Run Deep (New York: Henry Holt & Company, 1955).
**Captain Hazlett died 2 November 1958 at the naval hospital in Bethesda, Maryland.

all came back, "Oh, no, don't, please don't." And he finally picked out one of them and wrote back and said, "Well, I realize why you don't want it. I'll tell you what. I can probably keep you out of it if you'll only go to Guantanamo."

Whereupon, the guy came back, "I'd be delighted to go to Guantanamo."

One of the other ones I remember distinctly, because he showed it to me. He was trying to find somebody for the submarine job in the Philippines, and he picked out a number-one submarine officer that he felt would like the job, and it would be a great job for him. He wrote him a letter and said, "I plan to issue orders to you for this job out in the Philippines."

He received in reply about a three-page letter with all of the reasons he couldn't go to the Philippines--his children were the wrong age, the financial situation wasn't right, and his wife's health wasn't right. Everything was wrong. This whole letter, "Please don't send me." Then there was a small scrap of paper tucked in the envelope at the bottom, "Dear Swede, I'd love it."

He said, "Obviously he's going to say to his wife, 'That old SOB Swede Hazlett, I thought he was a friend of mine.'"

But anyway, Swede was a very, very--everybody loved him, but he was pretty astute as how to get people to thank him for things they didn't want.

Davidson #2 - 129

Q: So you apparently learned a fair amount of the submarine detail business along with the junior officers.

Admiral Davidson: This is the reason I was later ordered to be submarine detail officer, because I had been there and been all through it. During the tail end of the war, that's what Bob Rice was doing, and they tried to get him out of there.* I protested to Admiral Lockwood, because I had been promised a division and a wolf pack out in the Pacific. Instead, I was ordered to Washington. Lockwood said, "Well, you're going because you don't require any breaking in. You can go back there and relieve Bob Rice and just pick up where you left off years ago."

Q: We're about to talk about Murray, back in the late Thirties.

Admiral Davidson: Then Sunshine Murray came in. In many, many respects he was just another Swede Hazlett. He was just such a wonderful guy, and I thoroughly enjoyed working for him. He saved my neck once that I know of. Old C.S. Freeman, believe it or not, walked in the office one day and was looking for a flag lieutenant.** I think I was still a lieutenant then. He was looking for a flag lieutenant. He saw me there and he remembered

---
*Captain Robert H. Rice, USN. Davidson took over from him in the Bureau of Naval Personnel in early 1945.
**Rear Admiral Charles S. Freeman, USN, destined to be Commander Submarine Force U.S. Fleet in the latter part of 1937.

having had me as an ensign on board the battleship, and he knew I was a submariner, and he said, "Wouldn't you like to come and be my flag lieutenant?"

And Sunshine spoke up and said, "Well, you know how to pick 'em, Admiral, but he can't go. We can't spare him. He's half of the office." This is when I was a junior.

So the finale to that story was Freeman went to be Commander Submarines, and I went down to Panama to be the exec of the S-45 boat and later the skipper of the S-44.* Freeman came through on an inspection trip and said, "I thought you were indispensable in Washington."

Q: Any more on Murray, on how he ran the thing?

Admiral Davidson: No. He followed very much the same pattern as Swede did. There were some interesting things in the job with me as assistant there. Maybe this is worth bringing out. We had far more applicants for submarine school than we could handle, so we had a selection board to select, from the applicants for submarine school, those that we would send. In the Bureau of Aeronautics at the time, there were two commanders. One of them was Commander Sallada, and the other one was Commander

---

*Fifty-one S-class submarines were commissioned between 1920 and 1922, but were assigned numbers instead of the more familiar names which were given to the submarines constructed later.

Mitscher.* But in any event, they were concerned because they didn't have a selection board for Pensacola, and they learned that I sat there picking the class for Pensacola every time. So they decided to raise some objections. Sunshine was very good in defending me on this thing. What was going on was exactly this: aviators were taking, I believe, 80 a year at that time. I was able to show that every young officer who requested flight training, who qualified physically was being ordered. He might not be ordered to the first class he requested, but he eventually was ordered. So there was no need for a selection because they were all going to get there anyway, whereas in the submarine force, we didn't take but about 50 a year, I guess, and we had far more applicants than we could handle. So we were able to talk down Commanders Sallada and Mitscher. I think that was the beginning of my having a little bit of a reputation as anti-aviator, but I never was anti-aviator.

Q: You've mentioned this process where you had the big book and you jotted down the impending assignments. What was the basis for those assignments? How did you decide who went where?

Admiral Davidson: Trying to give each officer as good an overall experience as possible and still be somewhat within his desires.

---

*Commander Harold B. Sallada, USN, later admiral; Commander Marc A. Mitscher, USN, later admiral.

Very often an officer needed to be sent someplace for his own good that maybe he didn't want, but the main problem, of course, was to fill all the billets. That was the first item, fill all the billets somehow. Then, of course, the various demands for submarines and for aviation were going to deplete the ships each year, a certain number, and if you took them from destroyers to go to Pensacola, then you had to grab them from battleships to go fill up the destroyers, because the destroyers couldn't get along with any fewer officers. Then, of course, there was always postgraduate school coming along and shore duty. You were guaranteed, in those days, shore duty at the end of seven years.

Q: What percentage would you guess of the personal desires were fulfilled?

Admiral Davidson: I can't put a percentage on it, but very high, actually. We worked very hard to try to please people, and we wrote to them and found out their wishes in personal letters, which wouldn't be in their records, which was a good way to do it. They weren't able to do that on the destroyer desk, for instance, and the senior desk. After you got to be a lieutenant, you went on up to what they called the senior desk--lieutenants, lieutenant commanders, commanders. Then you went up to the captain desk. But you just couldn't possibly give somebody everything he wanted, because he might be too greedy.

I do remember one thing. Sunshine Murray won a bet off me one time. There was a young jaygee, I think, who was at PG school or someplace, and he was being ordered to the West Coast to a ship, and Sunshine said, "Why don't you call him up and ask him to give you a memo on how he would like to travel, how much leave he would like, and everything. Just make him real happy. Then I'll bet you that before he gets there, he'll ask for modifications to his orders." So we picked on somebody and gave him his choice, and he spelled it out. He wanted to travel by his own automobile with his wife, and he wanted X number of days' leave, and he was going to be in St. Louis for a certain length of time, which was his home. We wrote the orders exactly to fit everything. Sure enough, he telephoned from St. Louis and had to ask for a modification. Well, there was a real good reason--his mother was very, very ill and wasn't expected to live, so that wasn't really a fair test. But still, it was true so often. If you let somebody write his own orders, he couldn't do it without asking for some change.

Q: Was the Navy as good about taking care of dependents on these travels as they are now?

Admiral Davidson: I think maybe better. We were allowed to travel by automobile at no additional expense to the government. That's what it always read. But actually, you were much better off to drive. You weren't allowed very much, five cents a mile, but that was better than trying to come across with the government paying your way on a train. The other big advantage to traveling by automobile was, if you were ordered from, say, the West Coast to the East Coast and you were given 30 days' delay in reporting to your new job, part of it was not considered as leave, wasn't charged against you. I've forgotten. The part that it would take if you went by train or something. That didn't count as leave.

Q: Travel time.

Admiral Davidson: Yes. It was more travel time. I've forgotten some of those things.

Q: Probably more time was allowed if you were going by auto than by train.

Admiral Davidson: Right.

Q: The fleet was expanding in the late Thirties. How did you accommodate that?

Admiral Davidson: I was gone from the detail office by '38, so I don't remember what we did to get expanded. By the time I left there, the Navy was still fairly small. I seem to recall that when I first went back as an assistant in the detail office, we used to refer to the total Navy count of officers as 11,000, and that included doctors, chaplains, supply officers, and so on, which is nothing when you stop and think about it. Take the submarine force. I remember the figures on that. We had 50 submarines, and the allowance was four-and-a-half officers per submarine. There was a very definite reason for it. You had a division of six S-boats, and the allowance was four-and-a-half officers. What they did was, on three of them they put five officers, and on the other three they put four. And if somebody got sick on one of those fours, you'd move a person from one of the fives to fill the billet. That's the way it was. That was the allowance on the books--four-and-a-half officers.

Q: The Bureau of Navigation as a whole probably didn't have more than a dozen or so detail officers, did it?

Admiral Davidson: As far as the detailing of officers, I don't think but five of us. There was a captain, a commander, and his assistant was a lieutenant. In the submarine desk there was Commander Hazlett and I was his assistant. That was five. Then we did have an aviation desk, and I don't think he had an assistant. He was just a lieutenant commander without any assistant. So that's about all we had to handle the assignments.

The assignment of supply officers and chaplains and so on came on recommendations from the various bureaus: the Bureau of Supplies and Accounts, Medicine and Surgery, and so on. We may have prepared their orders for them over there. We had a pretty extensive order-writing department.

One of the big jobs, and I learned a lot from it, was the reviewing of fitness reports in order to select people for jobs. For the choice jobs that everybody wanted, you picked them according to their performance.

Q: Do you think that that insight as a junior officer helped you better on your own career, knowing what type of things people look for?

Admiral Davidson: Right. Right. Yes. I don't think there's any question about it. I think that it helped me, and it also made me realize, when I was writing fitness reports on other people, how important it could be, because a lot of fitness reports were written that didn't seem to mean very much. They were written by people who, to use the old expression, believed in never using one word when 16 would do.

Q: I've heard some detailers say that just by human nature an individual would come by and make a personal visit and express his desires, and so forth, that as often as not, you would try to take care of him.

Admiral Davidson: I think we did. Of course, we had a lot of help from the outside. Not only from congressmen, senators, and so on, but we had a lot of senior naval officers who thought they ought to have a hand in running the various things. For instance, we established a rule that before you could be ordered to command a fleet type submarine, like the ones we fought World War II with, you had to have been selected for lieutenant commander at least, not necessarily promoted, but you had to be selected. So Sunshine had selected Oz Colclough to be skipper of one of these boats that was building in Mare Island, I believe, when the president of the Naval War College, who was a rear admiral, asked for Oz Colclough to be his aide.* Sunshine told him that Oz had been selected as one of the exceptionally good people who was going to get command of a fleet type submarine just as soon as he was promoted. Therefore, he thought it would be best for Oz's career that he go on and take this command. Whereupon, the admiral replied, "You let me take care of Colclough's career." And it ended up, Colclough ended up to be his aide, but he later came back and got his command.

---

*Lieutenant Commander Oswald S. Colclough, USN. The president of the Naval War College in Newport, Rhode Island, was Rear Admiral Charles P. Snyder, USN.

Davidson #2 - 138

Q: And became a flag officer.

Admiral Davidson: And became a flag officer. So you had a lot of that sort of thing. I even found one a little bit like that on me. I had forgotten how many times I put in for submarine school, but I put in in '31 and in '32 and in '33, when they put out the call. I found in my record a letter signed by an Admiral Luke McNamee.* It was written to a Captain Johnson in the Bureau of Navigation, inquiring as to my prospects of being assigned to submarine school.** The reply to the letter said that a review of my record indicates that I was well qualified to be selected for submarine school with the exception that there was some doubt about my medical history. The same thing was plaguing me for submarines. So then I had to get a special exam for submarines. I'm surprised I'm still alive after reading all these medical reports on me. The very last one that I saw just said, "Following defect: underweight." I wish they could say that right now.

Q: There have been so many rumors about what role the Green Bowl Society played in assignments.*** You can address that because you were making the assignments.

---
*Rear Admiral Luke McNamee, USN.
**Captain Alfred W. Johnson, USN, was assistant to the chief of the bureau.
***The Green Bowl Society was alleged to be a secret Naval Academy club in which the members pledged to help each other's promotions and assignments.

Admiral Davidson: The first I knew of the Green Bowl was when there was an airplane accident of some sort, and in the possession of the pilot was a list of Green Bowlers. Somebody decided to send that to the bureau. It ended up in Captain Nimitz's office, as I remember. These are just faint memories. An order was issued that under no circumstances would anybody on that Green Bowlers list be ordered to any job where he could influence the assignment of officers, which meant that they couldn't be ordered to the detail office. One of my very closest friends was a Green Bowler. He denies that there was any such business at all, but in the detail office we all had the list in our desk of Green Bowlers that had come from this airplane accident. They were not to be considered as candidates for duty in the Bureau of Navigation. That's all I know about the Green Bowlers. I think one of the persons that tried to expose it was John Crommelin.*

Q: He made a big effort.

Admiral Davidson: Yes. John Crommelin made a big effort. Of course, I later in life worked for Henry Crommelin and knew him well, and I knew young Charles before he was killed.**

---
*Captain John G. Crommelin, Jr., USN.
**Rear Admiral Henry Crommelin, USN; Commander Charles L. Crommelin, USN, killed by enemy action in the Asiatic area during World War II.

Q: That became a virtual crusade with him in the late Forties.

Admiral Davidson: Yes. Well, I think John got a little bit excited.

Q: Do you think the whole business has been overrated?

Admiral Davidson: I think it was snuffed out, probably by Nimitz. I think it was actually snuffed out. I think that it could have been quite a thing. It started, apparently, mostly as a group of athletes at the Naval Academy to gather someplace, some house out in town. But the danger was that they were supposed to have taken some sort of an oath to always promote their fellow Green Bowlers.

Q: They could do that by fitness reports, even if not by assignments.

Admiral Davidson: Yes.

Q: Aggressiveness was very much prized in the wartime skippers. Was that an aptitude that was sought in the Thirties?

Admiral Davidson: In the Thirties, I think submarine skippers were evaluated on their ability to hit targets with torpedoes, only to find out after the war started that those that were hitting were missing, and those that were missing were hitting.

I don't know whether we ran through that story before or not. We found that the torpedo was running much deeper than set, and they were measuring the hits by the bubbles and how long it took the bubbles to come to the surface. If the bubbles came up in the right spot, you called it a hit. Actually, if the torpedo was 20 feet deeper than that, the bubbles would come up much later than when they should have. The British used to laugh at us a little bit in the early days of the war, but once a week we were given new instructions on how to adjust our torpedoes and how to aim them, and how to do this and how to do that. That's too bad that we didn't have that all ironed out before the war.

Q: Through your conversations, then, with Commander Hazlett and Murray, the ability to hit targets was the thing?

Admiral Davidson: That was the thing. For instance, in peacetime, one of the supposedly outstanding skippers was Mort Mumma, class of '25. Mort Mumma never missed. He was supposedly the hottest there was. Mort Mumma folded up completely during the war, turned his boat over to his exec.*

Q: He had the Sailfish, didn't he?

Admiral Davidson: I think he did.

Q: That was the old Squalus. What was the impact in the submarine community when the Squalus went down?**

Admiral Davidson: I was just reading a letter I wrote to somebody whom I was welcoming, Ian Eddy, to be my exec on the S-44, and I said I'd just read of the Squalus and it's a very disturbing thing.*** Actually, after studying all I could about it, it was no different from any other casualty. It was a personnel error, that's all. We have so many backup means for material casualties. If the personnel observed all of the safety requirements, Squalus should never have happened. He was diving the boat without making any effort to close the inboard inductions. The main induction failed, and if they had done what

---

*Lieutenant Commander Morton C. Mumma, Jr., USN, while in command of the USS Sailfish (SS-192), broke down mentally during a Japanese depth charge attack. He was credited with sinking a Japanese destroyer, but during the counterattack, he turned command of Sailfish over to his executive officer. Mumma was relieved of command, but he later went on to distinguish himself as the commander of the PT boats. He retired as a rear admiral.

**Squalus, under the command of Lieutenant Oliver F. Naquin, USN, was exercising dives, when she became partly flooded and sank in 243 feet of water on 23 May 1939. Twenty-three men died, but 33, including Naquin, were rescued by the McCann Rescue Chamber. The submarine later was raised, refurbished, and renamed the Sailfish.

***Lieutenant Ian C. Eddy, USN.

we were supposed to do, close the inboard inductions, the boat would have been very heavy, but it wouldn't have been flooded. And yet they made a hero out of Oliver Naquin in his hometown. He apparently was attempting to establish some diving time records. He was going to be the best boat we had when it came to diving. He was going to go down faster than anybody else.

Q: You said you went to be exec of the S-45. Was that an assignment you arranged for yourself in BuNav?

Admiral Davidson: Yes. The rule that we had established was that my class should serve one year as exec before we got command, and so I picked the S-45, and Sunshine Murray lived up to his promise and sent me as skipper of the S-44 a year later. While I was in the S-45, I was the exec and navigator. I guess I was even first lieutenant for a while until other people came along. Johnny Waterman was my skipper.* He indirectly always paid me a big compliment. Johnny Waterman was a PG engineer, and every time anything happened to the engine, he would send for me and say, "Take over the bridge," and he would run back and grab a monkey wrench and start repairing the engine.** I was always very sorry for his engineer officer, Bladen Claggett, later famed for being the skipper of the boat that took off the crew of the

---

*Lieutenant John R. Waterman, USN.
**PG--postgraduate.

Darter when it went aground in the South China Sea during the war.*

Anyway, I served as the exec of the S-45 for a year, and then I went across the pier and took command of the S-44. At the time I took command, the boat was immobile. It had the after soft patch off and they had pulled one cell of the after battery because it had a cracked jar. I think it took five or six days after I had command before we had it running again. But I think the day of the change of command was one of the real great thrills of my life. Right after the ceremony, Garcia, who was a Filipino mess boy, came up to me and said, "May I take your sword, Captain?" And that was the first time anybody ever called me captain. I was pretty thrilled to be the boss man for the first time, and sort of the answer to why you go in submarines--early command.

I had the S-44 boat for a year, I guess, just a year, and then we made some fleet problems in the Caribbean and did a lot of our cruising and torpedo shooting down in Panama Bay on the Pacific side, going through the canal a great many times. One of the interesting sidelights to going through the canal was we never could convince the pilots of the idiocyncrasies of S-boats. If you were in a normal ship and you wanted to come in alongside

---

*Lieutenant (junior grade) Bladen D. Claggett, USN. The incident involving the Darter occurred on 25 October 1944, during the Battle of Leyte Gulf, when she went aground on Bombay Shoal. Her crew was rescued by the USS Dace (SS-247), commanded by Claggett.

a pier at an angle, and you wanted to swing the stern in, to put your starboard side alongside, you would normally come in at a little angle, and then when you backed, you backed your outboard screw and put your rudder over and just slid in. Well, in an S-boat, you didn't do that. It was the opposite. You put the rudder over all right, but you backed the inboard screw. The pilots would never believe that. They would just not believe that that's what you did, so they would back the outboard screw and the tail would go out. I remember talking to this pilot until I was blue in the face. We called it a Chinese turn. If you wanted to increase the speed of the turn on an S-boat, you would back the outboard screw instead of the inboard screw. It didn't make any sense, but it had something to do with the stern planes and the rudder and all, and the way the wash hit it when you backed. We went through the canal a lot back and forth, and we all had very nice quarters there at Coco Solo.

It was during that period that my wife became quite ill, and I eventually had to take about ten days' leave and fly her up and turn her over to her family with the baby, and go back, and I lived alone. I moved out of quarters and moved into what was called the BOQ.* After a very short period of time, I found that the 7:00 to 1:00 working hours, followed by two beers and lunch and then a sound sleep until 4:00 was deadly, because it was hot,

---

*BOQ--Bachelor officers' quarters.

we didn't have air-conditioning. When you woke up, you felt like who-shot-John. So I started playing 18 holes of golf every afternoon without the beer and without the nap, and that was very good for my golf game, at least, and also kept me out of a lot of trouble, I'm sure.

Q: Fairly good for your health, too.

Admiral Davidson: Yes. Then after a year of that, which was pretty much normal operations, I think there's one little interesting antecdote. I had an officer, who was my engineer in the S-44, whose name was Mose House.* Mose was one of the people that couldn't smile to save his neck. The crew in the engine room detested him. They just thought, "How could he have such a disagreeable temperament?" Mose, when he had the duty, would be up at the gangway to meet me when I came on board in the morning. When he'd say, "Good morning," I took to saying to him, "Are you greeting me or bawling me out?" And then he would almost snicker.

Q: Almost.

Admiral Davidson: Almost. Well, we received a group of young

---

*Lieutenant (junior grade) Arthur C. House, Jr., USN.

officers who came down there from submarine school. Each boat got a new officer. I got one by the name of Barney Flenniken.* He had just been married and he had about the cutest little wife you ever saw in your life, practically on his honeymoon. Among other things, we were all issued bicycles there on the submarine base to provide the transportation--we lived in apartments or quarters--transportation to and from our apartments down to the piers. One morning we were to get under way at 8:00 o'clock, and young Tommy Baskett was the officer of the deck, and I was standing down on deck.** The submarine base struck eight bells, and I think it was a phonograph that played "The Star-Spangled Banner." We all stood at attention, and it was by then one or two minutes after 8:00 o'clock. The orders for the day said under way at 8:00 o'clock. Tommy Baskett leaned over the rail and said, "Captain, Barney has not yet come aboard. What are your orders?"

I said, "Under way on time, Baskett."

So he said, "Take in all lines. All back two-thirds."

About that time the exec said to me, "Here comes Barney down the pier on a bicycle." By that time we were about 15 feet from the side of the pier.

Tommy Baskett said, "What shall I do, Captain?"

I said, "Continue to sea." So we backed down and left old

---

*Ensign Clifton W. Flenniken, Jr., USN.
**Lieutenant (junior grade) Thomas S. Baskett, USN.

Barney standing there looking at us. He was fresh out of submarine school, dying, just dying. I'm sure he thought he was going to get a general court-martial for missing ship or something.

So when we came in, he was there to handle the first line that was sent over. He practically helped tie up the ship. When I came down from the bridge and walked across the gangway, I didn't say anything to him at all.

Q: The Comstock technique.

Admiral Davidson: Didn't say boo. About two days later, Ian Eddy, my exec, said to me, "Hey, captain, you've got to say something to Barney. His wife says he's going crazy. He can't sleep; he wonders when he's going to get his court-martial."

So I said, "Okay." When Barney came in the wardroom, I said, "Barney, I bet you'll never miss a ship again in your life, will you?"

He said, "No, sir." And that was the end of that incident.

Q: Eddy was a future athletic director at the Naval Academy. What do you recall about him?

Admiral Davidson: Ian Eddy and I grew up together practically. He and his wife were the godparents of my baby. We were in submarine school together. Ian Eddy was ordered to be my exec when I had the S-44, and then he subsequently became the skipper of the S-45. He relieved Johnny Waterman, to whom I had been exec. I remember him very well. He was always on a diet, not getting anyplace at all. He practically skipped lunch but by 4:00 o'clock in the afternoon he had the steward bring him two sandwiches. His wife was a lovely gal, Wings. We were together here at the Naval Academy when I was head of the English, History, and Government Department. He was the director of athletics. He was very hard of hearing in those days. He had a hearing aid, and when we'd sit in the academic board meetings, he'd turn it down until Admiral Hill would shout at him, and he'd turn it up.* His son once told me, when we were all walking to chapel, he said, "Daddy keeps that little thing in his shirt pocket, and when Mother starts shouting at him, he turns it off." This is a little boy, about that high, telling stories. I used to try to have a garden in back of my quarters there on Porter Road, and he'd come over every morning and help me dig in the garden and tell me all the stories about his father. So I was always up to date on Ian Eddy. God bless his soul, he's gone.**

Q: What do you remember about Panama and the area surrounding the base?

---
*Vice Admiral Harry W. Hill, USN, Superintendent of the Naval Academy from April 1950 to August 1952.
**Eddy, who retired as a rear admiral, died 30 December 1976.

Davidson #2 - 150

Admiral Davidson: I spent a good deal of time going back and forth to Fort Davis to play golf and to Gatun Locks, where there was a golf course, too. We played over the locks and all that sort of thing. What I remember are things that today people wouldn't believe. When my wife and I got down there, I was a lieutenant in the Navy. We had an apartment. We had three servants: we had a cook, we had a nursemaid for the baby, and a laundress. The laundress just came once a week, but the other two came every day. The nursemaid started work about 5:00 o'clock in the morning, whatever time a baby wakes up, and worked until we turned in. We paid those three a total of $33 a month.

Q: But you didn't have a lot to pay them with.

Admiral Davidson: That's true, but $18 for the cook, $12 for the nursemaid, and $3 a month for the laundress. Three dollars a month for the laundress, that's all she got. Well, they were mostly Jamaicans. They toted a lot, and it was just as well to overlook the toting. In other words, they thought it was their right to take home all the scraps of food, and we never had any leftovers.

Q: That was part of the pay.

Admiral Davidson: That was part of it. I learned to drive on the left. I learned that it's a more heinous crime to kill a dog than it is to kill a person while driving an automobile. I enjoyed Panama. We had the two seasons--the dry season and the wet season. In the dry season, the wind blew all the time. It was quite comfortable. I didn't mind the heat down there at all. Ian Eddy used to mind it more than I did, because he had a lot more weight. I didn't mind it much, because I was so skinny it didn't make any difference.

When you had the duty, the duty officer had the duty for six boats, and the enlisted crew were aboard. Those of the duty section would be aboard, but the duty officer would have the duty for all six boats. So each boat had to provide one every sixth day or whatever it was. We had one division commander, and I don't remember which one it was, who insisted that we inspect in white uniforms. This was before the days of the short sleeves in uniforms. We wore the high collar. You can imagine climbing through an S-boat in whites, and you had to climb through six of them, usually along about late afternoon. We all survived, and I enjoyed it.

We made a couple of cruises up through the Caribbean. We went to St. Thomas, the one I remember most. We later had a little submarine base there during World War II.

Q: How was the political situation? How were Americans received in Panama and these other countries?

Davidson #2 - 152

Admiral Davidson: At that time it was fine. We had no problems whatsoever. I don't remember when it started that we began to be sort of persona non grata. Actually, Panama was sort of dependent on us with all the traffic through the canal and so forth. We had our own shipyards down there where we did our overhauls.

Q: How much did the boats depend on the tender?

Admiral Davidson: We didn't have a tender in Panama. We used the submarine base. We had a rescue vessel, the kind that carried the diving bell.

Q: You talked about the screening that officers had to go through to get into submarines, and I presume it was similar for enlisted men. How good were the enlisted men you had those years?

Admiral Davidson: They were just excellent, just really top-notch, and they stayed that way. I think I mentioned the other day, we had the great authority of the commanding officer to declare anybody temperamentally unqualified, and that could cover a multitude of sins. It might be he was physically unqualified, temperamentally unqualified, maybe professionally unqualified, but all you had to do was say he was temperamentally unqualified. No, I can't remember having any real bad ones. Later, in the <u>Blackfish</u>, I had a chief petty officer who was as good a petty officer as I ever saw, who used to go ashore and drink a little too much. Occasionally he had a little trouble ashore, but aboard ship he was just great, until all of a sudden his drinking business caused one problem. The chiefs' quarters were very confined, and there were about four chiefs in this one small room. He started wetting the bunk night after night after night, and the others weren't going to have any of this, so we had to disqualify him. And yet if you wanted something done on that boat, he was the guy who knew how to do it. I don't know whether his drinking caused this or not, but it became a real problem and he couldn't do anything to stop it. He'd sleep too hard and not wake up when it was time to go.

Q: What was the relationship between you and the chief of the boat?*

Admiral Davidson: It had to be about as close, probably almost closer than between me and the exec, in a way. The chief of the boat was an extremely important cog. If you had a good chief of the boat, you probably were going to have a darn good crew. If

---

*The chief of the boat in a submarine is a senior chief petty officer who supervises administration of the crew and serves as a link between the enlisted men and the commanding officer and executive officer.

you didn't have a good chief of the boat, the chances are the crew wasn't going to measure up.

Q: Did you have a gauge on how disciplinary problems were in the submarine force as opposed to the Navy at large?

Admiral Davidson: I don't suppose I have anything. I would think we had less disciplinary problems than they had in big ships. In big ships, you had a conglomeration.

Q: You had people who wanted to be there, too.

Admiral Davidson: That's one of the big things.

Q: And with this threat of disqualification, they had a great incentive for good behavior.

Admiral Davidson: Right. The only time I ever had anything to equal it was later in the Albany. We can get to that later. The conduct of people aboard the Albany was fantastically good. I guess I was just fortunate. I had a lot of good people working for me.

Q: Then you went on from the S-44 and got command of the Mackerel. How did that assignment come about?

Admiral Davidson: According to my submarine friends, once a detail officer, you're always calling your own shots. This was not quite true, because I didn't know anything about the Mackerel, really. I think Sunshine might have been responsible for that. Sunshine is the one who issued my orders to go to the Mackerel. The Mackerel had the same silhouette as the fleet type submarine, but it had only two engines. It didn't have any legs at all. It could just about go to Guantanamo and back, maybe, something like that. It was about the same tonnage as the S-boat, a little bit more, maybe 950 tons, something like that, and it didn't have any speed to speak of. It did have four tubes forward, I believe, and two aft. It had NELSECO--that's the New London Ship and Engine--engines, the old NELSECOs which we had had in S-boats before, but these were modern NELSECOs that you could back down on.* I don't think we had any air-conditioning, but it was quite a comfortable boat, rode well, dove well. Its principal value and the purpose for which it was used was as a training boat for commanding officers. Admiral Tommy Hart had advocated for a long time--he thought the fleet boats were way too big.** This is before he knew how he was going to need them. He thought they were way too big, and he leaned to the smaller

---
    *The New London Ship and Engine Company was formed by the Electric Boat Company to build submarine diesels.
    **Rear Admiral Thomas C. Hart, USN, later admiral, was Chairman, General Board from 1936 to 1939. A submariner, he nevertheless was opposed to the development of newer and larger submarines as impractical and advocated the return to the medium sized submarines of World War I.

boat. He was able to convince somebody that we should build a couple of experimental boats.

Q: This is when he was on the General Board?*

Admiral Davidson: I think he was. I was always told that this was his idea. He came to ride the Mackerel with me one day and asked me how I liked it, and I told him its shortcomings, and he thought that I was probably wrong, that we would all learn to live with this smaller boat. But I was very proud of her as a command, and I took her out on some pretty good cruises--the only boat I ever survived a hurricane in.

Q: Could you describe that, please?

Admiral Davidson: Yes, I could give you an idea. We had been patrolling 450 miles east of Hampton Roads in the Atlantic in the year 1941, when World War II was raging in Europe, and we were loaded with torpedoes, with warheads, with orders to sink any German ships which came within this 400-mile line, whatever it was. I can't remember the exact mileage. The Marlin and Mackerel were out there. We were out there for about two weeks, just a modified war patrol, the U.S. not being at war.

Q: Neutrality patrol.

---

*The General Board was composed of senior naval officers. One of its functions in the period before World War II was to decide on ships' characteristics.

Davidson #2 - 157

Admiral Davidson: Neutrality patrol. So on our way back, I was roughly half a day ahead of Marlin, headed for New London, when the hurricane blew up. So we stayed submerged all day at 200 feet and rolled as much as 20 degrees down there, very miserable. When the battery was beginning to run down and it was obvious that we were going to have to surface--I preferred to surface with a little bit of daylight, so I could see what I was up against. I got the chief of the boat to round up the four or five oldest, most experienced submariners I had, enlisted, because the officers weren't experienced as much as I was. I asked them all to come to the captain's cabin, and I said, "Have any of you ever had to surface in a hurricane?" No, nobody had. But we all decided we would debate the various possibilities of how you would go about it. The consensus was that we should try to come up to periscope depth, get a periscope up, and see if we could determine the direction of the sea exactly, then head the ship into the seas at about two knots on the motors, and then take a chance and surface.

Well, we got up there and still had some daylight left. We picked a course. Everybody looked through the periscope. The exec and I took a look, and maybe one other officer, and we all said, "Well, let's say we ought to be heading northwest." So we put on that course at about two knots and surfaced. The first class quartermaster and I went to the bridge, and as we came out of that hatch and went to the bridge, I swear, I looked up at that angle, off the starboard bow maybe ten degrees, was a whitecap just about to break. It looked like it was going to land right on top of us. So I yelled to the quartermaster to shut the hatch. Well, he had been smarter than I was. I had gone up first. He had another man standing by there with a toggle ready to pull it. I thought he and I would be either washed overboard or crushed or something, but the old boat went right over in a roll. Then it sounded like it hit a stone wall. It stopped dead, then righted itself. As soon as I could possibly do it, I got word to the conning tower to alter the course about ten degrees to the left, and we were headed right into it. After that we rode it just like this--up and down. We eventually were able to ride out the storm that way. When the battery was really getting down, two knots was not using very much, so we were able to ride for several hours, and then we finally were able to get on the engines.

We had a mess down below. We had secured the ship for heavy weather. In spite of that, there were two boxes of tools just spilled all over everything, and we had taken quite a bit of water that had gone down into what we called the motor room, which was below the control room deck. But the worst thing we had done was, when we went over that 45 degrees, we had spilled a little bit of acid out of our batteries. However, we survived it all right. We got everything working, and I was able to report to New London, to ComSubLant, that I was en route at six knots, or something, and on course so and so.*

Shortly thereafter, the old Marlin came on the air. ComSubLant was asking him where he was and how he was doing. Well, I learned later what he did was surface with the seas, and he got pooped right away.** The seas went down the hatch and flooded his control room, knocked out his gyro. The pump room was all flooded, and he was a mess. His message, I always thought, was real wonderful. He gave approximate position, so many miles from New London, steering in the general direction of New London, pooped by the seas, gyro out of commission, this, that, and the other thing. I often thought afterwards, I wonder how he happened to pick to ride with it. Now, if he could have gotten up to about 30 knots, he might have done well to ride with it. But that was a great experience for me in the Mackerel.

Q: What was Admiral Hart's objection to the bigger submarines? It sounds as if he didn't want something as capable as it could be.

Admiral Davidson: I don't know. He was an old-time S-boat sailor, you know, and maybe he just thought they would be easier to handle in battle. I don't know. I don't remember why he felt

---
*ComSubLant--Commander Submarines Atlantic.
**A vessel is pooped when a following sea breaks over her stern and the waves land topside.

so strongly about it. I know he argued with E.J. King about it.*
King was Commander in Chief Atlantic Fleet at the time. He tried
to convince King that we should have a small one. The General
Board, I think, were the ones that determined that we would go
with the fleet type submarines.

Q: You must have had some of the famous World War II skippers
come through your boat as PCOs.**

Admiral Davidson: Oh, gosh, yes. It would be hard to remember
now. I remember Donc Donaho.*** I think he gained a reputation
for never letting any of his officers do anything. He tried to
do everything. I had had that experience a little bit with
Johnny Waterman when I was exec of S-45. He didn't like to let
his officers do much. He didn't trust me, and he didn't trust
most of the younger boys. Donc had that reputation, and I can
see Donc today in the Mackerel, when we were coming in after a
day's torpedo firing with the PCOs, and my officer of the deck
was a kid by the name of Peter Berry.****

New London was quite a tricky place to make a landing. The
piers are sticking out like so from the beach, and you come up

---

*Admiral Ernest J. King, USN, was Commander in Chief Atlantic Fleet from February to December 1941. The USS Mackerel (SS-204) went into commission 31 March 1941.
**PCOs--Prospective commanding officers.
***Lieutenant Glynn R. Donaho, USN, later a flag officer.
****Ensign Howard B. Berry, Jr., USN, later lost in the submarine Cisco (SS-290) in 1943 in the Pacific.

the river and the tide is running full blast this way, maybe, and so if you're going to this side, you've got to really hold it up there to get it alongside. If you're going to go to this side, you'd better come up pretty far off and drift in. Well, young Peter was bringing the boat in, and I was standing on the after cigarette deck talking with Donc. Before I knew it, Donc was jumping up there to tell Peter what to do. Donc was senior to me, but that didn't make any difference. I was the skipper of the ship, and he was a student. He was jumping up, so I had to say, "Leave him alone. Leave him alone, please." We got alongside, and Donc said to me afterwards, "How in God's name do you stand it when somebody's doing such an awful job?"

I said, "Donc, we're alongside. He hasn't nicked a thing. He's been doing this for me for weeks, and he's a real good shiphandler."

Donc said, "Well, I'm glad I don't have your job, because I could never let somebody do that." And I learned from his officers later, he never could let anybody do anything.

There were plenty of PCOs running through the school. Practically every skipper that was being ordered out to the Pacific took a refresher course. The <u>Mackerel</u> and the <u>Marlin</u> were the two PCO boats. We were taking people out all the time. Actually, we didn't have them doing any shiphandling. They were making the torpedo approaches and firing the torpedoes and so on out on Long Island Sound.

Q: What did you have for the target?

Admiral Davidson: We may have had destroyers. They were, of course, exercise heads, and we had to set them to run deep under the target. I think that was it. We used destroyers. It's funny how you can forget certain things.

Q: It would be interesting if you could remember some of the other names and any incidents involving them.

Admiral Davidson: Perhaps I can do that in the future. I've got a submarine history. It has the name of boats and skippers, and perhaps I can remember which ones went through.

Q: Who was running the school at that time?

Admiral Davidson: I wonder if Karl Hensel had gotten up there to the school by that time.* I wouldn't be surprised. My particular--experimental division--they called it, Bob Preacher was the division commander when I got there.** Then he was relieved by Frank Watkins.***

---

*Lieutenant Commander Karl G. Hensel, USN.
**Lieutenant Commander Robert M. Preacher, USN.
***Lieutenant Commander Frank T. Watkins, USN.

Davidson #2 - 163

Q: Frank Watkins spent some time in the detail business also.

Admiral Davidson: Oh, yes. It was later when I was squadron commander that Jimmy Fife was in New London.* It's funny, those names of those skippers, except for Donc Donaho. I probably remember him only because he didn't see how I could stand doing what I was doing.

Q: Didn't you have an encounter with something that either was or was not a German submarine while you were out there?

Admiral Davidson: I read something scolding me for including in a fitness report some mention of that very incident and calling my attention to the fact that such things as that were classified and shouldn't have been in the fitness report.

The Mackerel went down to Norfolk for some reason or other, and as we were proceeding on the surface--my memory's not going to be too good on this, Paul--but as we were proceeding on the surface going in to the entrance to Hampton Roads, the light was very poor and you couldn't see well. The lookout reported a U-boat. We swung around to head for it, and it immediately turned and started heading out to sea, as I recall. We ended up, I believe, firing a couple of fish in the general direction, but

---

*Rear Admiral James Fife, Jr., USN, was Commander Submarines Atlantic from 1947 to 1950.

we had no evidence that we hit it. Except we figured that he couldn't dive, because we were already in far enough so there wasn't deep enough water for him to do much diving, and we wondered what he was doing in there anyway, unless he was just reconnoitering. I was not on the bridge when it was sighted. By the time I got up there, we were ships passing just like so, and we had to swing around completely. Because the Mackerel didn't have that kind of speed, I don't know what this was. It could be it wasn't a U-boat either, but the lookout always thought it was.

Q: Did you get a look at it yourself?

Admiral Davidson: No, just the shadow. I realized it had not dived, but then it did disappear as we followed on out to sea. It disappeared, and I figured by that time it might be in deep enough water. We didn't have any way of locating him once he was down. I never was really convinced what it was, but I had to report what we saw and what we did, so on and so forth.

Q: Could it have been a whale?

Admiral Davidson: I doubt it. The whale would have had to have been riding on the surface, and also I don't know how fast a whale can go, either.

Davidson #2 - 165

Q: What was the atmosphere of that time? Did you consider that war was inevitable?

Admiral Davidson: Oh, yes. This was subsequent to the time that I had been on this patrol, I think, with the hurricane story. I'd have to look up dates to see if I could find out. Yes, there wasn't any question about it. In going to Norfolk, it seems I was forbidden to dive at the sign of an aircraft or something because it would invite attack by U.S. forces, because they were so sure there were U-boats in close to our beach. Later in the <u>Mackerel</u> I went hunting U-boats. I was there when the war started in '41 in Argentia on patrol against U-boats, of all things.* It's dog-eat-dog.

Q: That's quite a contrast to Panama. Could you describe Argentia, please?

Admiral Davidson: Yes. In Argentia we had a nice little closed harbor with a rather narrow exit, and we had two or three S-boats, I guess, and the <u>Mackerel</u> up there. We went out each night and patrolled. We were on the surface, patrolling with our sound gear, trying to pick up the possibility of any U-boat trying to penetrate what we called the exit to get into the inner

---

*Argentia, Newfoundland, Canada.

harbor, where we had quite a few surface ships. Let me tell you, the water was so deep out there that it was quite possible to have a collision with the land, because it went down so straight that you could run into it; and the snow was usually horizontal. It would blow so hard--oh, the most miserable conditions you can imagine.

We were up there when Pearl Harbor happened, and I was ordered back to New London from there, and it was a very miserable trip. We had a destroyer escort, and there were two or three other boats. There was one 24-hour period that making turns for ten knots, we covered exactly seven miles. We were bounding up and down. You couldn't go any faster. The destroyer was taking an awful beating even trying to make ten knots, you know.

Q: There was a PBY operation out of Argentia.* Did you work with them at all?

Admiral Davidson: We saw a lot of them up there, but no, I don't think we even had a communications setup with them. We went out and just did it at night. In the daytime we were tied up to a tender. The division commander was Ralph Christie.**

---
  *PBY--Navy patrol bombers which worked from seaplane tenders.
  **Captain Ralph W. Christie, USN.

Davidson #2 - 167

Q: What are your memories of him?

Admiral Davidson: Oh, the poorest sport I ever knew, really.

Q: In what sense?

Admiral Davidson: He lost 20 cents to me in a golf game one time. I was taking a shower, and he came to the shower and said, "You owe me ten cents from last week."

I said, "Well, that means you just owe me ten cents, then, Captain, because you lost 20 cents to me today."

So he went back to his locker, came back, and took ten cents and threw it in the shower and said, "An elephant never forgets, does he?" He was a real poor loser. A handsome guy, pretty good golf player. I think he should have had some of the responsibility pinned on him for the torpedo fiasco in the beginning of the war, although I couldn't prove anything.* He had a nice wife who left him, or he left her. He's remarried. I guess he lives in Honolulu.

---

*As a lieutenant in the Bureau of Ordnance in the 1920s, Christie became a recognized torpedo expert, making significant contributions, including development of the magnetic exploder. Controversy developed over the high failure rate of the magnetic exploders in torpedoes in the early part of World War II. Christie insisted that the failures were due not to the device, but rather to poor maintenance, improper settings, and errors by the submariners' commanding officers and crews.

Q: Yes, I think he is still alive.

Admiral Davidson: Merrill Comstock and I went to call on him once in Washington, and he asked us if we would have a drink. We said yes. Christie said, "I've got anything but Scotch. No Scotch." So we took some of his homemade bourbon or whatever it was. He was called to the phone, and Merrill went out to finish making the drinks, and there was a bottle of Scotch out there and Ralph's glass half full of it. But for guests, he didn't have Scotch; that was too expensive. We didn't have a very high opinion of his sportsmanlike conduct.

Q: What is your recollection of finding out about the attack on Pearl Harbor and the effect of that?

Admiral Davidson: Oh, we were just completely glued to radios, and we couldn't believe what had happened, because we didn't have any warning at all. We didn't know all the things that were going on between Washington and Pearl, or the things that should have been going on between Washington and Pearl. So it was quite a surprise. We were just in our own little bailiwick up there, thinking we were fighting some Germans and hoping that we would get to them before they got to us.

Q: Did your boat have radar for making these night patrols?

Davidson #2 - 169

Admiral Davidson: No radar until I got the Blackfish later. I had one of those first radars that wasn't the greatest thing in the world either.

Q: How did your mission change, then, when the war started?

Admiral Davidson: I was ordered back to New London and immediately got orders to put the Blackfish in commission. It was building there at Electric Boat Company. I thought, of course, that we would be going to the Pacific, but right after we commissioned, for some reason or other--I'm trying to think why--they changed all our allowances of certain things, issued a lot of cold weather clothing, all sorts of things, which made you wonder a little bit what was going on. Finally, I received in the Blackfish sealed orders with instructions that they were not to be opened until I was 100 miles at sea. At 100 miles at sea, we opened the orders, and it said, "Proceed to the Mediterranean, to the south coast to France, pick up General Giraud of the French Resistance forces, and take him to North Africa."* I forget which port we were to go to, but down there someplace. "Proceed at best possible speed to arrive there by such and such a time." So I sat right down with my navigator and exec, and we

---

*General Henri Honore Giraud had been Commander Allied Forces Northern France. After his escape to Algeria in 1942, he organized the French Colonial Army there in support of the Allies.

worked it out that even at our best speed it would take us two days more than we had to get there. This was a message from Ernie King that told us to do this, see, so I sent Ernie King a message and said, "Maximum speed of this ship 18 knots. Distance to port so and so. Under best conditions can arrive at such and such a time," which was 48 hours late. Whereupon I received a modified set of orders to proceed to Dakar and to oppose any sortie of the so-called Free French ships. The Richelieu and some battleships were down there. So we proceeded down there instead. I learned later that they drafted a British submarine from the Med to pick up Jerauld Wright, to proceed to the south coast of France to pick up General Giraud.* And I learned later from talking to Admiral Wright that the reason he had to go and the British couldn't do it was that the French didn't trust the British. And therefore it was a British boat and they wouldn't trust them. But if you had an American--I guess Wright was only a captain at that time--on board it would be okay. If you had an American Navy captain on board, he supposedly was in command of the expedition, even though he was riding a British boat, and the French would accept it. So that's what actually happened.

---

*Captain Jerauld Wright, USN, later admiral, was on General Dwight D. Eisenhower's staff, where he was ordered in November 1942 to the British submarine Seraph to evacuate General Giraud from southern France. According to Clark G. Reynolds in Famous American Admirals (New York: Van Nostrand Reinhold, 1978), Wright assumed temporary command of the submarine.

Q: The French Fleet had been shelled in Mers el-Kebir by the British, so they had reason to feel that way.*

Admiral Davidson: Yes. So I proceeded down there, and we patrolled off the coast of Dakar. That's when I first used the radar, a very interesting experiment. While crossing the Atlantic Ocean, we had our radar going, and we had had about a week when we had sent a chief petty officer to a school to learn all about it and how to operate it and how to maintain it and so on. He was manning the radar one evening when I sighted a cruise ship, fully lighted, a passenger ship, coming over the horizon. So I called down to the conning tower to the chief and said, "Have you got anything on the radar?"

He took a sweep around and said, "All clear, captain. Not a thing."

I said, "Come to the bridge." He came up, and by that time about 2,000 yards going down our starboard side is this lighted--and we're darkened ship--cruise ship, just as big as a battleship.

He looked at me and said, "Oh, my God."

So the next time he ever gave me anything to report, he

---

*On 3 July 1940, the British Royal Navy blocked part of the French fleet--under control of German-occupied Vichy France--which was at anchor at Mers-el-Kebir near Oran on the Mediterranean coast of Algeria. The British issued an ultimatum to surrender or scuttle the ships and when the French refused, opened fire.

picked up land as we approached the coast of Africa, and that turned out to be fairly accurate as to distance. You've got sort of blips on your radar screen and you didn't have a picture at all.

Q: An A-scope, probably.

Admiral Davidson: Yes, an A-scope.* Anyhow, we patrolled off there for quite some time. Nothing ever came out, but one ship tried to go in, and we decided that it was Free French, or whatever, included in our list of enemies. So we decided to attack it, and we attacked it with what we thought were pretty good results, but we couldn't see much. The only evidence I ever had on it was that many, many months later out in Australia, Jim Elliott, who had been my first lieutenant during this attack, ran into an officer from the merchant marine, and they started exchanging sea stories, and he said, "Well, I guess I'm lucky to be alive.** I was in a ship that was hit by torpedoes right off Dakar at such and such a time."

Jim said, "Where?" He asked him what happened. Well, they were able to beach the ship before it really sank. They beached it. He said, "We were all taken off, but somebody hit the hell out of us." That's the only story I ever heard that tied in at

---
*The A-scope radar gives range readings by vertical lines, or blips, on a horizontal scale.
**Lieutenant (junior grade) James F. Elliott, USNR.

Davidson #2 - 173

all, because it was the same time. So that's the only thing we ever got to shoot at down there.

From there we were ordered to proceed to Roseneath, Scotland, where we had a submarine base.

That was the beginning for the Blackfish. My first trip was over there to Dakar, then up to Roseneath, then we patrolled out of Roseneath into the Bay of Biscay, which was not a very happy hunting ground. We were operating under the British and we were told under no circumstances should we sink anything except a German-flag vessel, but in the same breath we were told that many of the German vessels were flying French flags or any other kind of flag they wanted to fly just to get through. So we ended up making one attack the whole time we were there, got some good, solid torpedo hits and then got the hell depth-charged out of us. We ended up on the bottom with the conning tower flooded completely and quite a bit of water down in the control room. One of the other restrictions was we were not to attack anything inside of whatever it was--12 miles off the north coast of Spain. Before we made the attack, I checked with the navigator and asked him if he knew where we were, and he said, "Well, we have to be more than 12 miles off, because we've got several hundred fathoms of water," or whatever it was. Well, when we hit bottom, we were in only 200 feet of water. So we had to have been inside when we made the attack. It was probably an illegal attack, but anyway, there we were lying on the bottom, and it was by that time almost nighttime. It became nighttime and the guy went away, stopped dropping his depth charges. We later learned that what we hit was a merchant ship, but he was being escorted by an antisubmarine ship of some sort, which did the depth charging. We learned that from the British intelligence later.

We then proceeded very quietly to pump out some water, get ourselves off the bottom, and started north while submerged to get away from the coast of Spain. Finally, late that night we surfaced and got the conning tower drained down, pumped out. We reported in to our base in Scotland, and were given orders to proceed to Falmouth on the south coast of England to the dockyard there, where we were repaired. One of the results of the whole thing was a modification to our fleet type submarines. We had a conning tower door, and we were flooded through a cracked conning tower door. They took out the door and welded it up eventually, and orders went out to all the other boats to weld them up. I believe that to be a fact. So we spent quite a lot of time in the dockyard there in Falmouth and became a great friend of Lady Astor's.*

Q: What nationality was this vessel that was attacking?

---
*Virginia-born Nancy Langhorne married Britain's Viscount Astor and became famed as the first woman to serve in the House of Commons when she succeeded her husband in 1919. During the war (1939-1945), she continued to represent in Parliament the district of the city of Plymouth, where her husband was the mayor. About 50 miles from Falmouth, Plymouth was frequented by U.S. military personnel.

Admiral Davidson: German. No question about it. I had my exec, Al Becker, look through the periscope before we fired, and said, "Al, you want to assure me that that's not a neutral ship?"*

He looked through it, and he turned to me and said, "Captain, if that ain't a swastika, I'm a horse and buggy."

So I said, "All right. Ready one," and we fired. He had the last look before we fired.

Q: You must have had better exploders then than some of the boats out in the Pacific.

Admiral Davidson: Yes. We were still getting dispatches, though, telling us what to do--inactivate the magnetic exploders and then activate them the next day. The British were laughing at us because we were getting orders every other day on what to do. Then it got even worse than that in the Pacific when they started telling us to no longer fire to hit at a right angle; you had to fire to hit at an oblique angle because the exploder wouldn't go off if you hit it straight.

Q: This is where you didn't develop too warm feelings for Admiral Christie.

---
*Lieutenant Albert L. Becker, USN.

Davidson #2 - 176

Admiral Davidson: That's right.

Q: Could you compare the building period in shipyard that you had in the <u>Blackfish</u> with what you'd known earlier in the <u>Cachalot</u> as a junior officer?

Admiral Davidson: Actually, it was being built at the Electric Boat Company. Of course, that's an entirely sort of different setup than we had up in Portsmouth. In Portsmouth the crew that was ordered to commission the boat did all of the trials, did everything. In Electric Boat Company, they had a trial crew. Old Captain Foster had been for years and years the captain of the trial crews. My crew went along as observers for all of this sort of thing. Mr. Johnstone, who was the sort of supervisor of the building of my particular boat, he was a great guy.* You might ask Admiral Joe Williams of him.** He's a submariner. I think he made rear admiral. His last job was Com Eleven in San Diego. Anyhow, my experience at Electric Boat was very good. I enjoyed my experience with them, but Captain Foster took the boat out, he did all the diving, put it through all the trials and all the tests, and scared the hell out of us most of the time. But he'd been doing this thing ever since--he used to tell fantastic

---
*Harold Halleck Johnstone, who was in the Naval Academy's class of 1907; he resigned while a midshipman.
**Rear Admiral Joseph W. Williams, Jr., USN(Ret.), who married Johnstone's daughter Madeleine.

stories about how in World War I a boat was built out in the state of Washington, perhaps at Bremerton or someplace, a submarine was built, and the British wanted to buy it before the U.S. got into the war. And the U.S. said, "Well, we're neutral. We can't sell it to you." So they hired Captain Foster and his crew to steal it, and they delivered it to Canada. They delivered it to Canada and turned it over to a British crew. Then he couldn't return to the United States for fear he'd be put in jail. This is the same guy that was still trial captain when I was with the Blackfish.

Q: How did he scare you?

Admiral Davidson: Some of the things he did diving the boat we considered very dangerous tactics. He authorized all sorts of things not to be closed, and all that sort of thing. But every member of his crew was an ex-chief of the boat, just about. They had retired and gone there, so there was no question about it; he had all the skill he could need.

Q: You also had the thought that he was going down there with you.

Admiral Davidson: Oh, yes, yes. I liked old Captain Foster. Some of the skippers used to argue with him a little bit about things, but I sort of liked him. I suspect that I learned a lot from him, too.

Q: How did you then provide training to your crew that you pulled together in shakedown and so forth?

Admiral Davidson: They rode with the trial crew and for every position you had somebody observing, practically. And, of course, the crew that was ordered to the ship with me were all experienced submariners. They came from other boats. I had a very inexperienced officer that later became a vice admiral, the first skipper of the Nautilus, Eugene P. Wilkinson.* He was a reserve ensign, fresh out of sub school at the time when Karl Hensel was head of the school. Wilkie came to my boat with tears in his eyes because he stood two in his submarine class and he thought he could have stood one. God, he was a brilliant kid.

Q: That's what someone else said. He said you could play poker with him and he'd always win.

Admiral Davidson: Yes. Same thing. I had the same experience. We sat on the bottom in Long Island Sound once testing the effect of exposure of torpedoes to pressure in the tubes with the tubes

---

*Nautilus, the world's first nuclear-powered submarine, was commissioned 30 September 1954 with Commander Eugene P. Wilkinson, USN, assuming command.

open--how long could you sit down at a couple of hundred feet and expose those torpedoes to sea pressure and still count on them performing properly when you fired them when you came up. We sat down there and played poker, and I think we played from 8:00 o'clock one night to 2:00 and Wilkie hadn't won a hand, and by 3:00 he was the big winner. He never lost when he didn't have anything, and he won big when he had something. It was all mathematics with him. I was very fond of Wilkie. I don't know whether I've talked about him or not.

Q: No, you haven't.

Admiral Davidson: The <u>Blackfish</u> went from the dockyard there in England to our base in Roseneath, Scotland. The next time we went on patrol, we were again down in the Bay of Biscay, which was not a very happy hunting ground. There were too many ifs, ands, and buts. We were told don't attack this guy, don't attack that guy, be sure you identify this guy, and yet you knew damn well that if any of the enemy saw a submarine out there, they knew pretty well it was us. So it wasn't a happy hunting ground at all, but while we were down there, we got the hell depth-charged out of us one time. This may have been the time that sent us to the dockyard. I think it was. The diving officer at the time was my engineer whose name was Clay Tucker,

I believe.* Anyway, he cracked up under fire. He just went all to pieces. After our repairs in the dockyard, we went back to Roseneath, Scotland. And when we were about to sail on the next patrol, I was standing on deck with the boss, who was Norman Ives, the division commander, and young Clay Tucker, who was still the engineer on my boat, came up and said, "Pardon me, Captain. I can't go on this patrol. I can't go because I'm frightened to death."**

Knowing what he'd been through, I said, "Clay, have you packed up your things?"

He said, "Yes, sir."

I said, "Okay. I'll send you over to the squadron office and they'll give you some orders of some kind."

And Norm Ives said to me, "What are you going to do for an engineer?"

I said, "Oh, I've got a kid here that can do anything. His name is Ensign Wilkinson. When he came aboard, I asked him what his particular forte was, and he said, 'Oh, nothing in particular. Just general all-around handyman. I stood second in my class in submarine school." But he was a reserve ensign. I said to Norm Ives, "I'll use Wilkie as my engineer." Because I'd watched him standing watches as diving officer and he'd done very well. I watched him teaching enlisted men why this valve

---

*Lieutenant Houston C. Tucker, Jr.
**Commander Norman S. Ives, USN.

Davidson #2 - 181

did that and why this machine did that, and he was so brilliant.

So we went on that patrol, and then Wilkie was my engineer for one more patrol, I believe. Then we went on a patrol up in the Denmark Straits, up around Iceland and Greenland, looking for U-boats. Of all the places to send anybody--24-hour-a-day daylight. You'd go up there on the bridge and you watch the sun at midnight dipping down to the horizon and starting up again. Well, for a submariner, that's terrible, because you had to have some time to charge those batteries; the only thing to do was to take a chance and be on the surface and charge those batteries. In any case, while we were on that patrol, which didn't result in any sightings or anything, Wilkie was--there wasn't any question in my mind he was the most outstanding young officer I had ever run into, and as far as I was concerned, he was more outstanding than my exec or any first lieutenant or any of them. So I had always said in the wardroom that if they started sending orders to send one person back to new construction or one enlisted man to this or that, I was going to reward the guy that I thought was doing the best job. Even though it may hurt me a little bit, I'm going to give a reward to the guy that's doing the best job. It's like giving a medal to inspire somebody to do more than he's capable of. Well, anyway, sure enough, coming back in to the Shetland Islands--that's where we made landfall, about that time I got a dispatch, "Transfer one officer to commission the USS Darter." So we got in. I said, "Wilkie."

He came into the wardroom and said to me in private, with no other officers present, "Captain, do you have any parting words of advice?"

I said, "I have some parting words of advice, Wilkie. You're one of the finest officers I ever saw in my life, but you're also the most conceited."

And he said to me, "Captain, that's not conceit; that's self-confidence. After all, I never try to do anything I can't do better than anyone else."

Davidson #3 - 183

Interview Number 3 with Rear Admiral John F. Davidson,
U.S. Navy (Retired)

Place: Admiral Davidson's home in Annapolis, Maryland

Date: September 4, 1985

Subject: Biography

Interviewer: Paul Stillwell

Q: Admiral, we finished up last time talking about Eugene Wilkinson.

Admiral Davidson: I remember saying that I detached him because he was the best officer I had. I sent him back to new construction. I remember I told him he was the most conceited youngster I ever knew. His response was, "Captain, I'm not conceited. That's just self-confidence. After all, I never try to do anything that I can't do better than anybody else."

Q: Was that justified?

Admiral Davidson: I said, "Well, Wilkie, there's only one subject that I've never heard you say that you excelled in. When we have discussions in the wardroom about women, you're strangely silent."

And he said, "Well, that's because when I was at San Diego State, the women almost wouldn't leave me alone. I almost failed

Davidson #3 - 184

there." That's about all I can remember about Wilkie.

Q: What was the rest of the Blackfish's cruise, then, after he left?

Admiral Davidson: Wilkie left after a cruise we made in the Arctic Ocean. The main thing I remember about that was that we made a discovery during that cruise that the gyro compasses did not have a latitude corrector which would take care of latitudes above five degrees, or something like that. So that we were not having much luck with our gyro compass once we got up there in the Arctic Ocean. I had a chief on board who was so good that he was able to use a tachometer, and by introducing new resistances into the supply of current, as I remember it--I don't know much about electricity--but he introduced new resistances so he could speed up the gyro compass, and we then were able to have an approximate gyro course. We tried leaning very heavily on our magnetic compass, but, of course, it had never really been compensated for anything like that. I finally hit upon the best idea of all--if we were told to go someplace, always steer into the sea, which was the most uncomfortable course, and you would always get where you were supposed to go. Sure enough, on our way back to Scotland, we set a course from the Denmark Straits back to try to pick up the Shetland Islands on the very northernmost point of Scotland. We headed into the sea for a couple of days, and then one morning the officer of the deck called me and said, "Captain, the seas have shifted and they're now on the starboard bow."

I said, "You'd better steer into them," and he did.

Somewhat later in the day, he said, "The seas are shifted and they're now on the starboard bow again."

I said, "We better steer into them." Well, believe it or not, we did. That had us going south instead of east, and we picked up the Shetland Islands right on the button, all by steering into the sea, on the most uncomfortable course you could be on.

Q: How did that work?

Admiral Davidson: It couldn't. I'm just telling you the story we talked about. We talked about it all the time. We said, "All you have to do is steer into the sea."

Q: What made that the most uncomfortable course?

Admiral Davidson: Pitching. We were pitching all the time.

Q: That was worse than rolling?

Admiral Davidson: Well, worse than a gentle roll, but not worse than a heavy roll. But it was uncomfortable and it slowed you down. You didn't make the progress that you might.

Q: What was your mission that far north?

Admiral Davidson: Anti-U-boat patrol in the Denmark Strait. As I recall, the Denmark Strait was north of Iceland, really. It was a very, very uncomfortable patrol. The weather always seemed to be a little bit rough, and the spray over the bridge would freeze on your outer clothing, so that when you came down, you had a little coat of ice all over you. We reduced the officer of the deck watches to about one to two hours at the most, instead of the ordinary four-hour watch. Also I had a supply of medicinal brandy on board, and I used to give each man that came from the bridge a good shot of brandy when he came down. It was pretty miserable. We were looking for U-boats. We had daylight 24 hours a day, which was terrible, because we didn't have any time to charge our batteries. And the decks would get coated with ice, and when you dove, it took considerable time and effort to get the boat under, because with the deck covered with ice, the air would get trapped between the hull and the deck, and it would tend to hold you up there. We finally had to go down and melt it off. We took to diving two or three times a day in order to melt off the ice, because if you'd go down to 100 feet you could get the ice melted off the boat.

Davidson #3 - 187

Q: Was there reason to believe there were U-boats that far north?

Admiral Davidson: The convoys had experienced troubles up there, and that made a double jeopardy, you know. We were submarines, and we weren't too different looking than the U-boat would be. I always felt it was double jeopardy.

Q: Why was it considered useful to send American submarines as opposed to surface craft?

Admiral Davidson: I suppose the hope was that if we could spot the U-boat first, we'd have a chance to submerge and get in undetected. That's the only thing I can think of.

Q: Did you have any help from aircraft or other U.S. ships?

Admiral Davidson: No, not to the best of my knowledge. As a matter of fact, we considered every aircraft an enemy, because we didn't think that they would have time to identify us. So we would dive. If you had contact with an aircraft, you dove and got out of there. We assumed that the aircraft would be Allied aircraft, and we'd better not try to stay up there and identify ourselves.

Q: Was there any thought that any German surface ships might come out?

Admiral Davidson: No, not while I was up there, anyway. My history books tell me the Scharnhorst and a couple of others did make a run for it, but I wasn't up there at that time.*

We finally got back. We made a landfall on the Shetland Islands and then came down through what are called the Minches, first the North Minch and then the Little Minch, and back to Roseneath, Scotland, which was our base. I'm thinking that that's the last patrol that I made also.

I was relieved by one of the staff. This was Submarine Squadron 50, which was based in Scotland. One of the staff relieved me and took the boat back to the United States, and I flew back. Then I took it over again in New London. This was simply, I guess, to give me a rest, but also give him a chance to be skipper of a boat for a little while.

We had an interesting trip back, in that there were three of us, all skippers, doing the same thing. We were flying back via Pan Am from someplace, the south coast of England. I have a feeling it was a place called Bournemouth. We had engine difficulty over Ireland, and we put down in Limerick, Ireland.

---

*The German battle cruiser Scharnhorst operated as a surface raider in the North Sea and Atlantic Ocean. The ship was sunk 26 December 1943 by British battleships, cruiser, and destroyer attacks in the Arctic Ocean north of Norway.

Because of the neutrality agreements, the Irish couldn't allow us to come ashore off the plane in uniform. So we had to have civilian clothes. The only person with civilian clothes along was Sec Johnson, out of the class of 1930.* He was somewhat taller than I and considerably heavier. I was next in size, and then the next one was one of the skippers, and I can't remember which one it was. He was about 5'6". Sec was the only one with civilian clothes, so we all borrowed suits from him, and we turned the sleeves up, rolled the trousers up, and so on, and we had to stay three days there in Limerick in the hotel, having a great time and washing out our nylon shirts every night so we'd have a clean shirt each day. Finally, Pan Am managed to fly in an engine, which was offloaded out on the water somewhere and brought ashore, and installed it on our plane, and then we flew to New York.

When we arrived in New York, we went to the Commodore Hotel and went up to the desk to register, the most bedraggled-looking three people you ever saw in your life. The clerk did not wish to accept the fact that we were naval officers. We had quite a time getting ourselves accepted to stay at the hotel.

Then we went back to New London, and our boats eventually came back there. We had two or three weeks of recreation at that point.

---

*Lieutenant Commander Raymond W. Johnson, USN.

Then my boat was ordered to Brisbane, Australia. Before leaving, we discovered that the coils in our evaporators were worn out, and we very badly needed replacement coils for the evaporators. The evaporators were pretty important, because they made all the fresh water for the ship, not only for the crew, but for the water in the batteries, and so on. I was informed by ComSubLant's engineering staff officer that there were absolutely no coils available and we were going to have to make out the best we could to get to Australia.* So we sailed.

When we arrived in Panama, we were given a week in Panama at the submarine base there to get ourselves squared away for the long trip across the Pacific to Brisbane, Australia. We were in rather dire straits for water, so I asked the squadron engineer in Panama what he could do about it, and he said he couldn't do anything. If ComSubLant's engineer had said no, he couldn't do anything. Therefore, I couldn't induce anybody in Panama to send a message about it.

One day we went out for exercises in Panama Bay, and I instructed my radio gang to see if they could raise Cominch in Washington, who was Ernest J. King.** I sent a message and said that it was absolutely imperative that we renew the coils in our evaporators before undertaking the long trip across the Pacific.

---
*ComSubLant--Commander Submarines Atlantic Fleet.
**Cominch--Commander in Chief U.S. Fleet.

Two days later, an airplane arrived with complete coils. We took them on board, got under way, and my crew installed them while en route across the Pacific. I learned later that they were taken from the Electric Boat Company, where another boat was being built, and they took the coils from that boat and flew them down to us.

When I arrived in Brisbane, who should meet me on the pier but ComSubLant's engineering officer, who had been fired in the meantime and sent out to Australia for duty. He was little Shorty Nichols, and he said, "Damn you, Johnny. What the hell did you do to me?"[*]

I said, "Well, Nick, you told me there weren't any coils available, and I couldn't get to Australia without them, so I bypassed everybody and went to the head man."

Q: Did you get any flak for doing that?

Admiral Davidson: No, no, never got any. As a matter of fact, Jimmy Fife was the boss out in Australia, and he sort of complimented me for using some sort of ingenuity in getting us out there.[**] The only thing he didn't compliment me for--and I'll insert this one. It was a long trip across that Pacific,

---
[*] Commander Stanley G. Nichols, USN.
[**] Captain James Fife, Jr., USN, Commander Task Force 72.

and we were required to dive in the morning before daylight and then you'd take a look around and come up and cruise on the surface during the day, and then dive again just before dark to be sure you had the trim, and come up. We had been given a speed of advance; we were supposed to make so many miles each day, and we began to run into a little bit of weather halfway across. We were having great difficulty making our speed of advance with any economical expenditure of fuel oil. Someplace along about two-thirds of the way over, my engineer officer came with a very sad look on his face to tell me that they had just cut in another fuel tank only to find that it had nothing in it but saltwater, and that obviously somebody had made a bust while fueling in Panama, and one tank was not filled. Of course, as you use fuel oil in a submarine, you compensate with saltwater in order to keep the trim of the boat proper. So here we were, instead of 105,000 gallons, we had started with about 95,000 gallons. In an effort to try to keep up the speed, we were using it a lot faster than we needed to, so we had to slow down. We arrived in Australia about a day late. As we entered the waterway leading up to the port of Brisbane, there was a great big sign over on the beach that said, "Eight knots," I believe. I could be wrong. Maybe it said ten. Well, I went up the river at 15 knots. When I arrived alongside, old Admiral Jimmy Fife said to me, "Johnny, what the hell are you doing, coming up, violating all the speed laws coming up there? Didn't you see that sign there that said eight knots?"

I said, "Yes, sir. I thought that was the current. I thought I had to add some horsepower or I'd never get here."

He had the courtesy to laugh. But we were so tired of being at sea that I wasn't about to slow down to get up there. Also, I was going to get there with about a teacup full of fuel, which was just about what we did.

Q: Did you have any trouble keeping stores for all that time?

Admiral Davidson: No, no. The food part worked out very well. With our new coils in our evaps, our water situation was all right.* Our great danger there was running out of fuel, and that would have been disastrous to run out of fuel in the middle of the ocean.

Q: That isn't the sort of news a skipper likes to get when you heard about that tank.

Admiral Davidson: Yes. Right. He was a good officer. I don't know how they missed it, because we fueled in Panama and topped off. I don't know how they missed that one tank, but we started out with one 10,000-gallon tank full of saltwater.

---
*Evaps--evaporators.

We had about two weeks refit there in Australia. The men didn't get to go ashore. They had to work all the time to get the boat ready for patrol.

Q: Had the idea of relief crews not yet grown up?

Admiral Davidson: At that point, there wasn't a relief crew for my ship there. The next time we came in we had a relief crew. I think the time between patrols was only about two weeks. We had a relief crew when we came in. Then we patrolled up there. We had a base in New Guinea. We used to leave Brisbane and go up to Guadalcanal to Iron Bottom Bay, they called it, and we'd fuel there in Iron Bottom Bay and then go on patrol. I just don't even remember the names of the places. We did things like scouting before landings in New Guinea and various places. We didn't find much in the way of good hunting. I don't think I ever fired a torpedo without being depth-charged, which lots of ships did. Lots of submarines fired lots of torpedoes without any retaliation, but I don't think we ever did.

There's a retired minister down in Dallas, Texas, now who stopped by last year, and he said, "Captain, did you ever stop to think that we never fired a torpedo without getting blasted?"

I said, "You're probably right, Bob. We always did."

And the only time that we came close to having the end of the world, a depth charge damaged our rudder, and one of the men from the after torpedo room came up to the control room and said, "Captain, every time you move that rudder, there's a great big groan back there." All of a sudden I realized that's why the Jap--we were not getting away from him. He was following that with his sound gear. So we left the rudder on ten degrees right, just circled, and he went away. That's as close as I came. We had quite a bit of damage and had to go back to Brisbane, go in the dockyard and have our rudder repaired. I can remember seeing that Jap. He was in a Zero. I was on the bridge when all of a sudden, right out of nowhere came this Zero. I could see him with his goggles. He had the hood of his Zero open, and I could just see that guy. He made a terrible mistake; he didn't drop right then and there when he had us dead to rights. He decided, I guess, the tactics must have called for going astern and then coming up parallel to us so he could drop one after the other. When we dove, we turned immediately. One of them got pretty close, but the rest of them walked away.

Q: What is it like to be under a depth bomb or depth charge attack?

Admiral Davidson: Well, disconcerting, to say the least. I think the thing about it, Paul, that bothered me most of all was you don't feel you can shoot back. You know, if you're fighting a battle and you're shooting and they're shooting, at least you're doing something. But once you have to go down and don't have any offensive weapon, you just feel like you're a sitting duck, and if he happens to hit, he'll hit. The only good thing about it is you know that if you hear it, it didn't hit.

Q: I guess the compensating factor is that you get the first shot usually.

Admiral Davidson: Yes. Right.

Q: And you get to pick the time and place that's most advantageous.

Admiral Davidson: Right. I had a young officer by the name of Taliaferro, and I remember coming down from the conning tower one time, Taliaferro was stretched out, lying on his back, and looking up and saying, "Jealousy will get you nowhere. Jealousy will get you nowhere."* He was talking to some Jap up there that was dropping on the ship. Fortunately, the crew found that amusing enough so it took their mind off what was going on.

Q: How many attacks did you make on enemy ships?

---

*Ensign Philip B. Taliaferro, USN.

Admiral Davidson: I don't remember. I don't remember.

Q: What were your experiences with the torpedoes?

Admiral Davidson: I had two or three very, very discouraging torpedo experiences, torpedoes that went off within 300 or 400 yards of my bow, premature explosions. I don't recall that I ever knew that I had a circular run. A lot of people talked about circular runs and so on. I don't recall that I ever knew that, but I did have a lot of prematures.

Q: Did you have any cases where you felt you hit the target and didn't get an explosion?

Admiral Davidson: No. Of course, I didn't have enough real hits to know. I don't think I ever was lucky enough to be able to stay up there and see what happened. I don't ever remember attacking anything that wasn't heavily escorted. One of the greatest disappointments of my whole life was that we received one of these decoded Japanese Ultras, and we ran all night at top speed to get in a position dead ahead of a pretty good sized convoy.* Come daylight, we dove to wait for it. Sure enough,

---

*Ultra, for ultra secret, were decoded Japanese ship movement messages. The U.S. Navy early had broken the Japanese naval codes, but the fact remained secret throughout the war. See David Kahn, The Codebreakers (New York: The MacMillian Company, 1967).

exactly on schedule, on course, on speed and all, here comes this convoy over the hill. When he was still beyond torpedo range, the whole convoy turned to the right and went east, leaving me out in left field. After he had gotten far enough away, I took a chance on surfacing. Darn if he wasn't joining up with some escort vessels, maybe as many as five or six, seven miles to the east. What we finally found happened was that this Ultra showed that he had orders to rendezvous. It was a tanker convoy, I think three big tankers coming up from the south, laden with oil, headed for Japan. He had orders to join these escorts at a certain point, and that was the point that we went to. Well, apparently the escorts or the convoy--I'd like to think it was the escorts--had some errors in navigation, because they showed up about ten miles to the east. When the convoy spotted them, he turned and went to join them instead of letting them come to join him. I never got to shoot a single torpedo, because I was all the way out on the flank, and their speed was great enough I couldn't get ahead. I went down and went to bed. I was just sick.

Q: How could you sleep in this situation?

Admiral Davidson: I turned the boat over to the exec. Gosh, here we were. We thought this was going to be the highlight of our whole cruise, and we didn't get a thing out of it.

Davidson #3 - 199

Q: You had one claim, didn't you, that was later disallowed? I thought I read that.

Admiral Davidson: I don't remember it if we did. I was very careful not to claim things, because if I didn't see anything, all I could go on was what I heard. My exec used to argue with me a little bit. He said, "Oh, captain, you know damn well we got that."

I said, "Well, I didn't see it go down. I just didn't see it go down," so I wouldn't put it in there.

There were some embarrassments after the war, you know, embarrassing findings of their claims, after they'd been awarded all kinds of medals. I preferred it the other way around, myself.

Q: Could you comment on the value of patrol reports?

Admiral Davidson: I'm sure they had value, but I do feel that perhaps the ability of the author to write had something to do with what the report had to say. Some of them were able to build a great big story out of anything that happened. I don't remember having anything that I felt was worth a great big story. We had so few contacts. That was the disappointment to me, because when I went out there, I had a chance to read a lot of patrol reports, and gee, they'd been having a heyday out there.

Then when we started going out, there wasn't anything to shoot at. I guess my predecessors had knocked them all down.

Q: How useful to you was the torpedo data computer, the TDC?

Admiral Davidson: I'm sure it was a very valuable instrument in making the attacks. Otherwise it was like shooting a duck; you had to lead it. No, I think the torpedo data computer, the TDC, was a great invention. I never was much at being able to operate it myself, but I had some pretty good--Wilkie, to begin with--I had an expert, and then I had some others that were pretty good at it. By the time I was relieved of command, we didn't have a very effective radar. Certainly we didn't have very much in the way of a radar submerged.

Q: How do you keep the morale of the crew up when you've got that kind of frustration and bad luck?

Admiral Davidson: I don't recall that it ever became a problem. Not really. The only time I ever heard of the crew of the Blackfish having low morale was the patrol after I was relieved, and it was a sad thing that happened to Skip Sellars.* He went off on a patrol, and they didn't sight a target for 42 days. He

---

*Lieutenant Commander Robert F. Sellars, USN.

had left from Brisbane, and he went in to Iron Bottom Bay, I believe, to refuel, and his orders called for his patrol to terminate at Pearl, because the <u>Blackfish</u> was coming on back.* So when he went in to Iron Bottom Bay, he reported, after he had fueled, that he had a full load of fuel and had all torpedoes on board. The operations officer in Lockwood's headquarters in Pearl thought he had just started patrol, so he sent him out on another six weeks.** I was in Pearl when they arrived, and I knew all the men on board. I went down there. They were just incensed, to begin with. They'd been on out there 80 days, I think. I think it was the longest patrol anybody ever made. And they still hadn't had any great luck. Things were drying up about that time. This was '44, you see, and things were really drying up out there. I had almost more to shoot at over in the Bay of Biscay and there wasn't much over there either.

Q: I heard about the long periods without sleep. Did you experience that also?

Admiral Davidson: Not so much, no. The only time that worried me was when we were over there in the Arctic Ocean in daylight all the time. I had difficulty going to sleep over there,

---

*Iron Bottom Bay was the nickname for the area off Guadalcanal in which a number of ships had been sunk.
**Vice Admiral Charles A. Lockwood, Jr., USN, Commander Submarines Pacific.

because I would be imagining things all the time.

Q: Do you have any comparisons you could draw between the staff in Brisbane and the one in Hawaii?

Admiral Davidson: Not really. Jimmy Fife, who was a pretty tough taskmaster, was a teetotaler, expected miraculous things out of all his submarines and his skippers and so on, but he was extremely fair. There's another thing we always knew about Jimmy Fife--if we had to go in with a message about something, we knew that he was sitting at the other end of the telephone. He wasn't off with some wench some place. He was on duty 24 hours a day, and he was the first to respond. When I had this damage to the rudder and so on, and I finally decided to send in a dispatch saying that I could steer all right but had this loud noise that was making it very difficult to remain, he came right back and called me back in for docking.

There was another thing that was pretty good about Jimmy Fife, as far as I was concerned. One time I had gone up to do a reconnoitering of one of the beaches where we were going to make a landing. Where, I can't remember, except I believe it was up the Slot someplace.* We put a landing party in a rubber boat and

---
*Slot--the wide channel between the two chains of volcanic islands that make up the Solomon Islands. The group of islands is about 700 miles long from Guadalcanal in the southeast to Bougainville in the northwest.

sent them in while we were lying off, and somehow or other, they got in, got all the information we needed, came back, and early in the morning, we were just easing back out to sea, when all of a sudden there was a convoy going by. So we tore out at the best submerged speed we could and made this attack on this convoy. I think that's one that I remember definitely we got some good hits, but we weren't up there long enough to see any ship actually go underwater, but we got some good hits. We were pretty happy with the thing. But we took a hell of a depth charging afterwards, and we had gone to 200 feet, and we were trying to maneuver down there to avoid the depth charge attack. When I came in and Jimmy Fife read our patrol report, he said to me, "Johnny, why in the hell didn't you come up and shoot that guy instead of staying down there and letting him drop those depth charges?"

I looked at the admiral and I said, "Well, if you want to know the truth, I was scared to death, damn it. I wasn't about to come up there."

And you know what he said? He said, "For once I have a skipper who's given me a truthful answer." He said, "I've asked that question of skipper after skipper, and they've always given me some damn excuse. I know damn well that they were scared, and so were you. You were the first one to give me a real honest answer."

I said, "No, I didn't know who was up there or what he was

doing. I wasn't about to come up and stick my periscope up into the middle of that hornet's nest."

So he didn't relieve me of command, so I assume he approved of what we were doing.

Q: You said he expected miracles. Do you think his expectations were too high?

Admiral Davidson: No. I think he was just trying, in his way, to urge everybody to do even better than they were doing. Of course, the submarine force as a whole was doing a pretty fine job out there. I think that was his method of encouraging people.

Q: Any of the officers or enlisted crew members you especially remember from the Pacific phase?

Admiral Davidson: Sure. My exec was later a skipper and did extremely well--Bill Kinsella.* He had a very successful later career. This man who's now a minister down in Dallas, Bob Blakely, he was a reserve officer, but a real fine young officer and one of the good examples about how in the fleet we didn't pay attention to whether a man was a reserve officer or a regular.**

---
*Lieutenant William T. Kinsella, USN.
**Lieutenant (junior grade) Robert T.C. Blakely, USNR.

They were all just members of the team. Jim Elliott was another reserve officer; he was the one that ran out of gasoline going across the ocean, but he had been with me in Europe. He was a very fine officer. Of course, Wilkie. I didn't have Wilkie in the Pacific. I don't know whether it would have made my torpedo shooting any better or not. Probably not, because when we were able to get into position on anything, we got evidence that we had some hits. The biggest thing that helped was when they authorized us to shoot to hit rather than shoot to run under, and when they authorized us not to have to get an angle to shoot--just shoot whenever you had a good setup. That helped.

Q: Did you feel that the postwar evaluation was fair in regard to the Blackfish?

Admiral Davidson: I never paid any attention to what it was. I'll have to get the book out and read it. I've got the book back there, but I don't remember reading it. If I did read it, I've forgotten it already. But this torpedo business, I can remember distinctly one time I never was so disappointed. After maneuvering for an attack, I was dead ahead of the convoy. We fired a spread of torpedoes right up the throat, and the first two torpedoes exploded at about 500 yards ahead of me, and the whole convoy fanned right out and went in different directions. We never got a single hit out of all six bow tubes. That's pretty destroying morale-wise.

Q: You had taken a risk and had nothing to justify it.

Admiral Davidson: Right.

Q: Did you have any encounters with Commander Dick Voge?*

Admiral Davidson: No, but Dick Voge was the one that sent Skip Sellars off on a second patrol. I don't know that it was necessarily his fault. Somebody missed on the communications there, and maybe Skip should have gone back to him and said, "I've just finished." But he was a new skipper and he didn't feel that he could find fault.

Q: How much administrative work was there to do on patrol?

Admiral Davidson: Practically none. I think that's one of the things they managed to relieve us of. We kept a log and that's about all.

Q: Anything else about the Blackfish?

---
*Commander Richard G. Voge, USN, operations officer on the staff of Commander Submarines Pacific.

Davidson #3 - 207

Admiral Davidson: No. I turned it over to Skip, and then I flew back to Honolulu, where I was ordered to be on the staff of Admiral Babe Brown in training command as a training officer for new skippers.* I did that for six or eight months, I guess, all the time being told that I was about to get a division and I could have a wolf pack. I think I mentioned the other day, Charlie Lockwood said, "You're going back and relieve Bob Rice," the detail officer.** That's where I ended up.

Q: What do you recall about that period of training the new skippers? Who were some of the ones that came through?

Admiral Davidson: My memory is just no good at all, and I don't have any pieces of paper that would refresh my memory.

Q: Did they have some sort of PCO course on the East Coast?***

Admiral Davidson: I think so, but what we were doing there was taking them out for three or four days outside of Pearl, firing practice torpedoes, making approaches and things. They were just sending a skipper who had been in the war zone out to observe their performance as skippers, but not under fire. So really, I

---
*Rear Admiral John H. Brown, Jr., USN.
**Commander Robert H. Rice, USN, was the submarine detail officer in the Bureau of Naval Personnel.
***PCO--prospective commanding officer.

don't know that it was advantageous, except it gave the new skipper a chance to shoot the breeze a lot with somebody who'd been out there and maybe get some background that would help him someday.

Q: I would think it would be useful for Brown to have you there as an observer, just to get a feel for how good these were.

Admiral Davidson: There were several doing it. I was one, Gene McKinney was one, and I'm trying to remember.* Lou Chappel was one.**

Q: Roy Benson was there for a while, too, wasn't he?***

Admiral Davidson: Not while I was there, but I wouldn't be surprised. Yes. It was a place to sort of put skippers that had just been relieved on ice for a little while, give them a blow, and stand by to go out as division commander or wolf pack commander.

---

*Commander Eugene B. McKinney, USN, who had commanded the Skate (SS-305).
**Commander Lucius H. Chappel, USN, who had commanded the Sculpin (SS-191).
***Commander Roy S. Benson, USN, ran the PCO course at New London after a successful command tour in the USS Trigger (SS-237). Benson, a classmate of Davidson and now a retired rear admiral, is the subject of a two-volume Naval Institute oral history.

Q: What do you remember about Brown himself?

Admiral Davidson: Old Babe. He was just a real likable teddy bear type, and I always enjoyed Babe very much. Other than that, I don't know. Of course, he never made a war patrol in his life, but he was an old-time submariner.

Q: Any specific incidents that have any relationship with him?

Admiral Davidson: The only thing I was trying to remember was something that happened with Gene McKinney and Admiral Brown and Joe Grenfell, who was over on the staff of Admiral Lockwood.* We used to like to tease Joe Grenfell, and we would call him on the phone and we'd try to imitate Admiral Brown's voice, and we would say, "This is Admiral Brown. I want you to do so and so and so and so." Joe never knew whether to take it seriously or not. Finally he decided we were pulling his leg enough, so one fine late afternoon or early evening, Babe called down to the office, and Joe had the duty. Admiral Brown called down to have his car sent out to quarters to pick him up.

Joe said, "Ah, go on. I'm on to you." Whereby Babe had him up and dressed him down, and we all enjoyed that. That was the only thing I remember about any kind of incident.

---
*Captain Elton W. Grenfell, USN, later vice admiral, was strategic planning officer on the staff of Commander Submarines Pacific Fleet; Vice Admiral Charles A. Lockwood, Jr., USN.

Q: Did you have much contact with Admiral Lockwood's staff at all in that position?

Admiral Davidson: Not too much. We saw some of them every day, of course. No, I don't know that we did.

Q: Was there an effort to protect the results of the successful patrols and the successful skippers and put those back into your training program?

Admiral Davidson: Yes. There were two or three things. Babe Brown discouraged a couple of them. This business that Sam Dealey used, the business of deliberately putting your periscope up and holding it up until the enemy started coming right down your throat and then firing, we discouraged that a little bit.* We didn't think that was a great tactic. It served a great purpose for Sam Dealey until he was lost. That's probably the way he was lost, as far as anybody can tell. We later discouraged things like Gene Fluckey did of going into harbors where there might not be a chance of getting out, even.** Some of those things obviously worked quite well on a one-time basis, but once the enemy knows about them, they're liable not to work

---

*Commander Samuel D. Dealey, USN, a Medal of Honor winner for his exploits in command of the USS Harder (SS-257).
**Commander Eugene B. Fluckey, USN, Medal of Honor winner as commanding officer of the USS Barb (SS-220).

the next time.

Q: Did you have a means of disseminating the enemy tactics in the same way?

Admiral Davidson: No, no, not to my knowledge.

Q: I thought maybe some of the things that people had learned, ASW things that the Japanese had done, would be . . .*

Admiral Davidson: The only thing that I remember that we all believed was that the Japanese had set their depth charges to go off--I'm trying to remember now whether we thought they were too shallow or too deep. Probably we thought they were too shallow, and that a lot of them, if they had gone off a little deeper, might have gotten us. No, I don't remember much about that.

Q: Where were you living in Hawaii?

Admiral Davidson: We had a place in Makalapa. A set of quarters was assigned to Lou Chappel, Gene McKinney, John Davidson, and Charlie Jackson, the four of us.** I think we were all on Babe

---
*ASW--antisubmarine warfare.
**Lieutenant Commander Charles B. Jackson, Jr., USN, had been commissioning skipper of the USS Pampanito (SS-383) in November 1943 and was then relieved following her shakedown.

Brown's staff. I can tell you an amusing story about that. We were having lunch one day when about a 65-year-old formerly retired commander arrived at the door, and when Gene McKinney went to the door--and Gene, I have to tell you, was a graduate lawyer--Gene went to the door, and the commander said, "Is there a dog living in this house?"

And Gene said, "No, this house is assigned to Commanders Chappel, Davidson, McKinney, and Jackson."

About that time, the Filipino steward put his head over Gene's shoulder and said, "I think he may be talking about my dog."

So then Gene said, "Well, what about the dog?"

And the visiting commander said, "Well, I want you to keep that dog tied up."

And Gene said, "Why?"

The commander said, "He just came over and tore all the tail feathers out of my hen."

And Gene said, "Do you keep your hen tied up?"

And this commander said, "No. It's a pet hen."

And Gene said, "Well, this is a pet dog." The poor guy from next door walked off. He had met his match. That always tickled me that a lawyer could ask the best questions. Anyway, we did keep the dog locked up after that.

Q: That's an interesting mental picture of a chicken on a leash.

Davidson #3 - 213

Admiral Davidson: We lived very comfortably there. Of course, whatever they called the recreation organization there owned quite a few automobiles, and we could sign up to get a car and go places if we needed them, so that's the way we managed to go get gals and take them to the submarine base dances, and things like that. Of course, all of us were married, but we were all still dancing. There were lots of available gals there in Honolulu.

Q: That was probably early 1945 when you got back to Washington.

Admiral Davidson: Right. I got back early in '45. Shortly after I took over in '45, I was given a set of TAD orders to visit Pearl Harbor and Brisbane and Perth, to talk about the future officer assignment with all of the submarine commands of the Pacific.* This was before we realized the war was about to end. I made the trip out there and visited all of them. As it turned out, I was in Pearl in a conference with Admiral Lockwood when the word came that the war was over.

Q: Had you really done the detailing job at all at that point?

Admiral Davidson: I had taken over, but we hadn't issued much in the way of orders. It was to prepare for the following year;

---

*TAD--temporary additional duty.

that was the idea. We were trying to line up everything for the following year. I was trying to find out just what the force commanders wanted, because we were trying our best in Washington to cooperate with the force commanders. It was difficult in some cases. They were pretty unreasonable in some ways. For instance, if you had a submarine officer who happened to also be a postgraduate in some specialty and he was needed, perhaps, in Washington, the submarine force didn't want to let him go. But at the same time, the force commander wanted results out of that office in Washington. Lockwood could be very unreasonable. He once accused me of having round heels. I said, "What do you mean?"

He said, "You're a pushover for anybody in Washington." But he never made me feel like he meant it. He just jokingly said that, because we were detaching people that he didn't want detached.

Q: He couldn't corner the market. Surely he realized that.

Admiral Davidson: One of the things that had happened there was that Ernie King issued an order that no senior officer would be ordered to command a division or a squadron who had not made a combat war patrol.* Well, Buddy Yeomans was on Lockwood's staff,

---

*Fleet Admiral Ernest J. King, USN, Commander in Chief U.S. Fleet and Chief of Naval Operations.

and Buddy was a real fine submarine officer, one of the best, but he had never made a war patrol.* So Lockwood wanted me to see what I could do about getting Buddy a squadron. He was senior enough for a squadron at that time. So I took the bull by the horns and went over to CNO's office. Admiral Dickie Edwards was number two to Ernie King.** I had worked for and with him in New London in my submarine days and knew him quite well. So I went to see him first. He said, "Well, Johnny, if we were to give Buddy a squadron, which he richly deserves, and which I would be very much in favor of, we would have to make an exception." Then he stopped. I didn't reply right away. And he said, "And you know, an exception is sort of like the lovely 18-year-old from the lovely family who suddenly discovers she's about that much pregnant, not too much, but just this much pregnant." And then he didn't say any more. So I waited and I waited. Finally he said, "Well, is there anything else to take up today?"

And I said, "No, sir."

So I wrote to Charlie Lockwood and said, "Cominch said no, there will be no exceptions." I didn't tell him the story. I just said, "He said no, there would be no exceptions." And there were no exceptions. At one point, Ernie King stepped in and decided at that one point you had to have had a combat war patrol or you couldn't be a boss.

---

*Commander Elmer E. Yeomans, USN.
**Admiral Richard S. Edwards, USN, Vice Chief of Naval Operations.

I don't know whether I told this the last time you were here or not, but there was a boy in the class of '27--I think it was John De Tar--who had gone out and had a rather unproductive patrol, and his division commander was Marmaduke O'Leary.* Marmaduke O'Leary had never made a war patrol in his life, but he went over the patrol report of this officer, and he just really criticized, as strongly as he could, this officer for lack of aggressiveness, lack of this, lack of that, so on and so forth. So we were all down at the pier to see this next sailing of this boat when it was going on its next war patrol, and the skipper was on the bridge, and the division commander O'Leary was there on the pier alongside all the rest of us. Everybody was waving goodbye, good luck, all this, and so on. The captain said, "All right, take in all lines, all back two-thirds."

Whereupon the division commander yelled, "Boy, I wish I were in your shoes!"

And the skipper said, "All stop, all ahead one-third, get the lines over." He called over and said, "Okay, you brave son of a bitch, come and take it."

Well, it ended there. The skipper went on out. I can hear it today. "You brave son of a bitch, come on, you take it." That, I think, was the type of thing that King may have been

---

*Lieutenant Commander John L. De Tar, USN, commanding officer of the USS <u>Tuna</u> (SS-203); Commander Forrest Marmaduke O'Leary, USN.

trying to avoid. However, I don't think you had to have made a war patrol to be an understanding boss.

Q: They started out the war with seniors who hadn't made war patrols.

Admiral Davidson: Right. Right. And Buddy Yeomans, of course, was just really tops as an officer. I think he would have done well as a squadron commander, and I would have been happy to have him as my squadron commander.

Q: Were you frustrated and disappointed that you didn't get a division and a wolf pack?

Admiral Davidson: To some extent, yes, although I think, probably, when it comes to benefiting my career, the detail office did me just as much good, as it turned out, because I learned more about what makes the wheels go around in Washington and so on, and I think that's a necessity nowadays. You have to be able to understand what's coming from the front.

Q: How much different was the job then than the one you had been in six or eight years earlier when Hazlett had it?*

---

*Commander Edward E. Hazlett, Jr., USN, had been the submarine detail officer in the Bureau of Navigation in the late 1930s when Davidson served there with him.

Admiral Davidson: Well, we had all the machinery that you could imagine. I could just say to a director of a section, "Give me a list of all submarine officers and their qualifications," and it came out as a printed list, started right off with Admiral Chester W. Nimitz, qualified for command in such and such a year, and had the following commands, and right on down.* You had that all done for you, you see. Then that simplified the task. We still did the personal letter approach. It seems to me that there were times when I was dictating 30 personal letters a day to people about assignments and so on. Otherwise, perhaps it wasn't that different, because I had been brought up under the old system.

Q: Did you have a problem at that point in the war, of the skippers who were relieved for apparently not being able to do the job and any plan of what you'd then do with those people?

Admiral Davidson: No. By the time I got back, those people were already out and reassigned. People like Mort Mumma, who, strangely enough, made a great comeback by volunteering for PT boats, after cracking up completely in submarines.** Then he

---
*In 1945, Fleet Admiral Chester W. Nimitz, USN, was Commander in Chief Pacific Fleet and Pacific Ocean Areas.
**Lieutenant Commander Morton C. Mumma, Jr., USN, had been relieved of command of the USS Sailfish (SS-192).

volunteered for PT boats and was quite a leader. That's a strange comeback. I think all the commanding officers that they felt were not going to produce, they were all absorbed some place.

Q: People that were moving up then; these skippers had proved themselves as execs.

Admiral Davidson: Yes. We even had one boat where the skipper had been the junior officer at the beginning of the war, and he stayed on that thing, went all the way up the line, and finally became skipper. I think that was Kefauver, maybe.* I'm trying to remember.

I think the biggest problem I had in the detail office was when the war was over. When the war was over, the reserve officers went out on points. We ended up with all kinds of ships where the captain could just walk off and go home, and a lot of them were out in the Far East. We had to provide experienced commanding officers. One of the great sources was the submarine force, because even though they were young, a lot of them, they had all been commanding officers. So the captain detail desk, of course, was senior to the submarine detail desk, and you were all

---

*Lieutenant (junior grade) Russell Kefauver, USN, was in the crew of the submarine Tambor (SS-198) when she went into commission on 3 June 1940 and eventually worked his way up to take command in 1943. He was the skipper for her ninth and tenth war patrols.

in his organization. He could say to me, "I need four skippers and we've got to get them out to Manila to pick up four transports to bring back all of the people. The war is over, and they all want to come home, and there's nobody to bring the ships back."

I remember one case particularly, which I hated to do. Mike Fenno, class of '25, was a wartime skipper, and he had been relieved and he was on his way to the East Coast for duty.* He was driving across the country. We found him in St. Louis or someplace where he was visiting family, separated him from his family, sent him back out to San Francisco and flew him to Manila to take command of a transport to come back. I was very fond of Mike Fenno. I hated to do that, because I was the one who had to write the orders. But we did a lot of that kind of stuff. Right after the war, we had a great deal in the detail office, a great deal of this, trying to fill vacancies. My assistant, for instance, was taken away from me for a half of each day to go work in what they called shore detail office, trying to replace people who were going out faster than we could replace some of them. If the job could get along without someone for a while, well, you didn't replace him. But one of the interesting jobs I had was an extra duty. We had doctors leaving the service as fast as they could; they made so much money on the outside. That was one of my additional duties as submarine detail officer, to

---
*Captain Frank W. Fenno, USN.

pass on the release of doctors who were requesting retirement or wanted to resign. We had a case of a young doctor from someplace up in Minnesota. They had a senator who called up the chief of the Bureau of Personnel and practically demanded that this doctor be released. He said, "He comes from a town of about 1,000 people. They have no medical services. They have no doctors in town. He's badly needed to give them one doctor."

So the chief of the bureau finally said to me, "You're going to have to violate your rules, but let him go." And as it happened, at the time he was at an air station down in Texas somewhere. So we issued orders releasing him from duty.

Two or three weeks went by, and this senator called. I don't know whether the chief wasn't in or what, but the call was transferred to me, and the senator said, "Where in hell is that Dr. So-and-so?"

I said, "I don't know. We released him. He was detached about two weeks ago with orders to proceed to his home."

Well, he said, "The damn fool has never arrived."

I said, "Well, let me look into it." Well, you know where we found this doctor? He had set up practice down in Florida, where he had a very lucrative practice.

I called the senator and informed him that the boy had never gone home at all. He said--I won't quote him. He named him all kinds of things. He said, "I want you to get him back in the Navy as fast as you can."

I said, "Well, I don't think we have any way to do that. Everything's been accomplished." We couldn't draft him.

Well, he said, "That's the last time anybody ever pulls one on me." He thanked me for all our efforts, but that kind of stuff was extra duty. We were doing that kind of stuff all the time.

For a while after the war, it was very difficult to man the Navy, because the Navy didn't shrink as fast as the personnel did.

Q: Some ships, I guess, just had to be left where they were.

Admiral Davidson: Yes.

Q: Did you get into the political side of justifying how large a force the Navy should have after the war?

Admiral Davidson: No, no. I never got into any of that, and I suppose that went on over in CNO, plus in the planning groups, probably in BuPers, but I wasn't in planning or the operating outfits.* But I had gone to that job in '45 with the almost promise at the time, not knowing the war was going to end, but the promise was that I didn't have to stay but a year. It ended up I had to stay two years.

---
*BuPers—Bureau of Naval Personnel.

Davidson #3 - 223

Q: Had you been reunited with your family at that point?

Admiral Davidson: No. We were getting a divorce.

Q: I remember reading that that was the period when the economy was being transformed, and it was difficult to find a place to live, to get a car, and all that. Did servicemen have any advantages?

Admiral Davidson: No. I lived most of the time in Washington. The last year I was there, Roy Benson and I shared an apartment. Before that, I lived at the Army-Navy Club in town. As to the automobile business, I couldn't get one. I even asked my brother in Warren, Pennsylvania, to see if he could get a car for me. He said every dealer in Warren said they were very fond of me, but they had so many customers up there, that they'd take every car they could get. So I couldn't get one. No, they didn't give us any special advantages. Roy Benson and I used to walk down Connecticut Avenue in Washington with our laundry bags over our shoulder and go to one of these coin washer things, get our laundry done, and carry it back. We were always dressed in our best blue uniforms and wearing our ribbons. We just wanted the public to know that just because we were captains didn't mean we didn't have to do our own laundry.

Q: What do you remember about Benson from that period?

Admiral Davidson: He was quite a character. He had never been married, and I used to joke with him a lot about it. He was 40 years old, at least. "The first thing you know, you'll be so set in your ways, you'll never be able to get married."

He said, "I'd rather be set in my ways than in some gal's ways." Then he met Vida, the widow of Dave Connole, who was class of '36.*

Q: Being a detailer, did you get to detail yourself to your next job at that point?

Admiral Davidson: Yes, yes. I ordered myself to Panama as a division commander. I went down to the sub base, which was on the Pacific side by then. I was a division commander down there for a year with quarters, submarine pay, and no income taxes.

The only very, very unusual thing that happened during that year was that I rode Frank Lynch's submarine, which was my division flagship, and I believe the other two boats went along with me, and we went down around the Cape and then returned to the Pacific via the Straits of Magellan, and came back, came on up the West Coast and stopped in some of the ports.** It was a

---
*Commander David R. Connole, USN, commanding officer of the Trigger (SS-237) when she was lost in March 1945. Benson wound up being married to the former Mrs. Connole for nearly 40 years, until her death in the mid-1980s.
**Commander Frank C. Lynch, Jr., USN.

Davidson #3 - 225

very, very interesting cruise to make on a submarine in peacetime. One of the things I remember distinctly was coming back through those straits; you could have tied up to the bank. The water was deep right up to the bank, much the same as in Argentia. They say that when the sailing ships first went through there, that's exactly what they did. When the current ran the wrong direction, they eased over to the banks and got some line over and tied up to trees. That was the story they told me, anyway. I visited the very southern point of South America. It was Punta Arenas. I think that's Chile. We visited down there. We went into a port which was the port for Lima, the capital of Peru.* A very interesting cruise. That was the highlight of my year as a division commander.

Q: What was the purpose of this mission?

Admiral Davidson: I think just to make a cruise and demonstrate that we could go to sea at the time. Another interesting thing that happened, one of my skippers came in one day and said, "I have a chief petty officer who is just not qualified for anything."

I said, "Well, why don't you disqualify him?"

"This is the story. He was a lookout on board the USS

---

*Callao, Peru, is the port city for Lima.

Davidson #3 - 226

<u>Tullibee</u> when it was lost. He found himself swimming, and the Japs picked him up. He was in prison in Japan for the duration of the war and then was released. You probably remember the Navy then said to everybody that they were entitled to advancement to the rank they would have been in they had never been prisoner, and so he became a chief torpedoman, I believe. He was just worthless. Not only that, he refused to attempt to catch up. He said, 'Why should I work at it? I'm already achieved it.'" The skipper had to request his detachment.

Q: During the war, of course, there was a great motivator for submariners and skippers. I wonder if there was any sort of a letdown that you felt as division commander after that.

Admiral Davidson: No, no. It just seemed to me that that was the service to be in. That was the service to be in.

Q: Why do you say that?

Admiral Davidson: It just seemed to me that we were one great big, good family. We were very proud of our wartime accomplishments, and we were proud of each other, and it still had the great advantages of early command and pleasant duty, and so on, as far as I was concerned. There was never a question in my mind but that was the place to be, as long as you were young enough to do it. If there comes a time when you get to the point where there's only one or two submarine jobs left, why, you won't necessarily have one of them.

Q: What role did you have as division commander, training, inspections, and so forth?

Admiral Davidson: Inspections and training. That's right. Although not very much training. Most of the skippers were pretty experienced. The division commander was probably more administrative than anything else.

Q: Why did you not have income tax in Panama?

Admiral Davidson: That just happened to be the law. I don't know why that was passed. Perhaps when we were trying to build the canal and all that, an inducement to people to go down there. You had income tax on interest and dividends and things like that, but not on your government salary.

Q: Was the living still as pleasant and cheap as you had known it before?

Admiral Davidson: Not quite as cheap, but it was pleasant, and we had nice quarters. We had a nice quarters and a nice, friendly group. It was just like a little village, just about like this area right here. Lots of golf. As a division commander, you rode a boat down the bay once in a while, but you didn't have to do it all the time.

Q: Were there any skippers that you especially remember that were in your division?

Admiral Davidson: Frank Lynch was perhaps the most outstanding of my skippers.* Frank Lynch was the class of '38. He was the five-striper. He was a top-notch football player. He stood very high academically, and he was about 6'4" and probably very close to 240, something like that, which made him pretty large to get down a submarine hatch. He was married to an admiral's daughter, who was just about as thin and small as he was big and tall. Frank had been the exec to Sam Dealey during all those patrols. He's the one who told me he was sure how Sam went. He said Sam used to sit in the room and cry after those attacks and say, "Don't let me do it again." But he'd always do it again. I enjoyed him very much. He was the skipper of my flagship, and it was his boat that I rode around the horn. A terrible, terrible, terrible calamity happened to Frank. I don't know whether he was commander or whether he had already made captain, but he was in

---

*Commander Frank C. Lynch, Jr., USN, was commanding officer of the USS Cutlass (SS-478).

Colombo, Ceylon, and he was in a taxi being driven some place, and the taxi driver went berserk and put his foot on the gas pedal all the way to the floor and tore down the main drag. There was a horrible accident at one intersection, and Frank was left lying in the middle of the intersection and, I understood, given up for dead. Somebody managed to gather him up. They found he was alive and that started the wheels rolling, and he was flown to a hospital in Japan, and he recovered, but he lost the sight in one eye and didn't have very good sight in the other eye, and, of course, had to be retired.* The last time I saw him, he walked into my office when I was ComTraPac, after I left the Naval Academy, and my chief of staff came in and said, "There's a retired officer out here who wants to know if you are the same Admiral Davidson that used to get everybody to do all his work for him."**

I said, "You're talking about Frank Lynch," because Frank used to say that.

Q: On to the <u>Orion</u>. What was it like to command a big ship like that after having been in small ones?

Admiral Davidson: It was quite a thrill in a way for shiphandling purposes, but the funny part of that whole story was

---
*Lynch was retired medically on 1 September 1954 in the rank of captain.
**ComTraPac--Commander Training Command Pacific.

the skipper of the Orion that I was relieving was one class junior to me, Freddy Laing, class of 1930. Whether you know or not, class of '30 had to revert to commander after the war.* So I relieved Freddy when he was a captain. He became a commander the next day. I flew to Norfolk and went aboard, and rode him back to Panama and relieved him. Freddy was a little tiny guy and a great friend of mine, and just as cocky as the day is long. I very much enjoyed taking a ride with him, watching the shiphandling, so on and so forth.

Then I seized every opportunity to go out in the Orion in Panama Bay, and we cruised even down to Peru and took the squadron commander along with us. The squadron commander was originally Creed Burlingame, who was a famous wartime skipper, and then he was relieved by Gene McKinney.** Another submariner, a great friend of mine, Weaver Garnett, out of '33, was the operations officer on the staff and rode with us all the time.*** Elliott Loughlin was a division commander.**** Elliott relieved me as the division commander. Paul Schoeni had the other division.*****

We made a fleet problem in the Atlantic with the Orion the year I had her. I don't know what part. We were probably one of

---
*Captain Frederick W. Laing, USN.
**Captain Eugene B. McKinney, USN.
***Commander Philip W. Garnett, USN.
****Commander Charles E. Loughlin, USN.
*****Commander Walter P. Schoeni, USN.

the transport squadrons or something that were being convoyed someplace during the fleet problem. When we finished, we put into Norfolk. While we were in Norfolk, it occurred to me that it would be a nice thing to take my father and mother back to Panama with me. You won't believe it, but I managed it. We had on board the Orion, of course, staterooms for submarine officers. When they were in port, they could come over and sleep on board the tender. So we had ample room. I decided that with my old BuPers connections, I'd call George Mandley, who was the senior civilian in BuPers transportation. So I called George and said, "Are there any rules that say I couldn't take my father and mother back to Panama with me in Orion?"

He said, "I don't know why not. Go ahead."

So I called my father, who was then 75 years of age and had never seen the ocean, asked him if he and Mother could be in Norfolk in two days' time to come and visit me in Panama, and I'd take them down in my ship. That's just what happened. I met them down there in time, we got them aboard. I put my father in my cabin, and I put my mother in the squadron commander's cabin. And then Brooks Harral, Brooks and Sally Harral, Brooks was one of the division commanders, I guess--I guess he was before or after Schoeni--but Sally's mother was a Mumma, and she had two sons in the Navy--Mort Mumma, who was a submarine skipper, and Al

Mumma, who was later chief of the Bureau of Ships.* Somehow or other, we managed to have her aboard, too. She was in one of the division commander's cabins.

We made the trip all the way to Panama, through the canal. It was just a great experience. Every night the chief master-at-arms would come to the cabin and say to me, "Captain, your movie is ready," and my mother and father and Mrs. Mumma and I would follow him back to the fantail, and they would have six or seven chairs all lined up with white linen covers, and the crew was already seated. As soon as we sat down, the chief master-at-arms would say, "Start the movie." My father was pretty impressed about all of this. His memory of me was at age 16 when I wasn't quite allowed to drive the family car yet, and he wasn't sure I should be allowed to drive it, and then I'd gone off to the Naval Academy, and he'd never seen me really in operation since.

After we had been there about three days, we were having dinner one night, and during a lull in the conversation, my father suddenly looked at me, and he said, "All right, John. I'm now willing to admit you're old enough to drive a car." It was a great thrill. My brothers tell me that when he came home, he spent several weeks standing on the main street corner in Warren, Pennsylvania, telling his friends about his trip in his son's ship. Not many people have had that privilege, you know. It was

---

*Captain Brooks J. Harral, USN; Captain Morton C. Mumma, Jr., USN; Captain Albert G. Mumma, USN.

quite a privilege.

When my year ended in the Orion and it came time for me to return to the United States, the Orion was designated to act as a transport for dependents in the Canal Zone returning to the United States that year. My family, my dog, and my automobile were all duly loaded, and I thought this was really something, when I had a call from the Commandant of the 15th Naval District saying that he had a retired captain and his wife that he wanted assigned to the commodore's cabin. I said, "I'm sorry. It's already assigned to my family."

Whereupon, the commandant said, "You can't take your family. You can take a lot of dependents, but a captain can't take his own wife. It might be too disturbing."

So I was pretty disturbed. I finally dealt with Washington, and Washington wanted to know how many spaces were available. I listed everything except the commodore's cabin, the squadron commander's cabin. When I was asked why, I said, "Well, it's connected to the captain's cabin, and I think the captain shouldn't be disturbed." The next thing I knew, I got a call from the commandant's office saying he'd like to have his friend the captain and his wife assigned to the division commander's cabin, and it would be all right if my family accompanied me. We ate in my mess. We had a very nice trip up. The first lieutenant was a former enlisted man, lieutenant commander, who was just one of the greatest. His name was Bob Fisher.* He built sandboxes for the children and did everything to make it a perfectly happy cruise, unlike most military transports, so much so that one day one of the submarine skippers' wives and her little girl were walking the deck and they met me, and the mother said to the little girl, "Janie, you know who this is, don't you? This is the captain."

Little Janie looked up and said, "He is not. Uncle Bob Fisher is." He's the one who made the sandboxes.

Anyway, we had a pretty hectic finish to the trip. Twenty-four hours out of Norfolk, I had just gone back to the movies with my family, when a messenger came and had a dispatch which said that my wife's mother had had a very severe heart attack and might not live more than a couple of days or something like that. So I left the movies and went to the bridge, got ahold of the engineer officer and said, "What kind of speed can you put on?" We had diesel engines in the Orion. I said, "Boost it up as high as we can get it." So we did. Two hours later, we got an SOS. There was a freighter 100 miles astern of us, a man had been hit by the boom of a crane and needed immediate medical attention, and probably wasn't going to live. There I was trying to get my wife home to her mother. An SOS. We turned around, went back, something like 3:00 or 4:00 in the morning. We had them steaming

---

*Lieutenant Commander Robert Fisher, USN.

toward us and we steamed toward them, and we were able to transfer this wounded man to our sick bay. Then we turned around and started for Norfolk. Everything went swimmingly until we got about 50 miles out of Norfolk--pea soup fog. Radar was only just so good, you know. You couldn't feel very good. You couldn't travel very fast in pea soup; I was on the bridge all that night when we finally got in to Norfolk, got tied up to the pier at the naval base there. The first order of business, we hoisted my car over, and my family and the dog started for Baltimore. I finally got a chance to sit down. I was unshaven, dirty, just in terrible shape, and dead on my feet, when a messenger came and said Admiral Fife was in town from New London and he'd like to see me over in the bachelor officers' quarters right away.* So I took it to mean right away. They had brought a car.

Q: Was he ComSubLant at that point?

Admiral Davidson: ComSubLant, my boss. They had brought a car up, so they took me over to BOQ. When I walked into his quarters, his room, whatever it was, I was smoking. He said to me, "Is that a tax-free cigarette?"

I said, "Yes, sir." The only kind they had aboard ship was tax-free. I said, "Yes, sir."

---
*Rear Admiral James Fife, Jr., USN, Commander Submarine Force Atlantic Fleet.

He said, "You know better than to smoke tax-free cigarettes on the beach, don't you? That's against the law."

Good God. How inconsiderate can you be? So I had to put my cigarette out. I went to my conference with him, and when I finished, he was very nice. He said, "Now have one of my cigarettes," which were not tax-free. But he let me sit through the whole conference without a cigarette, and I was a great smoker in those days.

I was detached from the Orion right there in Norfolk.

Q: What was this urgency in getting to see him at that point?

Admiral Davidson: Only that he was in town and I was one of his fleet, and he wanted to see me. I was bound for New London anyway to become SubRon Two, which would be right under his wing.* As a matter of fact, his office window was just up above the pier where I was tied up.

Q: How was the Orion as a tender during your time in command?

Admiral Davidson: I thought it was great. Of course, I would say that. I thought it was great. I thought we did a great job. We had some very fine personnel. They did a great job. One of

---
*SubRon Two--Submarine Squadron Two.

the things that Jimmy Fife did to me while I had the tender--this will make an interesting story, too--he came to Panama on a visit one time while I had the tender, and he discovered that we had slot machines on board the Orion. Now, the slot machines paid for all our crew's athletics and recreation and everything. They just made money hand over fist. So old Jimmy Fife saw that I had these slot machines, and he didn't say anything to me. But when he went back to New London, he had Mike Fenno, his chief of staff, write me a letter and call to my attention that it was a violation of the Navy Regulations to have gambling devices on board ship.* Well, I wasn't going to give in too easily, so I went to the dictionary and looked up the definition of gambling. I found one that said words to this effect: something about participating in a game of chance where you had a chance of making a lot of money or winning. So I wrote back to Mike and said, "I don't consider our machines the way they're set as gambling devices, because we have them set and you can't win. They pay only 20%. The machine gets 80%, so nobody can win, really. He's going to pay 80% just to play."

Well, the next thing I got was a dispatch from Mike. It said, "Get rid of the slot machines anyway." So I had to get rid of my slot machines. But you know what the machines did; they funded our baseball team, our swimming team, everything we did

---

*Captain Frank W. Fenno, USN.

was paid for by men who were willing to put in nickels and dimes in a slot machine all the time, and they loved it. So Jimmy Fife had his way again with me. He always had his way with me, because he was the boss.

Q: How did you pay for all of those activities after the slot machines were gone?

Admiral Davidson: You had to draw on BuPers' generosity to get it, because most of the recreation funds came from BuPers, you know.* We just had a little nicer recreation than we could get with just what we got from BuPers.

Q: How much did you get involved in the repair department facilities?

Admiral Davidson: Very little. As I mentioned once before, I was not a nuts and bolts man. I was just an administrator, I guess, probably, a demonstrator who prided myself a little bit in my ability to handle a ship and knew how to go to sea, and enjoyed going to sea. I enjoyed it very much.

Q: You were probably only involved, then, when there was some

---
*BuPers--Bureau of Naval Personnel.

sort of problem.

Admiral Davidson: Yes. That's right. Then, of course, I left the <u>Orion</u> and went up to New London, where I became ComSubRon Two. We had two squadrons there--Two and Eight. The senior one of the two had an additional designation. It seems to me it was called development squadron or something like that.

Q: That sounds familiar. I think Admiral Benson had a hand in that.

Admiral Davidson: I had additional duty as that, and Chuck Triebel, a classmate of mine, was my running mate.* He had Squadron Eight. He was relieved by Rebel Lowrance, who later became ComSubLant.** I was relieved by Sandy McGregor, class of '30.*** But I had a squadron up there for a year. We lived in town in New London. I enjoyed it thoroughly. There was no going to sea then, except to ride a boat out into the sound once in a while.

The job of being a squadron commander was pleasant. The squadron commander was purely an administrative job, inspections, administrative work, and so on. Your two division commanders

---
*Captain Charles O. Triebel, USN.
**Captain Vernon L. Lowrance, USN, later vice admiral, was Commander Submarines Atlantic from 1964 to 1966.
***Captain Louis D. McGregor, Jr., USN.

took care of most of your load, and you had an operations officer, you had an engineering officer, and you had a communications officer. We had a perfectly good staff to do everything. Like Frank Lynch used to say, I managed to have everybody do all my work for me.

Q: Well, you must have done something in the role of squadron commander.

Admiral Davidson: I didn't find it a very difficult job.

Q: Was there any aspect of the developmental work that you got involved in?

Admiral Davidson: No, no. Of course, all the boats were the fleet type boats. My flagship was the <u>Flying Fish</u>.

Q: Were you getting any of the Guppies by that point?

Admiral Davidson: I didn't have a Guppy, no. I didn't have a Guppy. I'm trying to think whether Squadron Eight had a Guppy or not.* I don't remember that they did.

---

*After the war, fleet submarines were outfitted with greater storage battery capacity for more power and were called "guppy" for Greater Underwater Propulsion Power.

Q: Do you have any recollections of Admiral Fife when you were working that much more directly for him?

Admiral Davidson: Yes. He loved to play poker. He didn't drink. So when we were going to play poker with Jimmy Fife, he insisted that we invite him to come when we were ready to play and not to have a drink first. Or even if you were going to invite him to dinner, don't invite him in time to have a drink before dinner; invite him when it's time to eat, and then play poker afterwards. He had a favorite game, which he called "True S.O.B." I'm not sure that I can even remember, except that it always ended up with one person having all of the money after that hand. Then you had to get out some more chips, because somehow or other, somebody always had all the money after that hand. It wasn't a poker game. It was just a real game of chance. Talk about gambling! It was a game of chance.

Jimmy Fife was a bachelor. I cannot remember whether it was a result of his wife's death or what, but he had a couple of daughters, and he was very strict with them. They didn't like his restrictions. He still loved the Navy above everything else. He loved his submarines above everything else, and he was always on hand. He always would look after his people, so I had to take my hat off to old Jimmy Fife always, and I was very happy when he made admiral, because a lot of people with his sort of personality wouldn't have been sure candidates for flag rank, I wouldn't think.

Q: What do you mean by his personality?

Admiral Davidson: Sort of gruff in a way, and abrupt, quite often, quite abrupt. But all in all, I'll have to give him pretty good marks, far better than I ever gave his running mate out in Australia, Ralph Christie.*

Q: Did you run into Christie once you got out there?

Admiral Davidson: When I went out there, the only time I ran into Christie was when I made that trip after I took over the detail office. I went out and I was a guest in his mess in Perth. He soon learned what I thought about him. They had a habit after each luncheon, each person ordered a package of cigarettes from the cigar mess--or was it a carton. Whatever it was, it doesn't make any difference. Then they would roll the dice to see who would pay for all of them, and then they'd roll again to see who'd get all of them. So Admiral Christie rolled the dice at the head of the table, and I was his honored guest, sitting on his right. He handed the dice to me, and I handed it to his chief of staff. He said to me, "You're not going to roll?"

---
*Rear Admiral Ralph W. Christie, USN.

I said, "You know I never gamble with you, Admiral." And I just left that to his staff to think about. It was all based on previous gambling with him in golf, and how niggardly he was.

Q: What about Admiral Lockwood? What do you remember of him from your contact with him?

Admiral Davidson: Very pleasant. Except for the time when he told me I had round heels. When the war was over, we had this big party for him in Washington. We had a big dinner dance at the Statler. During his remarks, he said, "I actually have heard some of you, since I've returned, referring to yourselves as submariners, and I want you to know that you're submariners. A submariner is an inferior mariner." So I've been correcting people ever since. That's a British expression--sub-mariner. Charlie Lockwood was great, great.

Q: You were talking about your squadron command. What was the tender you were based in?

Admiral Davidson: We didn't have tenders. We were based on the base, my memory of it, anyway.

Q: Are there any skippers of individual boats that you recall?

Admiral Davidson: I'm trying to remember. I think there was a boy by the name of Freeland Carde, and he had been on my boat when I had the Blackfish operating out of Scotland.* I remember him probably because when returning from that long cruise where we steered into the wind all the time, we had picked up a landfall on the Shetland Islands, and then we were proceeding down through the Minches, and we had an escort vessel. I don't know if it was an antisubmarine vessel, but a British destroyer type, but smaller than a destroyer. It was escorting us down through the Minches, which were used also as a convoy route for big convoys. Freeland Carde was the officer of the deck, and the orders to the officer of the deck were we were never to lose sight of the escort vessel, never. I was to be called if there was any suspicion that they were getting out of sight. Well, the first thing I heard was a collision alarm. And I bolted to the bridge, and here we were in the middle of about a 25-ship convoy, which was engaged in making a 90-degree right turn. All these ships, spread way out, everything turning. I was in the middle of it going the other way. As soon as I got to the bridge, it was obvious that I couldn't turn to the left, I couldn't turn to the right, I would be crossing the bow of something. So what they were doing was, they were coming to a course that was opposite to the one that I was on. So I said, "All back

---

*Commander Freeland H. Carde, Jr., USN. Carde was a lieutenant (junior grade) while serving in the Blackfish (SS-221).

emergency." And I made a great discovery, that when you got up to speed, which was probably as much as ten or 11 knots astern, and the convoy speed was not over ten knots, you could steer quite well going astern.

Q: Just maintain station.

Admiral Davidson: So I maintained station going astern until the convoy completed the turn, and then when we were like so, I could just ease out and go down one of the lanes between ships. When it was all over with, I went down to the control room--he'd already been relieved--where stood Freeland Carde, leaning on the gyro. He said to me, "Captain, I was scared to death, but as soon as you got to the bridge, I knew everything would be all right."

I looked at him, and I said, "I'm sure you'll never let something like that happen again as long as you live, will you?"

He said, "No, sir."

I said, "Freeland, why didn't you call me?"

He said, "Well, the escort just sort of disappeared, and I speeded up twice thinking I'd catch up with her."

I said, "But your orders were simply don't lose sight. Call me even if you think you're going to lose sight."

Well, it was a lucky day for Freeland Carde that we didn't have a collision, or he'd have never been skipper of a submarine in my squadron later. He was one of them. Let me think. I don't know who all these kids were. Duke Ferrara was the skipper of the Flying Fish before I got there.* The thing I remember about Duke Ferrara is this, that he came into the detail office when the war was just over, and wanted to know what I had in mind for him in the way of a job. I said, "Well, I have you slated for a submarine command."

"Oh," he said, "no. Please, Captain, I've been out there fighting the war for four years. I want shore duty."

I said, "Duke, your class is just now getting command, and, gee, you're turning down a great opportunity to get command of a fleet type submarine."

He said, "I've got to have shore duty. I've been away from home so much."

So I said, "All right. I'll look and see what I can find for you."

As he was about to walk out of my office, he said, "Oh, I forgot to show you a picture of my family." He brings out a picture, and he has four children all four or under. The oldest was only four years old.

I said, "You've been away so much, eh?"

He said, "I used to get leave once a year."

Anyway, Duke eventually went to New London, and he was

---

*Commander Maurice Ferrara, USN.

skipper of the Flying Fish when Bill Irvin was the squadron commander.* Somebody up there sent me in the detail office a copy of an order issued by Bill Irvin, and this is what the order said. It seems that when we went to war, we took what they called the skegs off from the stern of the submarines, the things that protected the propellers when landing alongside piers and so on. We took them off for the war, and they hadn't been put back on again. So there was a rash of boats coming alongside the piers in New London and wrecking a propeller because there was no skeg to keep them fended off. Bill Irvin got out an order to Squadron Two that said, "In the future and until the skegs are replaced on the boats, no one but the commanding officer will bring a boat alongside, with the exception of the Flying Fish, when only the executive officer will bring her alongside." I always loved that. Somebody decided to send me a copy of that order to the detail office so I'd know what he thought about Duke Ferrara's shiphandling.

Q: What was the reason for taking the skegs off?

Admiral Davidson: Probably to help the speed, and we weren't tying up to piers very much. We didn't need them during the war. The ship didn't need them on long patrols.

---
*Captain William D. Irvin, USN, whose oral history is in the Naval Institute collection.

Q: Just something else to drag along.

Admiral Davidson: Right. That just about finishes my submarine duty, because I had my year there as squadron commander, and then, of course, there's nothing left to go to except force commander, and you don't do that until you make flag rank, so I had to go through some other duties first.

When I was leaving the submarine squadron job, I had requested National War College. I had a letter from Washington saying that I had been selected for National War College and that I would go on such and such a date. I've forgotten what time it was exactly. But just before time to receive orders for that, Frank Watkins, who was then the captain detail officer in Washington, and former boss of mine, called me and he said, "The Secretary of the Navy has stepped in and changed some of our plans.* The Secretary has discovered that there are a certain number of officers in the classes of 1925 and '26 who have never been to the National War College, and if they don't go this year, they'll be too senior to go. Therefore, we went over the list of those selected for the War College this year and those who were selected as alternates, and a decision was made by the Secretary that certain of the alternates would replace some of you that had already been selected." He said, "Therefore, Mike Fenno [my

---

*Captain Frank T. Watkins, USN.

old friend Mike Fenno] is to be ordered to the National War College. Where would you like to go for this coming year? You'll go to the National War College the following year."

I said, "Let me think about it." I called Frank back and I said, "I'll tell you what I'd like to do. I'd like to go to the southeastern United States someplace where I can have a set of quarters." This time I couldn't say no income tax. "A set of quarters near a nice golf course and lots of spare time, enough to kill a year."

"Okay." Well, he looked, and he called me up and said, "How would you like to be chief of staff to Admiral Hayler in Charleston, have a nice set of quarters and lots of golf?"*

I said, "Suits me fine."

So we picked up sticks, and we moved everything--baggage, furniture, and all. We arrived in Charleston at the navy yard there on a Thursday. The packers were there on Friday, unpacked everything, and we sort of settled the house and were still hanging pictures on Sunday. I had said, "Let's go play golf."

So Monday I went to my office. I had already made my call on the admiral. I walked in the office, and very shortly thereafter the telephone rang, and it was Frank Watkins. He said, "We're issuing orders to you detaching you next week to go to the Canadian National Defence College."

---

*Rear Admiral Robert W. Hayler, USN, commandant of the Sixth Naval District in Charleston, South Carolina, from 1948 to 1951.

I said, "Where did that come from?"

He said, "We had turned the Canadians down. We said we would not send a naval officer to their National Defence College, because we had not been in a position to invite them to send somebody to the National War College. The State Department has just interceded and said, 'That's not a good enough excuse. If the Canadians want a naval officer there, send one. Why don't you send one?' So the Navy relented, and said, 'Okay.'" So they looked down the list, and here I was. I had orders to the National War College and it didn't materialize, so they said, "Send him to the National Defence College."

So that was on Monday. Wednesday we had the packers pack up all the furniture and everything, and I was told that they didn't know of any place for me to live in Canada, but that I would be coming to Washington for duty after I left Canada. So we drove to Washington.

Incidentally, we had put one of the girls in school in Charleston, had to take her out right away. We drove to Washington and started looking for a place to live. I was given two or three weeks' delay in reporting to Canada. So we finally found a house and bought it. Furnishings were put in storage temporarily. When the time came, I went to Canada. Well, after I'd been there a very short time, I found a lovely apartment down on Lake Ontario, across the street from the yacht club, just the most beautiful setup you can imagine, and only about six blocks from the National Defence College. I could even walk to it. So I called Washington. Of course, we didn't have a phone in my house yet. They got the neighbors next door to answer the phone. "Come on to Canada."

So I said, "Well, the schedule up here shows that we're going to be in New York at the United Nations in a week or two. Why don't you meet me in New York and we'll talk it all over and see."

To make a long story short, the family came to Canada two or three weeks later, and we rented the house, furnished, to four WAVE officers.* We went to Canada. So do you think we came back to Washington after we bought that house?

Q: Of course not.

Admiral Davidson: No. We went to the Naval Academy to become head of the English, History and Government Department. That's the way life goes.

But the Canadian tour was, for my money, one of the real treats that I had in my career.

Q: Why do you say that? What was your feeling about it?

---

*WAVES were U.S. Navy women. The acronym, no longer used for active duty personnel, stood for Women Accepted for Volunteer Emergency Service.

Admiral Davidson: One, it was made up of Canadians and Great Britain officers, a couple of people from the Far East, Pakistan, and anybody that had ever been associated with the British in a way. It was Army, Navy, Air Force, and State or Foreign Office types. First rule of the school was, "There will be no rank. Everybody will be known as Joe, Bob, and Jim. You wear civilian clothes at all times. You don't have to study if you don't want to. You're here for what we have to offer, and for you to get what you want out of it."

So the program, we went to a lecture about 10:00 o'clock in the morning, which was a nice leisurely time to have to be there. Your lecture lasted usually 'til maybe 12:30. Then we all went to the mess and had pink gin and lunch. Then the afternoon was for the library, if you could stay awake. We were formed into what they called syndicates. When we had a problem in strategy, or a problem of any kind, economic or whatever it was, the syndicates were poised against each other. It was done by debate. The reason everybody worked real hard and studied real hard was because you didn't want to get up in front of the whole class and look to be perfectly stupid. You knew you were going to have to speak, probably. They were all canned programs that had been tried in previous years at the college. They were very good. The people we had as visiting lecturers were just really tremendous. One program there that went on for about four weeks, we had a minister or rabbi or whatever from every different

Davidson #3 - 253

religion the world knows, and it was usually on the subject of religion versus communism. We'd have those lectures, and we were able to ask questions. I found it absolutely fascinating, because there was never a dull moment. We had something new every week. Then we started traveling. We came to New York and spent three or four days at the United Nations. Then we came to Washington. We came to other places. I forget where else we went in the United States. We went to the West Coast. Then we toured all of Canada, Vancouver, the Yukon Territory, Alaska, flying in the Canadian aircraft. We did that for as many as four or five weeks of touring. Then the big show, we all took off, and we went for ten weeks to England, the south coast of France, the whole Mediterranean area, Egypt, Jerusalem, Aden, Nairobi, then up along the north coast of Africa, the Mediterranean, and finally back to Ottawa--ten whole weeks. That got to be a little bit tiresome. We'd get out of an airplane, have a lecture, and then the next day get back in an airplane, go someplace else, maybe have more lectures. One of the things that got tiresome was the cocktail party you had to have every place you went, plus keeping up with your clothes.

Q: They have a very similar tour program at the National War College.

Admiral Davidson: I didn't know. But in any event, I found it fascinating, and I made some wonderful friends up there and had a nice time, taught a couple of the British how to play poker, and had a lot of fun doing that.

Q: What are some of the things you learned during this course?

Admiral Davidson: I think I've forgotten them all. I've just been replying to the annual letter they send to keep in touch, and they want to know if we want to have a get-together every year. I said, "No, I don't think I want to do that." But they have reunions. I voted for not more often than every fifth year. I was in what was known, I think, as course four, so it had been going on for only four years when I attended it. We had some very interesting people with great senses of humor.

Let me tell you a cute little story that the Canadian Foreign Office type pulled on us. We had arrived at a Mediterranean port, the north coast of Africa, and we'd been out of touch with any mail for some time. It was the week before we were returning to Canada. We were all sitting in this beautiful garden outside of some sort of hotel, reading our mail, the first mail we'd had in all this time. All of a sudden, this Canadian foreign officer started to laugh his head off. Somebody said to him, "What are you laughing at?"

He said, "Oh, my wife. I can't teach her to speak English. I've been working on trying to teach her to speak English for months."

"What do you mean?"

"Well, listen to what she writes. She says, 'Just think, darling, next week you'll be home. I can hardly wait.'" He said, "I've been trying to teach her for a long time. She can barely wait. I can hardly wait." I always thought that was a real cute story.

But we had some good close calls flying in various aircraft. Still, we all made it. We took off from Aden one time for Nairobi, no more than airborne when we got smoke all over. As we were about to land, a Canadian aviator sitting next to me said, "Gee, I hope he's not going to try to land."

"Why not?"

He said, "Well, we've got a full load of gas, and this plane won't land that heavy. He couldn't possibly put this down that heavy. If we're on fire, it'll be even worse."

Sure enough, we got back to Aden to the airport there, and made the smoothest landing you ever felt, floated down. All the comments from the aviators aboard were that nobody ever made a more beautiful landing in an aircraft than that. It was a British light colonel flying it, and it was a British conversion of one of the British bombers of World War II, converted to a transport.

Anyway, what we found was that somebody had piled a whole lot of rubberized life jackets on top of a lot of radio equipment, and when the radio was lit off, it heated up and caused the rubber to smoke, and that got into the ventilation system and came back through the aircraft. It scared the hell out of us, but otherwise we were all right.

We landed once in Montreal on icy pavement and slid the whole length of the runway into a snow bank, came out of that one all right.

However, I clearly enjoyed that year. I enjoyed the people. Those were the years '50 to '51. For a number of years after that, I kept in pretty close touch. You outgrow people. I don't know what's happened to Brigadier Borradaile or what's happened to Captain Perry or any of them now. They're probably all still going strong.

One of the things I did learn was that the British don't have brigadier generals.

Q: They're brigadiers.

Admiral Davidson: They're brigadiers. I think that maybe they used to make fun of us, the rear admiral of the lower half and the upper half, but what's the difference? We could have been commodores and rear admirals.

Q: Did this course cover strategic issues and geopolitical things?

Admiral Davidson: Yes.

Q: Out of this assignment were the two countries brought closer together at that point, the United States and Canada?

Admiral Davidson: I think so. I'll tell you an interesting thing that happened during my time there. I don't know just when it happened. I was there during the Korean matter. Of course, the U.S. went out to Korea with the United Nations forces and so on and so forth. The Secretary of State for Foreign Affairs of Canada at the time was a man by the name of Lester Pearson, and he came down to Washington.* He conferred with Harry Truman and the Secretary of State, Acheson, and when he came back, the newspapers in Canada were full of criticism for the United States for our part in the Korean affair.** He came down to the Canadian Defence College. Incidentally, our lecture room there, I think the walls were four feet thick. It was really a super, super secret sort of thing. He came down to talk to us, and he said, "I want you to know, and I swear you to secrecy until hell freezes over. What you're reading in the paper is the result of my briefing with the press when I returned, but I want you to

---
*Lester B. Pearson was Canada's Secretary of State for Foreign Affairs from 1948 to 1957 and subsequently the nation's Prime Minister from 1963 to 1968.
**President Harry S. Truman served in that capacity from April 1945 until January 1953. Dean G. Acheson was U.S. Secretary of State from 1949 to 1953.

know what I really said to the President and to the Secretary of State. I said to them that the government of Canada was behind the United States 1,000%, about going into Korea with the United Nations and so on. But if that should become known in Canada, the government of Canada would fall the next day. We don't have the benefit of the U.S. system where you've got four years. We would fall the next day if the people of Canada thought that we approved of intervention in Korea. I want you to know."

Well, that was the first time that I really realized that what you read in the paper might not be representative; and that stood me in good stead when I was in political-military policy later in CNO, because very often we were privy to pretty hush-hush, most secret things, and often the press made us look real bad, because we couldn't divulge what was going on. That was the first time, I think, in my life that I ever realized how different it could be.

One of the interesting things I had happen to me was we had a Jesuit priest on the subject of religion versus communism. He was just absolutely adamant that we shouldn't even be studying communism. He said, "You just should not be studying communism. You're not equipped to understand it. You shouldn't be studying it."

Some young lieutenant colonel who was from Quebec, who was a Catholic himself, got up and asked the question, "Where will we find out about communism if we don't study? We're in the military, and we should understand our business. Where will we find out?"

He said, "The Pope will tell you what to believe. The Pope will tell you what to believe. He knows what's right and what's wrong, and he'll tell you."

I got up and said, "Well, would you tell me what the difference is between that and communism, where the Kremlin tells them what to believe?"

He looked at me for a minute and he said, "You're from the United States. You wouldn't understand anyway."

But these were very interesting discussions that we had, and things that I would never have gotten into if we hadn't been exposed to all these speakers. There were no holds barred. You could say anything you wanted to. As I say, I thoroughly enjoyed it. I think it was good for me, and it was very helpful. I wouldn't be surprised that it had something to do with my getting the political-military job later.

Q: Do you think it was more helpful than our National War College program?

Admiral Davidson: Not necessarily, no. With the exception of, perhaps, exposure to other nationals, which might have been a little added advantage.

Q: Why were the Canadian people so against the Korean intervention?

Admiral Davidson: Canadian people, I think, were influenced mostly by Quebec. None of the Catholic population, other than those that I knew in the military, felt that you should ever have to provide arms. They said, "When the enemy lands on your shore, it's time to grab your pitchfork and repel him." But as far as developing Army, Navy, and Air Force, in general, they weren't in favor of it. They weren't in favor. I think they've changed.

Among other things, I liked the systems I saw going on up there. They had all prospective officers, Army, Navy, Air Force, go to the same academic school, and then they farmed them out in the summertime to their services to get their identification with that service. But they took the same academic program. In other words, they didn't have a West Point and a Naval Academy, and so on. I don't think there was too much wrong with that system, because then I think they understood each other better than we do.

Q: From here you got thrown right back into our system at the Naval Academy.

Admiral Davidson: Right. Then when I came back here, I was here for three years. That, perhaps, ought to be the subject of a new time. I don't know if there's anything else to say about Canada, except that I really enjoyed it, I think it did me a lot of good, whether anybody else does or not. My family enjoyed it.

All of these stories are from memory. I want everybody who listens to this to understand that my memory could be foggy, but most of these things are from memory. But this is one that I remember quite well. I went to work one day when I was the submarine detail officer, and I believe at that time the number one man in the detail office was Roland Smoot.* He called me into his office, and he said, "Johnny, we're probably going to detach you tomorrow."

I said, "How come?"

He said, "The presidential yacht needs a skipper, and they say that he should be experienced as a commanding officer and have some diesel engine experience, and that's right up your alley as a submariner. So you may be it. You're probably it, and you have to be detached tomorrow."

I said, "Who's the skipper now?"

He said, "He's a captain, but he was a mustang. He was an enlisted man, and he came up through the ranks, and he's a buddy of Harry Truman's, and they play poker together all the time. He's quitting. He wants to retire. So we've been told to get a

---
*Captain Roland N. Smoot, USN, later vice admiral, is the subject of a U.S. Naval Institute oral history.

skipper there tomorrow."*

Anyway, I was very concerned, because I was told that by the next day, my orders would be issued. So the next day, one of the first things I did was get ahold of George Leahey, out of '25, who had been skipper of the presidential yacht, and he said, "Well, Johnny, if you have to go, go."** But he said, "Don't get off on the wrong foot. Don't get into their poker games, because they play for a hell of a lot of money. We Navy captains can't afford that kind of stuff. The President always invites the skipper to join the poker game."

I said, "Well, thanks for that advice."

So that day went by and I still hadn't heard anything, and I was not breathing any easier. The next day Roland called me in and said, "You're off the hook."

I said, "What happened?"

He said, "Well, apparently Mr. Truman talked the present captain into staying around for another tour." I can't even remember what that captain's name was, but he was an ex-enlisted man. But for 48 hours there, they had me shaking in my boots

---

*Commander John H. Kevers, USN, formerly a chief boatswain, took command of the USS Williamsburg on 8 November 1945, three days after she relieved the USS Potomac (AG-25) as the presidential yacht. On 10 November, the Williamsburg was reclassified AGC-369. Kevers served as skipper until 7 March 1946, when he was relieved by Commander W.A. Bartos, USN. Kevers retired from active duty in August 1946, at which time he received a tombstone promotion to captain.
**Captain George A. Leahey, Jr., USN.

that I might have to go to be the skipper of the presidential yacht. Of course, however much prestige or whatever went with it, I didn't want it. I just didn't want to be involved in that kind of deal. So I got through that bottleneck.

Interview Number 4 with Rear Admiral John F. Davidson,
U.S. Navy (Retired)

Place: Admiral Davidson's home in Annapolis, Maryland

Date: Wednesday, 11 September 1985

Subject: Biography

Interviewer: Paul Stillwell

Q: Admiral, you became chairman of what's known as the "bull department" at the Naval Academy. How did it get that nickname?

Admiral Davidson: That's obviously something the midshipmen gave it. It was known as the "bull department" when I was a midshipman. I suppose because in the English Department everybody shot the bull. It was known as the "bull department" when I was a midshipman and still was the "bull department" when I became the head of department. The department at that time was known officially as English, History, and Government. The faculty was probably about 75% to 80% civilian, and the other 20%, 25% were officers who had been ordered back. I don't remember the division between history and English. I soon discovered that nobody was looking for a particular qualification in me for either English or history. What they wanted was somebody who could get the English professors and the history professors all to go in the same direction, which was very difficult.

Q: Why was it difficult?

Admiral Davidson: Well, I suppose, simply stated, the history professor could grade a paper and if it was factually correct as far as history was concerned, it was a 4.0 paper, even if every word in it was misspelled and every expression was terrible. On the other hand, the English professor had no interest whatsoever in the accuracy of history, so if somebody wrote something for him, it didn't make any difference. One of the great difficulties was to get--one of the things that I tried to do-- was to get all departments to give some weight to the use of English in written papers. For instance, I didn't think that somebody should get a 4.0 in the seamanship examination if he murdered the King's English in so doing. It was very difficult to get all the instructors and professors in other departments to mark an examination and give any credit toward the English used. But I thought it was important that they should give some credit for English used.

Q: Did your fellow department heads share that concern?

Admiral Davidson: Yes, I think so. I remember one very amusing incident. The Commandant of Midshipmen at that time started a strong drive for better discipline to and from the classes. He thought that the sections that were marching to class were not being very military. He had a tendency to hold the instructors in the various departments responsible for not enforcing discipline when the midshipmen were in their departments.

Q: Was this Captain Pirie?*

Admiral Davidson: Yes. So Captain Pirie got out a notice to all heads of departments requesting that we pay more attention to military conduct of the midshipmen when they were under our supervision. So almost immediately thereafter, a first classman in charge of a section marching through the English department was put on report by a civilian English professor for not maintaining order in ranks, and the report went back to the Commandant of Midshipmen. The commandant required that the young midshipman, the first classman, should submit a statement. When the statement was submitted, the young lad misspelled about three or four words, and so Captain Pirie somehow decided that that was a great chance to make a point, that he could say, "What kind of teaching do you do in the English department? They can't even spell." And he wrote it all out longhand on a memo pad addressed to me. In it he misspelled two words. He had underlined the words that were misspelled by the midshipman in red, so I, not being a very diplomatic type, I took his memo and underlined his

---

*Captain Robert B. Pirie, USN, later vice admiral, was Commandant of Midshipmen from 1949 to 1952. His oral history is in the Naval Institute collection.

two words in red and sent it back to him, and I never heard any more about it. I don't know whether Bob Pirie would remember that or not. He probably would deny it now, but it actually happened.

Q: What else do you recall about him from that period?

Admiral Davidson: Bob was a good, tough disciplinarian. He had been company commander as a first classman when I was a plebe, so I knew him from way back. We had won the colors that year, as a matter of fact, under his leadership. But Bob was a strict disciplinarian and demanded high standards.

Q: Was he accurate in the perception that it had fallen off at that point?

Admiral Davidson: Probably, to some extent. I would think it would be fair to say that the average civilian professor found it more difficult to discipline or to require order in ranks, and things like that, than the average officer instructor. Perhaps because my department had a very high percentage of civilians, we probably were a little more guilty of a lackadaisical approach to this. However, I don't think we were bad, and the midshipmen weren't bad either. It's far different from anything you see nowadays. It's pretty casual nowadays.

Davidson #4 - 268

Q: Very much so. I wonder if you have a means of comparing the level of instruction when you were head of department and when you were Superintendent in that particular department.

Admiral Davidson: No, I don't really have any way of measuring that. I didn't get into it at all when I was Superintendent that I know of. As a matter of fact, I never was the academic type. I suppose that the only qualifications I may have had for either job were administrative. As I've said before in some of these interviews, being lucky enough to pick the right person and then rely on them to do what should be done.

Q: Is there any sense of awkwardness being a department head who's only there a few years while the professors are really the institutional and corporate memory.

Admiral Davidson: I don't think so. When I was a midshipman, the head of the English department was a civilian. Professor Alden was head of department.* He continued to be head of department until--I just don't remember now. I think that Bob Rice was the second military head of that department.** There was one before Bob, and I've forgotten who that was. But in the

---
*Professor Carroll S. Alden was head of the English Department at the Naval Academy from 1922 to 1941.
**Captain Robert H. Rice, USN, was Davidson's predecessor as head of the Department of English, History, and Government.

department, strangely enough, we had a full professor who was a graduate of the United States Naval Academy, and who had left the Navy and gone on and attained his doctor's degree and so on, and came back and was on the faculty. He was of the class of about '21 or '22. I think when Bob Rice became head of department, this particular professor found it difficult to work for somebody who was five years his junior as far as the Naval Academy is concerned. They did not get along very well.

When I became head of department, I began to have difficulties right away with him. I went up to the front office one time to look up his record, and I found that Bob Rice had written this about him, "This professor chafes under authority, and when given authority, is a tyrant." And that's all he said about him. Well, I thought that was very true and beautifully put. But I had difficulty with him, and, finally, at a meeting one time of the faculty, the senior professor at that time was Royal S. Pease, and I've forgotten what Royal S. Pease was espousing that day, but he made his little speech, and this other professor, who was chairman of the plebe English committee, got up and made the most terrible comments about he was sick and tired of being led by a pusillanimous old fud who didn't know what the score was, and so on and so forth, and so on and so forth. Before he finished, I finally said, "You may sit down. You are out of order, absolutely out of order."

Two or three days went by and my secretary came to see me and said, "Captain, Professor Cook is just absolutely beside himself waiting for you to send for him."

And I said, "Well, you can inform Professor Cook that I'm not going to send for him. I'm writing a note informing him that he's no longer chairman of the plebe English committee, that he is now simply a teacher of plebe English." Period. Which is about as low as you could go in the department.

I don't remember what I wrote in my efficiency report on him, but a long time afterwards when I was skipper of the <u>Albany</u>, my Marine orderly came to my cabin one day and said, "There's a Professor Cook to see you."

So I said, "Send him in."

We sat down for a cup of coffee, and he said to me, "Captain, I wonder now that a year or so has gone by, perhaps you might have mellowed a little bit and you would like to change the efficiency report that you put in on me."

And I said, "Well, no, I think not, because probably what I wrote at the time would be much truer than anything I might write today."

But actually, the people I had were really so good, people like Ned Potter and Bill Jefferies.*

Q: Neville Kirk?

---
*Professors Allen Blow Cook, William W. Jefferies, Neville T. Kirk, and E.B. Potter were members of the English, History, and Government Department which Davidson headed from 1951 to 1954.

Admiral Davidson: Neville Kirk, yes. All these people were just fine, as far as I was concerned.

Q: Do you have any memories about individual ones to contribute here?

Admiral Davidson: Not anything in particular that I remember. I'd have to get out the book and look down the names and see who all was there. One of the reasons I remember Potter very well is that one of the things I tried to do as head of department was to take the course, so I decided to take the first class history course. What I did was to try to attend a different instructor for each assignment. That gave me an opportunity not only to follow what was going on in the class, but to evaluate each instructor. I remember being very impressed with Ned, because he was a great actor. He could put on a cocked hat and a sword and stride up and down and be Horatio, somebody or other.

Q: Make it really come alive.

Admiral Davidson: Right. He's a great guy.

Q: Where did the curriculum come from in both English and history?

Admiral Davidson: It was there when I got there. Where it came from, I wouldn't know. I can tell you a couple of experiments that we ran and didn't work worth a darn. We decided to run an experiment with spelling, and we'd take 20 words a day, and the first five or six minutes of each period was supposedly used up in testing them on spelling of 20 words. By the end of the year we hadn't made any progress at all. We came to the conclusion that there were two types--those who could not spell and knew it, and those who could not spell and didn't know it. The ones who could not spell and knew it, looked it up in the dictionary. Those who could not spell and didn't know it, let it go through wrong.

Q: Well, presumably there's a type that can spell.

Admiral Davidson: Yes. We found some of those, too. The other thing we tried was speed reading. I've forgotten how many we took. We took a sample number and then we asked the other departments to help us in evaluating the results of this speed reading. In general, I think we found that there was a considerable loss of comprehension with speed reading. Now, maybe that isn't true every place, but we tried it for only one year, and there was a loss of comprehension. I can remember particularly in the courses in physics and chemistry, the heads of department reported to us that those boys that we had in the speed reading group were not doing as well as they did when they used to sweat it out.

Q: Do you have a feeling that you might have gotten that position because you had been better in the humanities when you were a midshipman?

Admiral Davidson: No. I think the only reason I was ordered to that job was Bob Rice recommended me. We were old friends, and he recommended me.

Q: Well, he may have known that about you.

Admiral Davidson: He may have. I didn't excel in anything as a midshipman, but I did better in the humanities than I did in math. I didn't have too much trouble with most of the science; it's when I got up into the higher math. We used to call it--it was electrodynamics, but we always called it "electrogoddamnics." I say that quietly.

Q: Was there any sense--since the Academy has a reputation as an engineering school with an emphasis on science and math--that English and history were not so important?

Admiral Davidson: To this extent, and I think I talked about this the other day. Every time some new technical development came along, the department that had that particular field wanted more time. The normal assault was on the E, H & G Department and maybe foreign languages, because we had just so many hours a day, and if they were to get more time for electrical engineering and physics, they had to take it away from somebody. That's the time when I had to go to bat and go into battle in the curriculum committee meetings and had the support of Admiral Joy, who had just come from being the negotiator out there in Korea, and he supported me.* He simply said that he always felt that he came off second best in many of the meetings simply because he hadn't had the humanities background that many of the others had had. Of course, we always knew that we couldn't outtalk the British; they always were way ahead of us in debates and so on. So with that in mind, we were able to stave off some of this robbing of time from the E, H & G Department. I understand now that they're trying to emphasize it even more, the humanities.

Q: I think they're coming back from the very heavy emphasis for a while they had on the science and engineering, the 80% required to major in that. Well, looking back at it from the perspective of an overall naval career, what benefit would you see from the various departments in your own Naval Academy education? Would

---
*Vice Admiral C. Turner Joy, USN, was Superintendent of the Naval Academy from 1952 to 1954.

you say that the humanities were as important to you as the sciences?

Admiral Davidson: In my case, yes, because somehow or other I was fortunate in avoiding assignments that required me to be very well versed in some of the engineering and science fields. For instance, I fired a lot of torpedoes in my life, but I didn't know how to sketch and describe a torpedo. I managed to avoid that. I always thought that I had a torpedoman who would take care of getting it ready to fire. All I had to do was push a button. The same thing in engineering. In submarine school I had learned a little bit about diesel engines, but I wasn't able to know too much about them. The same thing with electronics, radio, and so on. As I told Admiral Joy that day that we had the big battle with Professor Thomson, never in 25 years had I had to take a vacuum tube out of its socket and replace it with a new one, saying nothing of sketching and describing what goes on in a vacuum tube. I never felt that a naval officer needed to know that very much, unless he was going into engineering duty only or into design or something like that, maybe. I didn't think I needed it. Luckily for me, I got away with it. I don't say that it would have hurt me if I had known.

Q: Naval officers, especially senior ones, so often get into diplomatic type situations where I think that background would be very helpful.

Admiral Davidson: Right. I think that's the answer. The higher they go, the more important it is, and that's what Admiral Turner Joy was saying, when he was the chief negotiator out there in Korea, he found somewhere in his background, he felt there had been a lack of exposure.

Q: When he was in that billet, he asked for Admiral Burke just to come give him some help.* I figure maybe it was the fact that Burke had had that difficult beginning with Admiral Mitscher.** He figured if he could be diplomatic in that situation, he could deal with the communists.

What else do you remember about Admiral Joy? How was he in leading the Academy?

Admiral Davidson: Just terrific, and such a wonderful gentleman. One of the nicest things he did, as far as I was concerned, was when my three years were coming to an end in the E,H & G Department, we were all at a meeting at the Naval Institute one day, and I was on the board, and he was the vice president of the

---

*Rear Admiral Arleigh A. Burke, USN, later admiral and Chief of Naval Operations, was a member of the United Nations Truce Delegation in Korea in 1951.
**Vice Admiral Marc A. Mitscher, USN. In 1944, Burke, then a captain, was ordered to be chief of staff to Mitscher, then Commander Fast Carrier Task Force 58.

board, a messenger came in and told me I was wanted on a long distance phone call. I went out and it was the detail office. He said to me, "The Bureau of Personnel has assured Admiral Joy that they will not detach any heads of departments during academic year, that he can count on keeping them through academic year until after June Week. On the other hand, Bob Rice has to be relieved in May before graduation, and you can have command of the Albany if you can get Admiral Joy to say you can go." So I waited until the meeting was all over and walked back over to the office with Admiral Joy and told him of the offer.

He looked at me and said, "Never, never would I stand in the way of a young man getting a command like the USS Albany. You tell them you're available."

Q: You were ready to bless him from that day forward.

Admiral Davidson: Right. I never would condemn him after that. I was detached early in May.

Q: Were you there also part of Admiral Hill's tenure?*

Admiral Davidson: I was there with Admiral Hill. Yes. I'll have to tell you about my initial experience in the E, H & G

---
*Vice Admiral Harry W. Hill, USN, was Superintendent of the Naval Academy from April 1950 to August 1952.

Department. I think within two weeks of the time I arrived, Admiral Hill sent for me. He said, "John, we have these weekly lectures to the first class. They're very prominent people--ambassador to Russia, ambassador here, and many others, including some military, including the Chairman of the Joint Chiefs, but a weekly lecture. All this is held in Mahan Hall." And he said, "The introductions have been made by professors in your department. Quite frankly, they stink. They're the worst I've ever heard, the way they get up and introduce a speaker. So therefore, I want you to make all the introductions."

I said, "Oh, Admiral." Then all of a sudden I had a very happy thought. I said, "Admiral, I have another solution to this which I think might be worth your consideration."

"What is it?"

I said, "I think we should have a first classman introduce the speaker."

"What do they know about it?"

"That's the point, Admiral. If he does a real good job, we can say, 'See how we train them?' If he doesn't do a good job, we'll say, 'He's in training.'"

Admiral Hill looked at me and he said, "All right, you can try it, but it better work."

So I went back down to the department and I got ahold of two of the professors. I said, "We're going to have a first classman make every introduction for the lectures. You all have to pick the first classman for each one, and then you've got to rehearse him for a week so he'll be all ready."

It made the greatest hit with Admiral Hill you can imagine to see these first classmen get up there. He said, "They're so much better than those darn professors." Anyway, it worked. I got away with it. It's in line with that later remark in my life, "Is this the Admiral Davidson who always gets somebody to do his work for him?"

Q: It seems like superb training for the midshipmen.

Admiral Davidson: It was. It worked. I don't know whether they still do it or not. I don't have any idea. But that was one of the things I learned very early in my life as head of department. There were other things that Admiral Hill used to give me a hard time about. We had one boy who was unsatisfactory in English and he went before the academic board. I've forgotten. Maybe I shouldn't even start this story, but something about--he had done very poorly on a book review or something. I'm not sure it wasn't Pilgrim's Progress or something like that.* The admiral said to me, "Have you ever read that?"

I said, "No, sir."

He said, "Well, you go home and read it tonight and tomorrow

---

*The Pilgrim's Progress, the allegory of a Christian traveler, was written by John Bunyan in 1670.

morning you give me a report on it." It's about that thick, you know. Of course, I never accomplished it, but he thought we were being a little unfair with this boy.

One of the saddest cases I had involved a young plebe who failed in English at the end of the first term. I had him in the office to interview him, to see if I could find out maybe what happened to him. My memory tells me he was from some place in Colorado, and his father was German and his mother was Swedish, and I believe there were seven or eight children. The boy told me that in the home his father never spoke anything but German and the mother never replied in anything but Swedish. All of the children spoke both German and Swedish, but when it came to English--what I couldn't quite understand was how he got through his high school with a passing mark in English, because he had, but he didn't pass with any of the professors in the Naval Academy English department. What a sad thing for a poor kid. He had never been exposed to English, really, at home. I suppose he had to have English in high school.

Q: High schools can vary a great deal in quality.

Admiral Davidson: Right.

Q: What was the outcome?

Davidson #4 - 281

Admiral Davidson: We had to let him go. He just couldn't measure up to our requirements in English. We had to let him go.

Q: Could you describe the workings of the academic board in a little more detail, Admiral?

Admiral Davidson: The academic board was made up in those days of all heads of departments and the commandant and the admiral. The admiral didn't vote except in cases of a tie. The academic board started its meetings at the end of each semester, and all of the boys who were unsatisfactory came before the academic board and were given a chance to plead their case. Then the decision of the academic board could be several things--one, you could give him a re-examination after two or three weeks, or something like that, to see if he could pull it up; you could turn him back into the next class; or you could discharge him.

Now, turn-backs, when I first was in the department, we sometimes would turn a boy back at mid-year and he would go home, then come back with the next plebe class, or if he was turned back in the second class, he would come back with the next second class. Well, it didn't work. Some of them went home and got married. So we decided that we would do away with the turn-back in the middle of the year. If he failed in June, we could turn him back to start again in September. We took a chance on those. Some of them, as I say, were given re-examinations. If they passed, they were promoted with their class. If they didn't pass, then there were two possibilities--turn-back or discharge.

The only times I remember the academic board had some great difficulties happened when, as a result of Korea, we had a lot of boys come to the Naval Academy to avoid the draft. The law was such that after two years they could resign and they were given credit for their two years, and then they didn't have to enlist. We were able to prevail upon the Congress to change it and make them serve the rest of the normal four-year enlistment as an enlisted man. If they had started the second class year, they were not allowed to resign, so we had a lot of boys deliberately failing in order to get out. Over here at the naval station they had a barracks, just like a prison barracks, where we had these kids while we were waiting for some decision from Washington. But when Congress finally said that we could make them go through two more years as enlisted men, we didn't have any more trouble at all. Then they stayed on to graduate. But these were things that came before the academic board to determine whether a boy deliberately failed. For instance, a boy who for two years made himself a 3.4 average or something like that, and he suddenly gets 2.0, it's pretty evident that he is deliberately trying to get out of the Naval Academy.

Q: Were there cases of trying to provide special tutoring for individuals to try to get them over a specific hump?

Davidson #4 - 283

Admiral Davidson: I don't know of any where the board was concerned. I do know that we used to try to help the football team. Some of the professors would take on extra duty in order to help a boy, because he spent so much time out at football practice that they needed help. They very often traveled with the team and studied while they were in the airplane, wherever they were, but that was just a volunteer thing.

Q: This is a thing that Captain Cutter told me, that Coach Erdelatz took his people out of class so much that they needed some help.*

Admiral Davidson: Erdelatz overdid it. There was no question about it. Finally Wayne Hardin started doing some of the same thing.** For instance, on this first class lecture business that I mentioned before, first class lectures were normally on Friday night. It soon became apparent that none of the football team first classmen were ever present. So I went to a great deal of trouble by long distance telephone and letter writing and so on, to rearrange the lecture schedules to have them on Tuesday nights. The next thing I know, there aren't any football players at the Tuesday night lectures. So I asked the athletic director,

---
*Captain Slade D. Cutter, USN, was director of athletics at the Naval Academy from 1957 to 1959. Edward J. Erdelatz was Naval Academy football coach from 1950 to 1958.
**Hardin was head football coach from 1959 to 1964.

Red Coward, "What gives?"*

He said, "Well, Wayne Hardin has just changed his showing of the movies of the previous game and all of his preparations for next week to Tuesday nights instead of Friday nights."

And I said, "Well, you tell Wayne Hardin that I'm running the Naval Academy, he isn't, and I don't care when he has his pictures or when he does this. I want the team to win and all that, but I want those boys there on Tuesday nights, because I've rearranged the whole year's schedule. He's always done it on Friday night before. I don't see any reason to change." So Wayne finally got over it. That wasn't when I was head of department that I did all that. That was later.

Q: I've heard that Admiral Hill was very enthusiastic about athletics, so I think he might have been willing to help them.

Admiral Davidson: Oh, he was really gung-ho on athletics, no question about it. He was at every kind of a game that he could possibly get to. He was very vociferous. He'd sit in the front row at the baseball field and shout and yell. He was a great guy.

Q: What else do you remember about Admiral Hill?

Admiral Davidson: What I remember about him is mostly when I was

Superintendent. We should come to that maybe later. I enjoyed working with and for Admiral Hill when I was head of department. He seemed to always think kindly of me, and when I came back as Superintendent, he went so far as to say publicly that he was glad to see all the people he'd brought up coming back to take the job he'd once had. Charlie Melson had worked for him, too. He was my predecessor.*

Q: Was there much effort at all as far as encouraging blacks to go to the Naval Academy in that era, the early Fifties?

Admiral Davidson: I don't recall that we had any move. If we did, I wasn't aware of it.

Q: Was there, on the other hand, an attempt to discourage them?

Admiral Davidson: No, I don't know of that either. I think some of that came along later, sort of the idea of quotas, you know. I don't recall ever having any knowledge of anything like that back in the days when I was head of department, and really not later. I don't think it affected me, anyway.

---

*Rear Admiral Charles L. Melson, USN, preceded Davidson as Superintendent of the Naval Academy from June 1958 to June 1960. He is the subject of a U.S. Naval Institute oral history.

Davidson #4 - 286

Q: That period in the early Fifties was the era of McCarthyism and loyalty oaths, and so forth.* Did that have any impact on what was being taught? Was there any emphasis on the evils of communism, let us say?

Admiral Davidson: I don't recall that there was anything any more than just that we didn't believe in communism. I had just come from the National Defence College, where we spent our time learning about communism and how bad it was, so on and so forth. I don't think that it got into our course, although it could be in some of those Friday night lectures. I just don't remember them well enough to remember what happened.

Q: I'm interested in more on your association with the Naval Institute in those years, if you could describe some of the board meetings and some of the things it tried to accomplish.**

Admiral Davidson: I was on the board when I was head of department, and then much later I was vice president. The biggest job of being on the board was that you had to read all

---

*Senator Joseph R. McCarthy (Republican-Wisconsin) directed Senate committee investigations and hearings on alleged communist and un-American activities in 1954 and was subsequently censured by the Senate for his conduct.

**Davidson served as a director of the Naval Institute from November 1951 to February 1952 and from May 1952 to May 1954. He was vice president of the Institute (ex-officio as Superintendent of the Naval Academy) from July 1960 to August 1962.

the articles and vote on them. Sometimes that could get to be quite an additional chore, to have all your articles read and vote on them. The other things I remember--where we ever had any sort of a flareback--we attempted one time to stop putting out a magazine with sewed binding, and we went to staple type, and we had objections from all over. As I recall, our idea was to make the magazine as much like the National Geographic in quality as we could possibly do. That was sort of the sample we were following. Money-wise, we were making money hand over fist while I was head of department, I'm sure. Maybe I'm wrong, but I think that's when we first employed a brokerage firm in Baltimore to invest for us. We built the present museum building during that period, I believe, a combination of the Athletic Association and the Naval Institute.

Q: I think that was enlarged during the early Sixties. That was probably when you were Superintendent.

Admiral Davidson: Maybe it was. But didn't we build it originally?

Q: I thought that dated from the Thirties. There was a museum building there, I'm fairly sure.

Admiral Davidson: You might have a lot better information on that than I would remember. I just remember that it was a big thing as far as money was concerned, and the Athletic Association and the Institute put up money. Then I think we sold the building to the government for $1, so that we would have government maintenance. Something like that. All of these things that you're getting out of me--I think maybe if I'd done this in 1962, my memory would have been a lot better than it is. I think of things and then I forget them, and so on.

Q: What do you remember about the general prize essay contests and how those were judged?

Admiral Davidson: We read the essays and voted as a board.

Q: What were the criteria on what you would consider a best essay? Did it have anything to do with subject matter, how important the subject was? Did you look for original thinking?

Admiral Davidson: I know what I did. I just read the article, and if I thought it was real good, I voted for it. I perhaps didn't give any consideration to what the subject was. Just if it happened to be a very well-written, timely, a good article. There were lots of them that were submitted that weren't very up to snuff.

Q: How much disagreement was there on the board about various articles?

Admiral Davidson: I don't recall that we had very much disagreement. One of the members of the board was Brute Krulak.* He was always a little bit vociferous about this, that, and the other thing. But I don't remember that we differed that much. Apparently we were successful in having pretty good articles, because it seems to have stood the test of time, I think.

Q: How much involvement did you have in the book program?

Admiral Davidson: I didn't have any in that at all.

Q: That's always been the complaint of the Proceedings people, that they get a lot more scrutiny than the books.

Admiral Davidson: Could be.

Q: Are there any specific articles or decisions from that period with the Institute that stand out in your mind?

---

*Colonel Victor H. Krulak, USMC, was on the Naval Institute's board of directors from August 1952 to June 1955. Now a retired lieutenant general, he is the author of First to Fight: An Inside View of the U.S. Marine Corps (Annapolis: Naval Institute Press, 1984).

Davidson #4 - 290

Admiral Davidson: I don't remember any, so I can't help on that.

Q: It's a bit difficult to compare, because there wasn't nearly so large a professional staff as there is now. It was almost part-time work by many people involved, including secretary-treasurer.

Admiral Davidson: Roy Horn was it, sort of.* He ran the show. I've forgotten now who the treasurer was, but he was an important member.

Q: Joe Taussig had it for a while.**

Admiral Davidson: Yes, but I'm thinking before Joe. I don't know the name of the man. You mean Joe had the treasury job?

Q: He was the secretary-treasurer.

Admiral Davidson: I see. I guess Roy Horn was secretary-treasurer. I'm trying to think who was it who handled all the bookkeeping.

---
*Commander Roy de S. Horn, USN (Ret.), joined the staff of Naval Institute Proceedings in 1944 and later was managing editor until 1959.
**Commander Joseph K. Taussig, Jr., USN, was secretary-treasurer of the Naval Institute from 1952 to 1953.

Q: A fellow named Gordon Williams.

Admiral Davidson: Yes. Gordon Williams was a stalwart member of the team. Was he there with you?

Q: No, he was gone before I got there.
Now there is a considerable emphasis on the idea that the Proceedings serves as an open forum for expression of opinions about the profession and what's been written in the Proceedings. I wondered was there that much emphasis on it then.

Admiral Davidson: I don't recall there was any great emphasis, but it was supposedly always from the time it was founded supposed to be an open forum, an expression of your views with resepct to the service and national and international affairs and so on.

Q: Did you have a feeling it was more difficult to express an opinion that was counter to the prevailing official policy?

Admiral Davidson: No. I don't ever remember having any controversial opinions, so maybe I wouldn't have been involved.

Q: We have talked in some of the previous sessions about inculcating in the midshipmen notions of ethics and honor and so forth. Did you do that in the English department, English and history specifically, along with the other departments?

Admiral Davidson: I can't recall that we had anything to do with inculcating them with any of that. Most of that was supposed to come from the executive department. As long as they did their job, why, I don't think we were involved.

Q: Was there any attempt to compare the operations in the department with the comparable departments in civilian universities? That is, accreditation standards and so forth?

Admiral Davidson: I think the only times that I ever remember that we ever had any comparisons was when the board of vistors would meet. They pretty nearly always had some college presidents and so on, and we had a chance to sit around and discuss the programs here as well as how it compared with theirs. But I don't know how much of that was done. I know this, that whenever we had promotions among the civilian faculty, there used to be sort of a hue and cry, "Oh, you can't promote him. What would all of the other colleges in the country think if you promoted a man who didn't even have his doctorate degree?" And that sort of thing. We had a lot of that, but that was internal bickering.

Q: Was that one of your bigger problems?

Admiral Davidson: I was chairman of what was known as the civilian faculty committee, which represented all the civilian faculty in all departments--foreign languages and anyplace you had civilian faculty. I wasn't chairman because I was John Davidson; I was chairman because the head of the E, H & G department always was the chairman of that. I discovered early in my first year that the only way to accomplish anything with a civilian faculty committee was to call a meeting 15 minutes before the Army-Navy basketball game and have all proposals all written out, worded and everything, and put them before the committee, and they would vote immediately and go to the game. If you didn't, you were there til next week changings "ifs" and "ands" and "buts" and whatever that everybody had his own idea of how you should word this and how you should word that. So I learned my lesson after the first one. Work it all out, figure out what you think is best, or maybe with a couple of your most trusted professors, have it all written out and give everybody a copy and say, "All those in favor."

Immediately they'd say, "Yes," and go on their way to the game.

Q: The annual slate of civilian promotions is comparable to a selection board for the military, of course. What criteria did you use on who would get it and who wouldn't?

Admiral Davidson: I'm not sure what criteria were used across the board, but I'll give you one example of what happened. We were considering associate professors for promotion to full professorship, and one of the associate professors who was under the gun, was eligible, asked if he could come to see me. He said, "I've come not to ask any special consideration for myself, but I would want you to think very carefully before recommending Professor So-and-so for promotion, because that would be almost a blight on the Naval Academy, and I think all of the other colleges in the country would look down their nose and say, 'What in the world are they doing promoting that kind of a man?'" I learned that this one who was making the pitch and the one against whom he was pitching were great friends, they played bridge almost every night with their wives, they were old pals. He just said, "Don't promote him. He's a nobody. He doesn't have his doctorate degree, and he's not even working very hard toward it."

So then I started looking into the thing, and I found out that the one against whom he was directing his remarks was coaching one of the sports, I've forgotten, spending 90% of his time out of the classroom, he was coaching. He had a reputation of inviting midshipmen to his home regularly. He had a reputation of tutoring midshipmen. Everything. He didn't have time to publish or perish.

Q: But he was doing a great deal for the Naval Academy.

Admiral Davidson: He was extremely popular with the midshipmen, and he was doing a great job for the Naval Academy. Then when I really looked into it, I found that he had once been a midshipman and that he left the Naval Academy, and I think he went to Princeton. He got a degree there and came back here to teach.

So I went to Admiral Joy and I recommended very strongly that we promote the one that this man said don't promote, and I said, "And don't promote the one that said he didn't want his best friend promoted." And that's the way it came out.

Q: Maybe he wasn't his best friend after all.

Admiral Davidson: I couldn't believe it. In the first place, that is so contrary to what you would expect naval officers to do to each other. You might not be in favor of one of your friends being promoted, but you didn't go around and try to keep him from being promoted. This, to me, was just about as disloyal a thing to do to a friend that you could.

Q: I assume they didn't remain friends after that, since it

backfired so effectively.

Any more on your Naval Academy years during that tour?

Admiral Davidson: No, I think that sort of winds it up pretty much. As I say, I went over to Admiral Joy's office and he said, "Tell the bureau you're available." My orders were issued, and I was on my way to Norfolk to take command of the Albany.

Unfortunately--well, I felt unfortunately, but not very unfortunately--the Albany was due to go into the yard. I don't think it was a complete yard overhaul, but it was a pretty extensive overhaul. We were in Portsmouth, Virginia, which is known as the Norfolk Navy Yard. We were there two or three months. I was there May, June, and July, anyway, before we finally did a little shakedown to Guantanamo and then back to Norfolk. From there we deployed to the Mediterranean.

Of interest is that's when I met Arleigh Burke.* When I arrived to take command of the Albany, she was moored at the naval base in Norfolk, and Arleigh was the division commander. He was aboard one of the other cruisers. Right after the change of command, I went over and paid my respects. Then I never set eyes on him again as long as he was my division commander. I went to the navy yard, he went to the Med. Then he was suddenly

---

*Rear Admiral Arleigh A. Burke, USN, assumed command of Cruiser Division Six in 1954 and became Commander Destroyer Force Atlantic Fleet in January 1955. In May 1955 he was selected as the next Chief of Naval Operations and assumed that duty in August.

promoted from division commander to Commander Destroyer Force Atlantic. He went to Newport, and meanwhile, I was in the Med. From that job up there at ComDesLant, he suddenly was picked above everybody else to be CNO.

Q: How does a senior keep track of you if he never sees you?

Admiral Davidson: This is a good question. I'll tell you, to skip over a little bit, after I had command of the Albany, my next job was as deputy OP-61, which was politico-military policy. As soon as I got there, I went into the record section and pulled my own record to see if I was up to date on everything, because I knew I was coming up for selection. Here's one fitness report from Arleigh Burke. One--and he's CNO. It said, "I have not had any opportunity to observe Captain Davidson or his performance as commanding officer of the Albany, but I've heard he's doing very well." Period.

I went home and I said to my wife, "Boy, there's damning with faint praise. If that's all the CNO can say about a prospective rear admiral, we might as well pack our bags." So I was quite flabbergasted to learn two or three weeks later that I had been selected.

No, Arleigh and I never had any contact then. All my contact was later under him as CNO.

Q: What changes, if any, took place in the Albany during that yard period?

Admiral Davidson: Not much of anything. I had a very fine exec, Dick Colbert, who went on to be head of the Naval War College.*

Q: Admiral Rice spoke very highly of him. I'd be interested in your recollections of him.

Admiral Davidson: Well, for my money, Dick Colbert was just a topnotch administrator, a very capable gent, very popular with other officers, with the crew, and still no pushover for anything, ran the ship, as far as I was concerned, beautifully. As I say, I thought enough of him so that I tried to get him later to be my assistant in Washington.

Q: As a person who specialized in having others do things for you, he must have been a Godsend.

Admiral Davidson: He was. He was perfect. Actually, we deployed to the Med, and I sometimes wonder how a commanding officer gets through a Med deployment, because it's one fleet exercise after another, one after another. You're up there on

---

*Commander Richard G. Colbert, USN.

the bridge day and night, you don't seem to get much sleep, and you have some very close calls every now and then.

My immediate boss was Ruthven Libby.* I've forgotten which ship he rode. I think he was riding a battleship. In any case, the trying times for me, it's black of night, you can't see anything at all, and you're all making 28 knots, get a signal "Form 40," and everybody starts maneuvering, and all you have to do is make one little mistake, and everybody could cross on each other, and so on. It's pretty nerve-wracking to stand up there. I, on more than one occasion, had to back down. Ned Hannegan had command of a carrier.** I remember one time when we were making this run at 28 knots, all in formation, and all of a sudden the young officer on the radar screen said that we were closing this carrier very, very rapidly. It ended up that I turned on lights and backed emergency, and the carrier went across my bow. When we were finally straightened out again, I discovered that my maneuvering board officer had me take a course ten degrees to the right of the base course, and I was supposed to go ten left, which had caused the mix-up.

The very next night, almost the same thing occurred, except that this time we had done the right thing, and Ned Hannegan in his carrier had done the wrong thing. He sent me a very nice

---
*Rear Admiral Ruthven E. Libby, USN, Commander Battleship-Cruiser Force Atlantic Fleet, subject of a U.S. Naval Institute oral history.
**Captain Edward A. Hannegan, USN, commanding officer of the USS Lake Champlain (CVA-39).

message. He said, "Think nothing about last night. It happens in the best regulated families. I apologize."

Q: How did the Albany handle?

Admiral Davidson: Oh, beautifully, just beautiflly. It's a thrill to have that much power after being in submarines. We didn't have very much power nor very much speed. I think the hard thing to get used to is speed. I had never been a destroyer sailor, so I was not used to anything over 15 knots. In the old days in battleships, we didn't go over 15 either. To be making 28 knots and you have to back emergency, you lift every safety valve in that doggone boiler room.

Q: You must rely a great deal on your OODs.*

Admiral Davidson: Right. I was lucky. I had a pretty good crew. A couple of them were reserve officers, very good.

One of the interesting things about our cruise over there that had nothing to do with shiphandling or anything was that there was a great campaign on about conduct ashore in the Mediterranean. I had a chaplain whose name was Bo McMillen.**

---
*OODs--officers of the deck.
**Lieutenant Commander Gervase C. McMillen, CHC, USNR.

Q: Sounds like the football coach.

Admiral Davidson: Right. He had snow white wavy hair, about your size, looked like he could be anything from a Boston policeman to a football player. At the very beginning of my tour, I had been on board a week, I think, and I was holding mast. A little Italian boy about five feet tall had been over leave, and when I said to him, "What do you have to say for yourself?" he told a story about the length of this room as to why he was over leave.

After listening to him, I turned to Bo McMillen and I said, "Padre, would you like to say something for this young lad?"

And Bo was a Jesuit priest. He said, "Oh, Captain, he's a fine lad. Oh, he is a fine lad."

I thanked him, probably gave the boy a restriction instead of a court-martial, some minor punishment. When mast was over, the Marine said that the chaplain was at the door of my cabin and would like to come in. He came in, and we sat down to have a cup of coffee and to get acquainted. I had met him, but just to say hello. After a couple of minutes, he said to me, "Captain, you know, I'm a man of the faith. I have to believe these kids, but you don't." From then on, he and I were sort of like this.

Q: Two fingers together.

Admiral Davidson: So we went over to the Mediterranean, and the ship's radio call, the voice radio call for the ship was "Conduct." Bo McMillen sort of parlayed that into a campaign for good behavior ashore, be the ship that has the best conduct record ashore. He was so successful that we went through the whole Med cruise until the next to the last week, and we had never had a shore patrol arrest on the beach. And we had just been awarded the number one position for conduct ashore when all of a sudden two or three of our boys got plastered and got picked up at one of the last liberties. Actually, the crew took them back on the fantail and were about to beat the hell out of them for ruining our record.

But I had a chance to return Bo's favor. He came to me once while we were in the Med and said, "You know, Captain, the language in use by the young sailors of this ship is just terrible. It's just about as foul as it can be, it's blasphemy, it's four-letter words all the time. It's just terrible. I need some help." This is the chaplain. "I need help in stamping it out. You must hear it."

I said, "Well, Bo, would you give me any idea of any one particular culprit?"

He said, "Yes, the chief boatswain. The chief boatswain's all over the ship, but he's the worst one. He can't say five words without four of them taking the Lord's name in vain and some four-letter word here and there."

So I said, "Well, let me work on it."

All of a sudden I had a real happy idea. I sent for the chief boatswain, whose name was West. I said, "West, I sit here at my desk in my cabin when the boys are out there scrubbing down in the morning, and I never heard such talk in my life. It's just terrible language. I am hereby appointing you as a committee of one to stamp it out."

About a week later, Bo came in and he said, "Damn it, captain, what the hell did you do?" So I told him. We cut it down a lot, just by getting the boatswain to be--he was going around saying, "My gracious."

Q: He set a different example.

Admiral Davidson: What were some of the liberty ports you hit in the Mediterranean?

Admiral Davidson: The south coast of France. We went to Naples originally, and we went to Beirut, of all places. We went to Villefranche. When we could get into port, we had quite a pleasant stay.

Q: What was the role of the ship?

Admiral Davidson: Just part of the Sixth Fleet.

Q: Was the idea to provide antiaircraft protection?

Admiral Davidson: You know, our cruising--we were with the carrier task force, which had destroyer screens and, I suppose, just AA protection.* I don't recall we ever did any shooting.

Q: Did you have any practice shoots?

Admiral Davidson: No. The only practice shooting we did was down in Guantanamo.

Q: Would that be, then, the shakedown?

Admiral Davidson: Yes.

Q: Did you get to use your 8-inch guns much?

Admiral Davidson: Not very much. Some.

Q: Was there a great emphasis on the smartness of appearance?

Admiral Davidson: Yes, yes. That was the big thing, and proper uniforms. This was really before the days when everybody seemed

---

*AA--antiair.

to be in dungarees, baseball caps. We didn't wear baseball caps when I had that ship, but that became the uniform of the day, baseball caps. To me, it was a beautiful ship, a great thrill to have it. But you have it just one year. That's it, you know. We came back to the Med and tied up, and before I knew it, I was relieved.

Q: Did you have any discomfort handling a ship that big and that fast?

Admiral Davidson: I got a little experience when I had the Orion, the submarine tender, which was the first time I ever handled anything bigger than a submarine, also the first time I had anything that went over about--in the submarine, with all four on, we could get up to 18 in a smooth sea. To get in a ship that had the capability of 30 knots and handled so beautifully, it was always a thrill for me to get up there on the bridge and think, "Gee whiz. This is something."

Q: Quite a number of flag officers have said that their greatest satisfaction was in a big ship command.

Admiral Davidson: Yes.

Q: Was that the same thing?

Admiral Davidson: Well, you start in and that's what you're working for. It seems to me that's your goal in life from the time you leave the Naval Academy, is command, to begin with. Then the larger it is, the most satisfying thing in the world. I will say this at this point--I later was a cruiser division commander, where I had three cruisers, and it isn't anywhere near the same thrill as being the skipper of a cruiser. There was not the satisfaction in it. As a matter of fact, one of the difficulties is keeping your hands out of the pie, which is inexcusable, to my way of thinking, to interfere with the skipper.

Q: Even so, I would think you would feel some isolation from the crew. You couldn't have the closeness of a submarine.

Admiral Davidson: No, no. Yes, there is some isolation, I suppose, because you almost never see any of the engine room force. Most of the people in gunnery or communications have also watches on the bridge, and you see those, but you don't see much in the way of the engineers.

Q: What do you remember about personnel inspections?

Admiral Davidson: I remember that I probably wasn't the best inspecting officer that anybody ever had. Somebody had to be pretty bad for me to stop and try to take him apart. Arleigh

Burke later told me that one of my troubles was that I couldn't take somebody apart.

Q: What do you remember about the ship's Marine detachment?

Admiral Davidson: Like everything else when I ever had Marines-- they were always excellent, always excellent. I never remember having any dealings with Marines that I didn't think they were tops.

Q: Did the ship have any sports teams?

Admiral Davidson: I don't believe we did during the year I had her. Not much opportunity over in the Med to do anything, because you aren't in port very much. We bounced from one port to the other. When we were in the navy yard, we didn't have any athletic teams. I don't recall that we did.

Q: Do you have any special memories of underway replenishment experiences?

Admiral Davidson: Yes. That's the first and real scary thing that happens to a new skipper, because somehow or other one of the things you've always tried to do is stay away from another ship, not get too close. It takes a little bit of getting used to. Admiral Libby was encouraging all the skippers not to come up too gingerly, come on up there and get in position and, if necessary, back a little bit and get those hoses over and get going.

Q: He's an old destroyer man.

Admiral Davidson: Yes, I guess so. And probably Arleigh would have been the same way. But I liked to come up there knowing that I had full control. One of the things I learned in submarine handling was you're in far better position if you don't have to back, because ships don't steer astern anywhere near as well as they do going ahead. So if you get in a position where by kicking ahead with one screw and using your rudder you can control your movement, you're better off than having to back one screw and handle your rudder. So the idea was to never get ahead of yourself; always be in position to go ahead. Because that's where the rudder takes effect, when you're going ahead.

Q: Any other memories of Admiral Libby? I understand he didn't have any trouble taking people apart.

Admiral Davidson: No. Well, Admiral Libby and I were to become great friends after this tour. I just knew him and wondered what in the world he was doing, ordering 28 knots and dark as pitch, ships all over the place, and he was in a battleship. I can remember riding--it seems to me I was practically on his fantail, and if his ship had turned, I don't think I could have avoided it, because I'm sitting right here making 28 knots and not far enough apart, so if he had done that, or if they had lost steering or anything, which reminds me of a cute little story one night when we were doing all of that. You know, all the ships had voice calls on the radio. One night here we all go, hell-bent, 28 knots, when all of a sudden on the voice radio comes--I won't remember his voice call, but I'll just invent one--the message was plain English, addressed to all ships in the formation. "This is Charlie C. My rrrrrrudder is jammed full rrrrrright. I am experiencing some steering difficulty."

Q: That's an understatement.

Admiral Davidson: All lights went on in the whole fleet, and here comes this tanker on opposite course. He had already got all the way around once. He came down. Well, it relieved all the tension on the bridge. In the first place, the lights were on, we saw where we were, and I wasn't in particular danger of having a collision with him, but somebody else was. "This is Charlie C. My rrrrrrudder is jammed full rrrrright. I am experiencing some steering difficulty."

Q: It sounds almost like a British officer would say it.

Admiral Davidson: Well, we came out of it all right, but you were right. Some of things got to be pretty hairy. Of course, here's your life's career. That's the thing about it, see. There's your life's career. Either you make a mistake, or you make a mistake of having confidence in somebody who makes a mistake.

I remember taking the <u>Albany</u> into Guantanamo Bay with the Secretary of the Navy aboard one time. It was Bill Franke, and we went into Guantanamo Bay.* Everything under the sun was anchored in there. There was a carrier anchored, and it was swung sort of across the path of my course, and this young j.g. reserve was my officer of the deck, and I had watched him; he was very good. So he headed about ten degrees to the right of the bow of the carrier which was anchored there and swung to a little current. As we proceeded on this course, it was obvious we were being set down onto the bow of the carrier. I stood there with Mr. Franke, watching very carefully, thinking he should say right, ten degrees rudder, to allow a greater clearance. Instead he said, "All ahead standard." He practically bent us around the bow, just barely. And then he said, "All back full." Then he

---
*William B. Franke was Assistant Secretary of the Navy for financial management in 1954, was then appointed Under Secretary of the Navy in 1957, and then Secretary on 8 June 1959, serving to 20 January 1961.

let the anchor go, and by golly, we were within ten yards of our proper anchorage.

I remember Mr. Franke saying to me, and also Dick Colbert, "Good God, Captain, how in the world? I almost jumped in there. How in the world did you keep quiet?"

I said, "Well, there were only two ways to get by. One was to speed up and one was to turn, and then you had to turn right back again. I guess I just trusted to luck." But he got it in there and we were right where we belonged. But I'll tell you...

Q: You aged.

Admiral Davidson: That could have been the end of my career right there.

Q: Especially with a high-ranking witness.

Admiral Davidson: Yes. But I think it eventually had something to do with my getting the job as Superintendent of the Naval Academy. I think it had something to do later when he was Secretary when I became . . .

Q: Just the fact that he had gotten to know you then.

Admiral Davidson: Right. We had discussions after that incident about the training of young officers, and I think I held forth my old song that you can't train them if you take things away from them all the time. You have to let them make some mistakes. My theory was always that you have to have enough confidence in your ability to get them out of a jam, or you take it away from them before there's any chances of them being in a jam, and if you do, they don't learn a damn thing. That was a theory I had when I had submarines, in training people in submarines. I let them come alongside, maybe too fast, and see if they could handle it, but you had to be confident that you could jump in just in time to avoid complete disaster. I think the poorest skippers that I observed under me as a division commander and as squadron commander and so on, were those who couldn't let the officers of the deck do anything because they became too nervous. The reason they became nervous was they didn't have confidence in themselves to the extent that they could get it out of the jam. I may be bragging, but I always had confidence I could do it. Somehow or other, shiphandling to me was just a beautiful way of life. I liked it.

Q: You have to have people who are trained when to call you at night.

Admiral Davidson: Like I wasn't called up there coming down through the Minches with that submarine. I wasn't called. Yes,

Davidson #4 - 313

you have to write your night orders, write your orders, and then you have to have confidence. However, the minute you see that you can't have confidence in one, why, you've got to push him aside.

Q: Do you think there are some innate abilities that go into being a good shiphandler?

Admiral Davidson: You suggested the possibility, but I don't know. There are none of us born with it, I'm sure, unless we are the offspring of somebody who was a real good shiphandler. But my father never even saw the ocean. I don't know that I was considered a topnotch shiphandler, but I always had confidence in myself. It never worried me. The times I worried was when I told you Libby was in that flagship going there at 28 knots and I'm so close, that even instant action might have been too late.

Q: I'm sure in your mind you knew what you would have done.

Admiral Davidson: Oh, yes, I knew what I would do.

Q: Did you get into any social situations in foreign countries with foreign nationals?

Admiral Davidson: Not really. One time only that I remember, I went to a dinner party in one of the ports on the south coast of France, and my dinner partner was a lady who spoke only French. She did not speak any English, and I did not speak any French, but here I am with a lovely lady next to me and no way to make conversation, until all of a sudden we discovered that she spoke rather fluent Spanish, and I had four years of Spanish in my background. She had to help me quite a bit, but with her help, we managed to carry on a conversation all during dinner. It's the only time I ever used my Spanish in my life, and not very well at that.

Q: Do you have any recollections of the period when you got back to home port after the cruise?

Admiral Davidson: My only recollection is that we tied up to a pier at the naval base in Norfolk, and my wife came aboard, and very shortly thereafter, she and I were leaving the ship. As we went down the brow, I said, "Where did you put the car?"

Dick Colbert and, I think, my first lieutenant and a couple of the mess boys said, "Welcome home, Captain." And they opened the door to this brand-new automobile. This is the way that happened. My wife had been visiting in Washington, and she was to drive down to meet the ship in Norfolk, and the car wouldn't start. She called a gas station and they brought her a rental battery and started the car for her, and she drove on down to

Virginia Beach, then sat there worrying about an unreliable automobile, that she should not meet me with an unreliable automobile, so she went downtown and traded it in and bought a new one. The only thing I can tell you about it was that on our way to Virginia Beach, after I left the ship, there wasn't very much gas in the car and we had to stop to get gasoline, and when I got out of the car to talk to the man at the gas station, the door handle came off in my hand--a brand-new automobile. That's what I remember of my homecoming.

Q: She must have developed a fair amount of self-sufficiency to go ahead and do something like that on her own.

Admiral Davidson: Yes. Incidentally, one of the things I left out. During the navy yard overhaul, we had a hurricane. Did we cover that the other day?

Q: I don't think so. No.

Admiral Davidson: I was moored to a pier at the navy yard in Portsmouth, Virginia, when we had this warning that a hurricane was going to strike, and the senior officer present afloat ordered all the ships to get under way to go to sea and ride it out. I had already defueled, so I'm sitting there about six or seven feet out of the water, and I considered it absolutely unsafe to get that ship under way. I think Arleigh had left by then. I got in touch with Admiral Libby and asked him to intercede with the senior officer present afloat, to get me excused from going to sea. Whoever it was that excused me said, "However, if something happens, it's your responsibility. You should be at sea." But both Admiral Libby and I agreed that a cruiser sitting there almost six, seven feet above, with the waterline that high above the surface. So we put over every kind of cable we had, and we warmed up the engines and stood by. They gave me two tugs, and we stood by and rode it out. The only damage we had was the roof blew off of a building on the pier and wiped out my stern deck where the helicopter flight deck was, did a lot of damage back there. We held her alongside that pier. That's the worst experience I ever had. I didn't know what was going to happen to that darn ship.

Q: How useful were helicopters to the ship? Did they do most of the logistic type things?

Admiral Davidson: We put them up during the day for so-called scouting, so on and so forth.

Q: They probably did some spotting for you, too.

Admiral Davidson: Right. But let me tell you, they're tricky to launch. You have to get the ship on the right course to launch those darn things. I had one tip over on deck one time. Fortunately, there was nobody hurt.

Q: Did you have any association with the city of Albany? Did they sponsor or do things for the ship in any way?

Admiral Davidson: No. It seems to me we had a set of silverware which had been presented to the ship from the city of Albany. She was a beautiful ship when I had her.

One of the things we did while I was in the Med--I forgot this one completely. We were visiting the Italian Naval Academy, which is in Livorno. At a dinner party being given by the head of the Italian Naval Academy one night, the aide for the admiral came in and whispered something to the admiral. The admiral said to me, "There has been a terrible earthquake in Volos, Greece, practically wiping out the town, and they're in desperate need of assistance. Orders have just been received through my office for you to load several hundred tons of tents and proceed at best speed to Volos, Greece."

So I had to get up from the table and head for the ship. Fortunately, most of the liberty party was back. We got under way shortly after midnight, and we ran at 28 knots, making the best speed we could. Sometime during the night, all of a sudden, lights went on all over all around--fishing boats, all out there fishing without any lights on, and suddenly they see this monster coming, tearing down there, they all turned on their lights at once. There was no place to go. So I said, "Left full rudder, all back emergency." We did that. We tripped all of the safety valves on the boilers, everything, and got dead in the water. I don't know whether it was Dick Colbert or the chief quartermaster said, "Where did you learn that maneuver, Captain?"

I said, "I didn't."

Q: You invented it.

Admiral Davidson: I invented it. So we didn't hit a thing. Then we proceeded to get clear of all of them and proceeded to Volos, Greece. We got there, we offloaded all these tents, and the crew, by that time, had taken up a collection, because it turned out we had on board a young sailor in my crew whose family came from Volos, Greece. He had come to the United States some time before, and his father said to him--his father had once been in the United States--he said to him, "When you get there, join the Navy." This boy had joined the Navy, and the crew were very fond of him. They all chipped in practically all their monthly pay, and we contributed this vast amount of money to the mayor or whatever he was there. Then the crew went ashore and tried to help people with their torn-down homes and all that business. We spent about four or five days there and practically saved the lives of the whole town. Then we proceeded to return to Italy.

Q: I imagine there was a considerable sense of disappointment when you left that ship, then.

Admiral Davidson: Yes, yes. That's about the end of the Albany. There might have been some other things happened. I'm sure there were things that happened.

Q: Then it was back to the Pentagon.

Admiral Davidson: This is the time that Admiral Holloway had decided that I should come to BuPers, but Smedberg was able to work on Admiral Holloway and get him to say I could come and be his deputy in OP-61.[*] That's when I went to be Deputy OP-61, and started learning a little bit about how the Pentagon works and also how Arleigh Burke worked, and how Don Felt worked.[**]

Q: I understand that wasn't an easy experience, either.

Admiral Davidson: No. He is quite a character, but there's one

---

[*] Vice Admiral James L. Holloway, Jr., USN, was Chief of Naval Personnel from 1953 to 1958. Rear Admiral William R. Smedberg III, USN, later was also vice admiral and Chief of Naval Personnel.
[**] Rear Admiral Harry D. Felt, USN, later admiral, was Assistant Chief of Naval Operations (Fleet Readiness) from 1954 to 1956.

thing you had to learn. Somebody told me, and I found it to be true, you had to be sure you were right and then you had to talk back to him. If you were right, why, fine. If you were wrong, he'd put you under the heel and grind away.

Q: Do you remember any instances of dealing with him?

Admiral Davidson: Yes, one in particular. I guess this didn't happen until I was OP-61. I don't know that I had this happen when I was the deputy. We had a problem over in Malta some place along the line, and we had an air wing, I believe, based in Malta at one time. The prime minister of Malta suddenly decreed that all Americans who had their cars over there were to pay an import tax, and it turned out to be the same as the value of the automobile. In other words, if you had a $2,000 automobile, the tax was $2,000. This caused a big hassle, and Arleigh Burke said to me, "What are you going to do?"

I said, "Well, I think we should get a couple of LSTs and back them up to the piers over there, load all the automobiles on board and then detach the whole group and send them someplace else."*

He said, "Well, you'd never get away with it."

I said, "Well, I think that's what we ought to tell the prime

---

*LSTs--tank landing ships.

minister that's what we're going to do, just pull out altogether." The prime minister had given us 30 days to comply with this order.

Arleigh said, "You'll never get away with it, but you can try if you want to. But where the hell are you going to put them? We haven't any place to send them."

I said, "Well, we'll work on that, Admiral, as soon as find out what this man says."

So we sent the message as to what we were going to do. We were going to pull all U.S. Navy out of Malta and we were going to send in a couple of LSTs, and all the cars would be loaded aboard and they would all be vacated.

Arleigh said to me, "Now, if we get an answer, I want to know immediately. I don't care what time it is, day, night. I want to know." So about 5:00 or 6:00 o'clock in the afternoon, the answer came in.

I ran down the passageway in the Pentagon, went in, and there was a young WAVE lieutenant there in one of the outer offices. She said, "You can't go in."

I said, "Why not?"

She said, "Admiral Felt is in there, and when he went in, he left orders under no circumstances was anybody allowed to come in there and interrupt his conference with Burke."

I said, "Well, I have orders from Admiral Burke to come in no matter what."

She said, "You're taking it on your own head, Admiral, if you go in there. Expect a blowup."

So I took a chance and went through the door. I'm looking right at Arleigh sitting over at his desk, and in a big leather overstuffed chair, something like this, is Felt, with his back to me. Felt was talking, and obviously he decided Arleigh was looking at something over his shoulder. So he turned around and stood up and said, "What in hell are you doing in here? I left orders that nobody's to come in here."

Arleigh said, "I sent for him."

And Don Felt had the courtesy later to call me and say, "I'm sorry. I realize now what you were doing." That was the closest I ever had--I thought I was going to have a showdown with him right there, but I didn't.

Q: Burke did a nice job of protecting you.

Admiral Davidson: He sure did.

Q: How much personal concern did Admiral Burke have in the work of OP-61?

Admiral Davidson: Daily, from morning til night, because almost every paper that came up in the Joint Chiefs had a political angle to it. He wanted to be briefed always. OP-61 was always one of the briefers that briefed him before he went to JCS meetings.*

Q: By the way, what did the Malta Government say?

Admiral Davidson: They backed down. We stayed. Yes, they backed down. I can't remember what that guy's name was. He was well-known, though, throughout the world as being a so-and-so, but he backed down that time.**

Q: Could you sketch in some more detail the functions that OP-61 performed, and maybe some examples along the way?

Admiral Davidson: OP-61, in a way, is the liaison between CNO and the State Department, ISA--I guess it is, down in Defense-- and the other service political setups.*** I believe I'm correct in saying the first OP-61 was in about 1945. Bob Dennison was given the job.**** Just one officer was ordered in to worry about politico-military things.

---

*JCS--Joint Chiefs of Staff.
**Dominic "Dom" Mintoff was prime minister of Malta from 1955 to 1958 when the constitution was suspended and he resigned. He became prime minister again in 1971 when his Labor Party won election.
***ISA--International Security Affairs, an office under the Secretary of Defense and headed by an Assistant Secretary of Defense, often referred to as the "state department" of the Department of Defense.
****Captain Robert L. Dennison, USN, whose oral history is in the Naval Institute collection.

Q: Before the war, there had been what was called the Central Division that fulfilled that function.

Admiral Davidson: I didn't know about that one. I know that Denny had come to see me when I was the submarine detail officer--he had a lot of submarine background--and said he had just learned that he was not on the slate to get a big ship command, and he thought that was the end of his career. He was a captain. I was in BuPers. He thought maybe I was here on the inside track. He wondered why didn't he get command. I couldn't tell him, of course, but he was from my hometown, and I had known him when I was a little boy. He was in Arleigh Burke's class, six years ahead of me. So he wanted to know. He said, "Well, what would you do? Here I am a captain, and really they're telling me I'm through."

I said, "Well, Denny, I guess the advice I would give you from where I sit is why don't you go over to CNO and see if there isn't a job over there that you can get where you can be spared, because every so often they need a captain for something." So that's what he did. He went over there and somebody got the idea of setting up this OP-61, politico-military business. He got the job over there, and then they gave him a commander assistant and a couple of lieutenant commanders, then a couple of lieutenants, and pretty soon he had a full-blown crew called OP-61. Sure enough, they had to have a captain for the Missouri, and there he was available to go right away.* He got the ship, and then Truman went to South America and wanted him as his aide. That's the story of Dennison.

Q: That was the making of him.

Admiral Davidson: Right. I was just lucky in my guessing at what advice to give an old friend. In any event, where were we otherwise?

Q: We were trying to describe the role of OP-61.

Admiral Davidson: OP-61, I think, was just to cover all of the possible political angles that the Navy might or should consider in everything they did.

Q: Was it more of a reactive type organization or a planning organization?

Admiral Davidson: Reactive. Because planning was all done, I believe, in OP-60. OP-06 was all plans and operations, I suppose, and OP-60 was strategic planning. OP-61 was politico-military policy.

---

*Captain Dennison was commanding officer of the Missouri (BB-63) from April 1947 to February 1948.

Davidson #4 - 326

Q: You said you developed a good relationship with Admiral Libby in that job.

Admiral Davidson: Libby was OP-06. I had been with him in the Med, and then he came back to be OP-06. He relieved an aviation admiral, Matt Gardner.* Of course, Dennison was later OP-60, too, I believe. He started as OP-61, and then somewhat later in life he was in OP-60. Almost everything had some sort of a possible political angle to it. We developed quite an organization there. We had the Far East desk, the European desk.

Q: What do you recall about the reaction to the Suez Crisis in 1956?

Admiral Davidson: It seems to me--and this is a very, very faint memory--that we were involved to the extent that we made recommendations that the White House call the British. I forget what was the story now, Paul. It's just sort of escaping me.

Q: That was a thing that just sort of collapsed, because we wouldn't support the British and the French.**

---
*Rear Admiral Matthias B. Gardner, USN.
**The crisis began with Israel's invasion of Egypt's Sinai Peninsula on 29 October 1956. When a demand for a cease-fire by Britain and France was rejected by Egypt, the two countries landed forces--with disapproval from the United States--to secure the Suez Canal. A United Nations cease-fire was effected on 7 November.

Davidson #4 - 327

Admiral Davidson: That's right. We did not support the British and the French. I believe what we recommended to the White House was that we tell them that we were opposed to something, but if they got into the thing and the Russians came in, we would be in there 100% with them. That's my memory of what our policy said as far as the Navy was concerned.

Q: Do you have any recollections about nuclear weapons policy?

Admiral Davidson: No. I don't think we even thought about it.

Q: What about the Far East--the Formosa situation?

Admiral Davidson: I wish I had Red Baumberger here.* He could tell you all about it. He was my deputy for the Far East. My memory is too foggy there. I don't remember much about it.

Q: There was still in that era the idea that Air Force had that strategic bombing could win anything. Had the Air Force-Navy rivalry cooled by then?

Admiral Davidson: At least some, I think. Of course, I don't think the Navy ever believes strategic bombing can cure

---

*Vice Admiral Walter H. Baumberger, USN (Ret.), who was a captain while serving with Davidson.

everything.

Q: No.

Admiral Davidson: We sided a little with the Army on matters like that. It's hard to remember all those darn papers we had and studied them far into the night.

Q: Was that a very demanding job in terms of hours?

Admiral Davidson: Oh, yes. Just to give you an example, I left the office one time at 7:00 o'clock, and it didn't take me more than 20 minutes to get to my home in Arlington, and the phone was ringing. I picked it up, and Arleigh Burke said, "Where the hell have you been? I've been trying to get you all afternoon."

I said, "I didn't leave the office til 20 minutes ago."

He said, "Well, I've got to brief the President tomorrow morning on such and such a thing." I'm trying to remember what it was that he had to brief the President on. He said, "I've got to be there at 8:00 o'clock in the morning, so I want a position."

So I got busy and telephoned all my troops that night, and we got to the office at 5:00 in the morning and worked up a position paper for him to go to see the President, and delivered it to his office in time for him to go to the White House by 8:00 o'clock, only to find out it had just been cancelled, that he didn't have to go. Instead, I was to go and brief the Under Secretary of State, by the name of Bob Murphy, on the Navy position.* For the life of me I'm trying to think of what the problem was and what the Navy position was. I can't come up with it right this minute, except that right in the middle of my briefing of Mr. Murphy, somebody interrupted, one of the State Department people, and made a statement that I thought was about as pink as anything we'd ever heard, because we were a little worried about some of the State Department positions in those days. I can't remember what it was now.

Q: I hope it will come to you at some point. Were there policy aspects that you considered in connection with the deployment of the Polaris submarines?

Admiral Davidson: No, I don't think. There were some places we weren't allowed to send them. No, I don't remember any. If there were policy decisions on that, they must have come after my time, because I don't think we had any Polaris by 1960, did we?

Q: The first one went into commission in 1959. There had been a

---
*Robert D. Murphy, Deputy Under Secretary of the Department of State from 1954 to 1959 and then Under Secretary in 1959. He is the author of *Diplomat Among Warriors* (Westport, Connecticut: Greenwood Press, 1976).

Davidson #4 - 330

lot of the planning for it before then.

Any recollections about living in Washington--the social life in those years?

Admiral Davidson: In these particular years we're talking about, most of that time the only social life I remember much about was that we had lots of good friends around Washington, the usual cocktail parties, and so on and so forth. Nothing very big, nothing very special.

Q: What was your status as a submariner then? Had you lost some of the closeness you had with them previously?

Admiral Davidson: No. I tried to keep pretty much in touch with all the submariners. As far as what type of duty, one of the things that bothered me when I was OP-61 was this business of--if one person, like the Superintendent of the Naval Academy, if he's a submariner, then the commandant had to be an aviator, or vice versa. If he was an aviator, the other could be a submariner. They couldn't both be the same. If one was just a plain old ordinary blackshoe sailor from the destroyer force, then there was a battle between the submariners and aviators as to who was going to take the number two spot, and so on.* I think what

---

*"Blackshoes" were surface officers, distinguishable from aviation officers who were known as "brownshoes."

bothered me in OP-61 was that when I was fleeted up from OP-61B to OP-61, initially, when Smedberg left, he recommended that I relieve him. Matt Gardner said no, because I had not yet been selected, and he didn't want anybody in OP-61 who hadn't been selected for flag rank. So they cancelled Herb Riley's orders.* He had been OP-61B before I was, and he was ordered to a carrier division. They cancelled his orders and brought him back to be OP-61, which left OP-61 as an aviator, and OP-61B was a submariner. Okay. Then when I was selected, then Matt Gardner said okay, I could be OP-61. That's when I asked for Dick Colbert, and they said no, I couldn't have Dick Colbert. The reason I couldn't have Dick Colbert was that he was married to an English girl. I never thought that was the reason at all; I thought the reason was that they were insisting that an aviator be OP-61B if I was going to be OP-61. So they sent me Red Stroh, and he was an aviator, but he hadn't been my choice.** No criticism of Red Stroh; it's just that he wasn't my choice. But anyway, this sort of thing went on.

An interesting sidelight, just something that was told to me, and I don't know whether it's worthwhile to put in here or not. I wonder if Chester Bruton was ever interviewed.***

---

*Rear Admiral Herbert D. Riley, USN, whose oral history is in the Naval Institute collection.
**Captain Robert J. Stroh, USN.
***Rear Admiral Henry C. Bruton, USN.

Davidson #4 - 332

Q: Yes.*

Admiral Davidson: Admiral Bruton. I wonder if he's still alive.

Q: As far as I know, he is. Yes.

Admiral Davidson: I've tried to find out. Chester was an aide to Nimitz after the war, you know, when Nimitz was CNO. According to Chester, who was a very close friend of mine, when Arthur Radford was OP-05, he insisted that all aviation personnel assignments be made by OP-05. They were running the show. According to Chester Bruton, Admiral Nimitz sent for Radford one day and said, "Look. The Chief of Naval Personnel is charged with the responsibility of the assignment of personnel. Now, you can have all the people you want from OP-05 over in his office working for him. He'll make their fitness reports, not you. They will work for OP-01 or whatever he is, the Chief of Naval Personnel. So I want all of this personnel business closed out of OP-05, except as you see fit to recommend to one of your people who's on duty in BuPers."** He issued such a written directive.

Well, after about two or three months, nothing had happened, and according to Chester, Admiral Nimitz sent for Radford and said, "What have you done about it?"

---
*Rear Admiral Bruton's recollections of service with Fleet Admiral Nimitz are included in the Naval Institute oral history collection.

**Vice Admiral Arthur W. Radford, USN, was Deputy Chief of Naval Operations (Air), OP-05, from January 1946 to March 1947.

And Radford said, "I put it in my bottom drawer."

He said, "What do you intend to do about it?"

He said, "I don't intend to do anything about it."

After he left, Admiral Nimitz said to Chester Bruton, "I have two choices. I can either order a general court-martial or I can forget the whole damn thing." And nothing ever happened, so I assume he forgot the whole damn thing. That's the story that Chester once told me. I don't know anything about it, but I'm sure there was something to it, because that was the battle that was going on. Nobody disagreed with having equal representation in BuPers, but whoever the chief of BuPers was, the guy was supposed to be making fitness reports on those people working for him, not somebody over in OpNav controlling it.* So, you see, there's not only politics between Air Force and Navy; there were politics right inside the Navy. I objected to being told, for instance, that you had to have somebody of one particular branch of the service. I still held to the same thing later in the Pacific when I was a cruiser division commander; namely that if a person has been promoted to flag rank and he's in command of a task force, I don't care whether he's an aviator or a submariner or destroyer sailor or amphibious, or what. He was selected on the basis of his ability to command--supposed to be--and therefore he should be allowed to command. If necessary, you

---

*OpNav--Office of the Chief of Naval Operations.

give him a staff with all the special talent to advise him. If he's any good, he'll take their advice. That's been my theme all the way through, but it hasn't always worked.

Q: What do you recall about Admiral Smedberg as a boss?

Admiral Davidson: Excellent. Excellent. I always got along fine with Smeddy.

Q: Any particular incidents that involve him from that period?

Admiral Davidson: I don't remember any, Paul. I wouldn't be looking for anything wrong with Smeddy because he worked hard enough to get me to work for him.

Q: What do you mean, he worked hard enough?

Admiral Davidson: Well, Holloway said I was going to have to go to BuPers when I came from Albany. Smeddy wanted me to be his deputy in OP-61, so if you can convince Holloway of something, it meant he had to argue a little bit to get me.

Q: Was that considered a pretty good promotion-maker, if you would get in OP-61?

Admiral Davidson: Yes. I think it was. Everybody that I knew--let me tell you one who really got promoted. My assistant was a lieutenant when I was OP-61B--Stansfield Turner.*

Q: I guess he did. Tell me some more about him.

Admiral Davidson: He's a smart boy. I tell you, he was a crackerjack. He used to brief every morning not only all of the OPs, but Radford would send for him.** A lot of people would send for him from the Joint Chiefs because he was considered such a top briefer. In order to do that, he had to go in early every morning and read all the dispatches, make up a briefing, and get on his feet and give it. Stan, of course, was a Rhodes Scholar, ex-football player, one of the top in his class. There wasn't any question about it, as a young lieutenant he was a crackerjack.

Q: You said you were flabbergasted when you found out you'd been selected for flag rank. What was your reaction when you came down to earth?

Admiral Davidson: The reaction was that I found an aviator

---
*Lieutenant Stansfield Turner, USN, later admiral. He was appointed Director of the Central Intelligence Agency (CIA) in 1977 by his Naval Academy classmate (class of 1947), President Jimmy Carter.
**Admiral Radford served as Chairman of the Joint Chiefs of Staff from 1953 to 1957.

friend and got a little airplane that flew me to New London to see a brand-new grandson. I celebrated up there and then I flew back and went to work. I was selected then, but I didn't actually put it on for some time. As a matter of fact, after I was selected, I was moved into OP-61 and took over from Riley.* About that time they wanted to send two flag officers to London to some sort of a conference. I can't even remember what it was all about. They selected Charlie Buchanan, who was in OP-60 at the time.** Then Holloway said, "We'll frock you for the trip."*** So I had to have my uniform converted to a rear admiral's uniform, and when I came back, I had to go back to captain because I hadn't made my number yet.

Q: Anything about the tour in OP-61 that you haven't touched on?

Admiral Davidson: No. I think it was a good education, because I learned a little bit about the workings of not only the Navy Department, but also a little bit about the other services and State Department.

Q: I think you said previously that your time in Canada came in useful then.

---
*Rear Admiral Herbert D. Riley, USN, whose oral history is in the Naval Institute collection.
**Rear Admiral Charles A. Buchanan, USN.
***Frocking--authorization to wear the rank and carry the title--but not receive the pay--of the next higher rank for which one has been selected, but not yet attained.

Admiral Davidson: Yes. Of interest, perhaps, would be this sort of an anecdote. Felix Stump was the Commander in Chief Pacific.* Somehow or other, he got the idea that his dispatches to the State Department were not getting beyond a very low level member of the department and were being pigeonholed or not acted on. So Arleigh said to me one time, "Let's see if we can't get Felix to send his dispatches to you, and you carry them over to Bob Murphy, the Under Secretary." We started doing that, and we discovered that it had been true. There was a State Department officer who had been in the Far East, who felt that he knew better than the ambassadors out there, who were advising Stump. So when Stump's dispatches would come in, he would just pigeonhole them and take any action he thought should be taken. He decided he knew better what was going on than the man out on the spot. So we uncovered that. That was done by the Navy, uncovering it. Bob Murphy was pretty incensed when he learned that underneath him was somebody diverting messages that should have come up the line to him.

Q: You went on to take command of the cruiser division. What was your flagship?

Admiral Davidson: The <u>Los Angeles</u>. I drove to California, and

---
*Admiral Felix B. Stump, USN, Commander in Chief Pacific and Commander in Chief Pacific Fleet from 1953 to 1958.

then I flew out to the Far East and I relieved Mike Fenno as ComCruDiv Five.* The flagship was the Los Angeles, and the other ships were perhaps the Roanoke--well, I'll have to look them up. I've forgotten. There were a total of three cruisers. It's nowhere near the thrill of being the skipper.

Shortly after I took over out there, I developed my second hernia. It finally became so uncomfortable that it was decided that I should go into the naval hospital in Yokosuka and have it repaired. While I was in there, the situation down in the South China Sea began to look rather serious, and they wanted to send a task force down into the South China Sea. They picked the Roanoke to be the flagship of it, and then all kinds of other types of ships. I think there were as many as 30 ships all told involved. I was to be the commander of it, and here I am in the hospital. So they flew Roy Benson out, and he took over my division temporarily.** As soon as I was able to walk, I requested that I be flown down to the Philippines to rejoin the task force. I've forgotten who the admiral was who had his own plane out there. The doctor said if I would be willing to be strapped in the bunk on takeoff and landing, I could go. So I flew to the Philippines and got aboard, relieved Roy, and proceeded down in the South China Sea. Jack Chew was my flag

---
*Rear Admiral Frank W. Fenno, USN, Commander Cruiser Division Five.
**Rear Admiral Roy S. Benson, USN, whose oral history is in the Naval Institute collection. Admiral Benson was then Commander Cruiser Division One.

skipper in the Roanoke.* He and I had several weeks of very pleasant cruising, with almost impossible orders. It said, "Remain undetected." Thirty ships, remain undetected in the days of airplanes and so on. They thought we might have to go in and evacuate people from Indonesia. We were going to have to go in and evacuate people, but it never developed. We didn't have to do it. Then I eventually rejoined my own flagship, the Los Angeles, and came back. I returned to the United States. Anyway, it was just a one-year cruise. We did visit Hong Kong, which was nothing but a shopping spree. We visited Subic Bay. That was standard. That's where I got aboard the Roanoke, I think, in Subic Bay. But of all the various commands I had in my life, I think the cruiser division was the least satisfying, really. You could almost get along without a division commander. It's just a job to give a rear admiral something to do at sea.

Q: Well, it depends on the situation. If you had a crisis there, you could have ...

Admiral Davidson: Right. But there wasn't any crisis. We were prepared for the crisis, so it didn't happen. That's the point, I guess.

---
*Captain John L. Chew, USN, whose oral history is in the Naval Institute collection.

Q: Sure. There is also an administrative side to it.

Admiral Davidson: Yes.

Q: What did that involve?

Admiral Davidson: Not very much. Make fitness reports on the captains.

Q: You probably conducted some inspections.

Admiral Davidson: Some. Flew back and forth between ships in the chopper, that sort of thing.

Q: Was it a disappointing tour of duty for you?

Admiral Davidson: The only disappointment was when I got my orders to come back. My orders were to go to Turkey, and I didn't want to do that. I was just reading through the orders, and I find orders from the Chief of Naval Personnel to Rear Admiral John F. Davidson to Turkey, and at the bottom it said, in pen and ink, "Delivered with regret, W. Smedberg."*

---
*Vice Admiral William R. Smedberg III, USN, Chief of Naval Personnel from 1960 to 1964.

Davidson #4 - 341

Q: Well, he'd been kind to you before.

Admiral Davidson: Actually, I can tell you a little bit about the story--I was told about that by Mr. Bill Franke. Gates was the Secretary.* You were right about that. When Mr. Franke told me later on, he said, "You weren't supposed to go to Turkey; you were supposed to go to the Naval Academy to be the Superintendent. I thought it was all arranged. Mr. Gates said that he thought that Charlie Melson was deserving of a crack at Superintendent and that he was two years senior to you, and therefore you had two more years in which you could perhaps get the job.** So he preferred to send Charlie to the job that particular year," which was 1958. "Therefore, we had to look around for a place to put you on ice. We needed somebody on the Joint Staff in Turkey as the senior Navy member of JUSMAT, and so he thought maybe that was a good place to send you."*** He said, "I knew you'd be disappointed, and Tom Gates says to tell you he knows you're disappointed. I didn't tell you this beforehand because you'd be really disappointed if you thought you'd just missed the Naval Academy and had to go over to that God-awful

---
*Thomas S. Gates, Secretary of the Navy from April 1957 to June 1959, was succeeded by William B. Franke, who served until the end of the Eisenhower Administration in January 1961.
**Rear Admiral Charles L. Melson, USN, Superintendent of the Naval Academy from June 1958 until relieved by Admiral Davidson in June 1960.
***JUSMAT--Joint United States Mission for Aid to Turkey.

place, Turkey." So I didn't know about it until afterwards, til I came back to the Naval Academy.

Anyway, I came back here to Washington and attended about a three-week course of some kind that they send people to who are going to be involved in overseas aid jobs. The only thing I remember about it, I lost my best Borselino hat there. Somebody decided they liked it better than I did.

Then I went to Turkey. I had a two-engine R4D, or whatever they called it. I guess the Army called them Dakotas. Anyway, the old standard two-engine DC-3. My aide was a pilot, and they had him meet me in Naples, so I flew from Naples to Turkey. We flew into Turkey and took over the job there. Except for living conditions and getting used to dealing under the table, I think it was a very educational tour. I became very fond of Admiral Koruturk.* Admiral Koruturk was the Chief of Naval Operations over there. He later, after their revolution, which happened just before I returned from Turkey, was sent to Russia as ambassador to Russia and then returned to Turkey and was President of Turkey. I have this model of a Turkish galley that sits right inside the door here that he gave to me.

My experiences in Turkey were far different from some of my predecessors. I heard great stories about how much money you could make over there, and how you could do this, and how you

---
*Admiral Fahri Koruturk, Turkish Navy, later was president of Turkey from 1973 to 1980.

could do that. By the time I got there, everything had been tightened up to the point where they were working real hard to stamp out black marketing. They were trying to stamp out this business of taking an old car over there and selling it for $10,000, and all that sort of business. So when I arrived in Turkey, we were looking for a place to live, the first order of business. We found that there was a national Turkish law on rent control, and every apartment had an established amount of rent. We went to a hotel where it was very disagreeable living, the odors were terrible, our room was small. When you went in the bathroom in the morning, you sort of got sick at your stomach, all that sort of thing. You couldn't eat anything that you weren't sure about, which was difficult. But we started looking for an apartment, and we found a lovely apartment. We thought this was just great. The established rental was 2,000 lira for a month. Well, 2,000 lira wasn't bad because the exchange rate was nine to one. We didn't think that was too bad. Then the landlord said, "Well, that's 2,000 lira that you give me over the table, but there's another 1,500 under the table."

So I said, "Thanks very much. I am not going to violate Turkish law as the senior Navy representative to Turkey." I wasn't going to start off by violating the law. So we kept looking and we weren't getting anyplace. The hotel was more and more miserable. One night we went to a party and met General Erdelhun, who was chief of the general staff, the senior military man in Turkey.* His wife was at that time in a U.S. military hospital in Germany. She had been horseback riding, and she'd fallen off and been injured, and our Air Force had sent her up to get better medical treatment. He was very friendly to the United States. I said to General Erdelhun at this party that night, "We've been here a month. We can't find a place to live, and we can't take the hotel anymore." He agreed that the hotel wasn't very good.

"Well," he said, "why can't you find a place?"

I said, "Because you have a law that says I'm not allowed to pay but so much."

He said, "That's the problem? Don't get hasty, please."

So the next day Admiral Koruturk called me and he said, "Have you found nothing at all?"

I said, "We found an apartment at such and such a place. The owner, I understand, is one of your wealthiest citizens, but he wants an extra 1,500 lira under the table."

He said, "Don't do anything now."

The next thing I knew, a young rear admiral came to call on me, a Turkish rear admiral, and he said, "I've just talked to the landlord, and he's agreed to let you have the apartment for the established national rent."

I said, "I'll take it." To this day I think the Turkish Navy

---

*General Rustu Erdelhun, Chief of General Staff.

paid under the table.

Q: But your conscience was clear.

Admiral Davidson: My conscience was clear. When I left Turkey, to show you, for example, how that kind of stuff worked--and this is the kind of stuff I didn't like--we had Chinese rugs all over our house at home; we didn't take them to Turkey with us. It's a good thing we didn't. When we got there, we bought quite a few rugs. When it came time to leave Turkey, I discovered there was a Turkish law that said you could not export more than 1,000 lira worth of rugs, or something like that. Oh, my God, at nine to one, that's practically nothing, and here I was with all these rugs that I'd bought. So once again, in talking to General Erdelhun, I said, "Well, I've got to do something. I've got to get rid of these rugs, but also the law says I cannot take but X number of lira out of Turkey. So I'm sort of hung up. I have to give them away, I guess."

He said, "Oh, no, no. Just hold on."

So the next day, the director of customs called on me, and he said, "I have a letter here from General Erdelhun, and he advises me that you have very kindly offered to take X number of rugs back to the United States for friends of his with your shipment. This is the clearance for customs for you to take them." So I got the rugs. Still I had a guilty conscience.

Q: I can see why.

Admiral Davidson: And that's the way they live over there. The actual civil servants and the military, they're not paid enough, so they live under the table. They live on what we call cumshaw. I found it very, very difficult, and also I found it difficult to accept our ambassador's insistence that we Americans were the guilty people, with the black market, for instance. He said it was all the Americans' fault, the black market.

I can tell you a story that finally developed there that gives a perfect example of it. Down in Izmir we had a black market scandal. Involved, when we first learned about it, was a U.S. Navy lieutenant commander; I believe he was a chaplain. There were some others involved in this black market scandal of selling lira, not nine to one, but probably 20 to one, something like that, and all this money was changing hands, and so on and so forth. So the ambassador called in the country team. The country team consisted of one of his representatives from the State Department, someone from ISA, I guess, and others including the military. I was the senior military at that moment, and I was on the country team. We had a meeting. He said, "I want the following procedure carried out. I want you to require everybody under you to submit every month his total expenses and where he got the lira to pay for them, the cost of your maid, your chauffeur, the whole works, your food and liquor. That will be submitted to you, and that way you'll know how much he draws American and how many lira he had to spend, and so on. Where is he getting them?"

We said, "This is an invasion of privacy. We can't do it. It's an invasion of privacy."

He said, "It will be done."

Well, about a day went by. We were all just really teed off about it. All of a sudden, he called another meeting and said, "I retract all my orders."

Someone said, "Why?"

He said, "It's just been discovered that the leader of the Izmir black market is one of the highest officials in the Turkish Government, and he's the one that's making the money out of it."

I said, "Mr. Ambassador, what's that got to do with calling this off?"

He said, "Do you realize, Admiral Davidson, that if it comes out that involved in this black market is a Turkish government official, the Turkish Government will fall the next day?"

John Davidson said, "Would that be bad?" Whereupon, I was scolded for being a little bit impertinent. Anyway, that kind of thing I couldn't buy.

One other story if we have time on our tape. We had an Air Force major, maybe lieutenant colonel, crashed and killed over there. His wife was left there with two children, and she had an automobile and she had a whole house full of furniture that had been taken in on what they called the Bayanomi. That's your customs list when you go into the country, and you either take it out or you pay the customs. By law, she had to turn her lira into the embassy for American cash, and the limit was 11,000 lira at nine to one, whatever that comes out to be.

Q: A little over $1,000.

Admiral Davidson: She applied for an exception, because the Turks wanted to buy her car for $4,500, and all her furniture came up to quite a good sum. I've forgotten. I think the whole sum came to around 40,500 lira. We had a meeting of the country team, and one of the rules of the country team, the vote has to be unanimous. So here was her request and the vote in the country team was John Davidson, yes, all the rest, no. The poor widow was stuck with all this stuff. Within a week, one of the high-ranking people on the embassy staff who had a Chrysler Imperial over there was offered $8,000 for it when he was leaving to come home, and the country team was voting on it. The vote was John Davidson, no, and all the rest, yes. The ambassador said, "You're being an obstructionist."

I said, "No, Mr. Ambassador. I'm perfectly willing to change my vote if you'll all go back and change your vote for the widow of last week."

He said, "This is different. This is the Turkish Government

that wants to buy this car, and they want it as the official car for the Minister of Finance. That makes it an entirely different thing."

I said, "It doesn't to me, because the law says that no American can turn in but so much."

Well, he sent his deputy around to see me a couple of days later. "The ambassador wants me to tell you that you and Mrs. Davidson are just a lovely couple, they love having you over here, but you are an obstructionist."

Well, this is the kind of stuff that burned me all the way through, and that's what ruined my whole year over there. There was always something like that going on.

Q: What was your mission over there?

Admiral Davidson: It was a military aid program. We had to develop a five-year plan for the Turkish Navy, and which ships we would sell to them or loan to them, where they would get all of their supplies, so on and so forth. And an educational program—we were teaching English. One of the problems over there was this. You give them a modern airplane and you give them a manual. And they can't read English, and you can't translate the manual into Turkish because there aren't any words in Turkish for a lot of words that are in the manual. Then you have to teach them English. That was one of our big jobs, teaching English to all of these people. There were a lot of other things about it. I loved a lot of the Turks that I knew, but, you know, one of the laws of Turkey says that if you graduate from high school and go in the armed forces, you must be an officer. Period. A high school graduate may not serve in the armed forces as an enlisted rating. The result is that many high school graduates do not serve because there are not enough billets for all graduates. Also many of the non-graduates who can read and write must be assigned as chauffeurs in the armed forces because the law requires car drivers be able to read and write. The end result is that the only ones left to be trained as petty officers and technicians are non-high school graduates who cannot read or write.

Admiral Koruturk used to agree with me. If we could just induce this Turkish Government to change because they were wasting their best manpower. They don't even have to go into the service if they graduated from high school and there aren't any billets for officers. If the officer billets are all full, then they escape service altogether. You could at least use them as drivers of automobiles. I could go on forever on that subject, but it was an education to be over there.

Q: Do you remember any of the specific weapons programs that you were involved with?

Admiral Davidson: No, I don't really remember anything in

particular. I remember one thing I did over there that helped me personally. Admiral Koruturk and I used to have a conference once a week, and he spoke Turkish, and I spoke English. To the best of my knowledge, he didn't know a word of English, and to the best of his knowledge, I didn't know anything except "merhaba," which is "hello," or something like that. Anyway, I had a Turkish lieutenant as my Turkish aide. We were going to have a briefing, and I put an introductory five minutes in English on a tape, and then my Turkish aide put that in Turkish on a tape, leaving a gap between each sentence, almost, and gave it to me. I took it home, and every morning of my life I played that thing. I was reading the Turkish, and when the tape would hesitate, I'd read that line. I got up before the whole Turkish Navy, all these admirals and Admiral Koruturk and all, and started right off in Turkish. Everybody damn near dropped dead.

Then we had an enlisted man who was married to a Turkish girl, and he was fluent in Turkish. He made the presentation with the slides and graphs and all that sort of thing. When we sat down, Admiral Koruturk got up, and in the most beautiful English I ever heard in my life, he said, "I now know for the first time in over a year what the U.S. Navy is planning to do for the Turkish Navy, because I have heard it from Admiral Davidson in my own language." And don't think that didn't pay dividends for me. I worked awful hard on it. It took me a month to get that thing down. Of course, my pronunciation must have been lousy, but still.

Q: How was life off duty once you got into the apartment?

Admiral Davidson: Very nice. Other than going to the embassy, most of our associations were with the rest of the American colony. You see, there was a major general in the Army who was in command of the whole unit, and then we had a brigadier Air Force, a brigadier Army, and a rear admiral Navy from the various services, and then they had their staffs. We had a nice big PX, commissary.* The Air Force established a small hospital over there, which was helpful, because so many people had some sort of ailment from food they ate. You had to boil everything.

The worst thing about living over there was that you had to fill your bathtub every morning, because you never knew what time of day they were going to cut off all the water. In order to flush the toilet, you had a bathtub full of water, and you had a bucket there, and you could pour into the john after you used it. Sort of hard living that way, you know, after what you're used to in this country. However, I suppose it's a good experience for everybody to try it once.

Q: And you've done your duty in that regard.

---
*PX--post exchange, a small department store operated for U.S. military personnel and their families. The commissary was a grocery store for the same customers.

Admiral Davidson: Yes. I'll tell you what happened the day we got there. We were having a departure ceremony for my predecessor. We were all at the airport, and all of the top-ranking military in the Turkish Navy and Army and Air Force were there. The wife of my predecessor turned to my wife and said, "This is the happiest day of my life."

Davidson #5 - 354

Interview Number 5 with Rear Admiral John F. Davidson,
U.S. Navy (Retired)

Place: Admiral Davidson's home in Annapolis, Maryland

Date: Wednesday, 2 October 1985

Subject: Biography

Interviewer: Paul Stillwell

Q: Admiral, we talked last time about your tour of duty in Turkey, and then Secretary Franke came through for you, and you became Superintendent of the Naval Academy. When did you take over?

Admiral Davidson: I arrived here in June of 1960, and I relieved Admiral Melson. I believe it was on the 20th of June, 1960. Then began one of the most beautiful two-plus years of my whole life, being Superintendent of the Naval Academy.

Q: Why do you say that?

Admiral Davidson: I was convinced before I came, and then after I had been here, that there isn't another job to equal it in the Navy. You could go on and become CNO, and it wouldn't be as gratifying as being the Superintendent of the Naval Academy.

Q: Admiral Kauffman said very much the same thing about his

experience.*

Admiral Davidson: Admiral Smedberg said the same thing. Admiral Smedberg sent me a message, something to the effect that this was perhaps the most important job in the Navy.** I have here what Admiral Burke said, a letter that might be worth my putting in here.*** This is a message I received. "Personal to Rear Admiral Davidson from Burke. Propose to order you as Superintendent of the Naval Academy this summer. This is one of the most important jobs in the Navy and has been superbly handled by Charlie Melson. His relief must be an exceptionally good officer who can instill in midshipmen all knowledge, integrity, and willingness to work hard that they will be required to have. I have searched the flag list, and you are by far best qualified. Ann will also have tough and strenuous jobs which she can do exceptionally well. I hope you will like this duty, for it is important. Smeddy will send you further information later. Do not yet know who your relief will be." Well, that was the beginning of this wonderful tour.

---

*Rear Admiral Draper L. Kauffman, USN, Superintendent of the Naval Academy from June 1965 to June 1968. Kauffman's oral history is in the Naval Institute collection.
**Rear Admiral William R. Smedberg III, USN, Superintendent of the Naval Academy from 1956 to 1958. His oral history is also in the Institute collection.
***Admiral Arleigh A. Burke, USN, Chief of Naval Operations from 1955 to 1961.

Q: What was the date on that message, admiral?

Admiral Davidson: The date on that message seems to be 27 February 1960. Of course, I didn't come back then. That was followed up by one from Smedberg, saying, "SecNav with CNO concurrence has approved your assignment as Superintendent of the USNA in June." Then telling me that R.C. Johnson had been approved to relieve me.* "Congratulations and best regards." That's about all he had to say at that point.

Anyway, I don't know how much I can remember about that wonderful two years. There are humorous things, extremely, to me, interesting things. One of the things I might start in on is the system in use at the time I arrived, and a system which I was used to from my days here as a head of department. The various departments had a number of civilian faculty in addition to officer instructors, and so on. These ranged in rank from assistant professor, through associate professor and finally, I believe, we had about six who had the rank known as senior professor. I believe that's what they called them--senior professors. The Superintendents before my time, with perhaps, at the most, one exception, and I don't remember who that might have been, were inclined to take the advice of the senior professors

---

*Rear Admiral Ralph C. Johnson, USN. Rear Admiral Charles C. Kirkpatrick, USN, followed as Superintendent, serving from August 1962 to January 1964.

on all academic matters. I certainly didn't consider myself as an academic expert. Therefore, I continued with the same system.

We had a committee of senior professors who advised the Superintendent on academic matters. Of course, the Commandant of Midshipmen and other heads of departments who were officers advised him on military and administrative matters. During my tour here, the Secretary of the Navy came up with an idea that we should have a civilian academic dean, and most of the faculty were opposed to it. In fact, all of the civilian faculty were opposed to it. They liked the system that we had. I supported them 100%.

Finally, Mr. Korth, who was then Secretary of the Navy, asked to come down and have a briefing on the general situation and what we thought about it.* Admiral Smedberg told me Mr. Korth had assured him there would be no drastic changes made without further consultation with the Chief of Naval Personnel, Admiral Smedberg. Well, Mr. Korth came down, and we had the meeting in the Superintendent's quarters one afternoon. The senior professors all had a crack at presenting their views.

When the meeting was over, the Secretary said to me, "Admiral, I have to congratulate every one of you. This has been a perfect meeting, wonderful presentations. It appears to me that the Naval Academy is operating as it should be, and no

---

*Fred Korth, Secretary of the Navy from January 1962 to November 1963.

changes should be made. Absolutely, I think this is a fine system." So he left about 5:00 o'clock.

The next morning about 8:30, his aide called me from Washington to say, "Admiral, you may want to look at the <u>Washington Post</u>, because today's <u>Washington Post</u> announces the appointment of Professor Drought as the academic dean at the Naval Academy."*

So I called Admiral Smedberg, and I won't repeat his expletive, but we had just been taken. I mean, it turned out it was really a falsehood to tell us that nothing would be done, and then something was done without our knowledge. At the time, everybody was distressed here at the Academy. Now, looking back on it, Drought turned out to be a very fine man, and his successor, Bruce Davidson, turned out to be just as fine or better.** I think it has worked beautifully. I still don't give Mr. Korth credit, because I don't think he handled it properly, but as it turned out, it's been a very fine thing. That was one of the big things that happened during my tour as Superintendent.

Q: That had been picked up when Secretary Connally was in office there.*** There had been a study. I interviewed Captain Kerr,

---

*Dr. A. Bernard "Ben" Drought became the first academic dean of the U.S. Naval Academy in 1962. He had been the dean of engineering at Marquette University in Milwaukee, Wisconsin.
**Dr. Bruce M. Davidson, academic dean from 1971 to 1985.
***John B. Connally, Jr., Secretary of the Navy from January 1961 to December 1961.

who was on his staff, and he had conducted a number of interviews and so forth.* He said that recommending and approving a change was one of the last official acts that Connally performed while he was in office.

Admiral Davidson: Of course, Connally told me some things that didn't stand up. I can see Connally and his lovely wife standing in the rose garden and saying to me and my wife, "I have reached the ultimate in my life. I aspire to nothing higher. I think being secretary of the most wonderful navy in the world is as far as I want to go, and I'm very happy."** Two weeks later, he announced that he was going to run for governor of Texas. So I began to wonder about Secretaries of the Navy. They seem to use words to sort of avoid letting anybody know what they were going to do.

But in any event, it turned out well, and I am happy that it did turn out well. We continued the progress that had already been started before I came here, the progress of establishing degrees and things like that, which we didn't have in my day. When I went through here, we didn't get any kind of degree. I was graduated in 1929, and I think it was at least 1939 before

---
*Commander Alex A. Kerr, USN, was special counsel to the Secretary of the Navy and is the subject of a Naval Institute oral history.
**The rose garden of the Superintendent's quarters. A Democrat at the time, Connally was in the car with President John F. Kennedy when Kennedy was assassinated in Dallas in November 1963.

somebody suddenly said, "You now have a bachelor of science degree," which was made retroactive. Then they began validating previous high school courses and other college courses, permitting a boy, if he could pass certain tests, to skip taking what was the old standard course. When I was here, we all took the same thing, all four years, with the exception of the foreign language. We had French and we had Spanish. Well, we continued this validation program, and then we set up the major program so that they could major in this and that, and that grew. That was just beginning when I took over, and it grew during my tour. I don't remember just how many we established, but I understand now that it's very extensive, the different degrees you can get.

Q: Who was the ramrod on that curriculum revision?

Admiral Davidson: I have a feeling that that started maybe under Admiral Smedberg and was passed on down to Melson. I can't be positive about that.

Q: I was wondering who on the faculty worked with you. Would it have been in the committee of senior professors?

Admiral Davidson: Probably. I could find out things like that, probably, by asking people like Bill Jefferies, whom you know, and Ned Potter, the senior professors, I guess. Ed Cook, do you know him?

Q: No, I don't.

Admiral Davidson: Ed Cook was a senior professor in the electrical engineering department after my old friend Thomson.* I don't know who was the honcho. I think perhaps something like that sort of evolved. Whenever they could set up a program, they did it. I don't remember much about it, and certainly I was not the instigator, because I didn't know enough about it to try to convince anybody.

Q: As the curriculum was changing and the civilian dean coming in, wasn't one of the concerns that the military education aspect would be slighted?

Admiral Davidson: It might have been a concern of people not here, but I don't think we ever let it concern the people here, because we were not slighted in the military end of it, I don't believe. There were things that happened. I don't know that I've mentioned any of these before in connection with my correspondence with Admiral Nimitz and so on, but, for instance,

---

*Professor Edward Cook was in the Engineering and Aeronautics Department in 1929. Professor Earle W. "Slipstick Willie" Thomson was in the Electrical Engineering and Physics Department.

along that line--whether or not we were sacrificing anything in the military, we stopped marching to class. This was an absolute necessity, because the commandant and I discovered that we were losing about 20 minutes out of every recitation period because we were mustering and marching to class and running into traffic jams. Sections were returning and sections going, plus the fact, instead of sections being made up of all one class, like all first classmen, second classmen, and so on, you had mixed sections. We had plebes who had validated courses and were taking classes with second classmen, and the other way around. All sorts of things were going on.

The commandant and I finally decided to make a test run. After we had built the new wing, the one that extends to seaward and in between which you have the brigade library and all that down there, you know.* Those wings were finished during my early days here, and one day the commandant and I decided to go to a room on the top deck nearest the sea wall and walk from there by the most direct route we could take to Isherwood Hall, which was the engineering building, the one that's recently been torn down. We walked at a reasonable pace and found out how long it took. Well, this just meant that much time, if you had to fall in, muster, march over there, march in, and so on. We found that we were losing about 20 minutes per recitation hour. So we decided

---
*The new wing was in Bancroft Hall, the dormitory for the midshipmen.

that we could require the midshipmen to be military, but proceed on their own, make them responsible for being in class on time, and for being there. They didn't have to be mustered.

The upshot of that was a rather large expression of concern from graduates. They thought the place had really gone to hell-- no more military bearing or anything. The only real good letter I had was one that came from Admiral Nimitz, and he simply said, "Knowing you, there must be a good reason. Everybody's asking me what I think about it, and I don't know what to tell them because I don't know the reason."[*]

So I wrote back and told him just what I told you, and that satisfied him, and apparently it satisfied a lot of people that he talked to, because it dried up and we didn't hear any more about it. But that's the only thing about the military end of it that I can recall.

Q: What were your reasons for opposing the adoption of a civilian dean? What arguments did you use with Secretary Korth?

Admiral Davidson: I think we were really arguing that the status quo was perfectly good. Here we had the benefit of about six senior professors, who had been here for a considerable number of years and worked steadily right up through the system, that they

---

[*]Fleet Admiral Chester W. Nimitz, USN.

were the best advice the Superintendent could get. As I look at it now, and having attended Bruce Davidson's retirement and heard all the wonderful things about him, perhaps the drawback, which I didn't see at the time, was that the committee didn't spend its time trying to establish new ideas. They just advised the Superintendent on the way things were going rather than suggesting new ideas and new plans. As I gathered, listening to the kudos about Bruce, he established a whole lot of new things while he was here, which have been well accepted and considered excellent.

Q: I guess that the philosophy up to then contended that if it isn't broken, you don't fix it.

Admiral Davidson: That's right. That's right. If it isn't broken, don't fix it.

Q: What would you say was the most important role for you as Superintendent? You've spoken so frequently about your talent for getting subordinates to do things for you, and yet Admiral Burke had specifically spoken in that message about how well qualified you were. What did he expect of you?

Admiral Davidson: I think he expected me, maybe, to be a role model or whatever you'd call it, and to set an example in everything from military bearing to enthusiasm for this, that, and the other thing. I was always very, very enthusiastic about all the athletic programs. I don't suppose a day went by that I didn't either go down to the football practice or do something. I tried to keep myself before the midshipmen all the time. In those days, I smoked a pipe. I don't think they would have known me without it. I traveled with the teams when they went places, and I spoke at all the pep rallies. I think that that probably was why I eventually was dubbed as "Big Daddy," and my wife as "Big Momma." When we were leaving here, they had suits of white works converted which said "Big Daddy" and "Big Momma" on them.*

Q: Could you compare it at all with the father figure and leader in the ship as a skipper?

Admiral Davidson: To some extent, yes. No question about it. You had to maintain the military discipline and so on, and still not be considered a sundowner or something worse.**

We had a lot of things happen. One of the interesting things I recall that happened with respect to Army-Navy game tickets. One day while I was sitting down at practice with the football team, less than a week before the Army game, I believe, the

---
*White works--summer weight white uniform with the traditional Navy jumper.
**A sundowner is an especially demanding naval officer, a martinet.

commandant arrived and said he needed to talk to me privately, that we had a terrible scandal on our hands. Is this new to you?

Q: Yes, it is.

Admiral Davidson: He said, "We have just uncovered a scalping operation which involves all of the football team, a large number of first classmen, and not of their own volition, a large number of plebes."

I said, "What happened?"

He said, "Well, we discovered that a large number of first classmen have been prevailing upon the plebes to get their two tickets to the Army game and turn them over to them, and they had a system set up where they were sent to a scalper in Philadelphia, who was selling them at very, very high prices. The football team is involved to the extent that each football team member was given eight free tickets to the Army-Navy game for his friends, and most of them had turned them over to the scalpers and are receiving very high prices."

I said, "What's your recommendation, Captain?"

He said, "I recommend that we put them all on report."

I said, "Do you realize we won't have an Army-Navy game next Saturday if you do that?"

He said, "Well, that's the only thing to do."

Q: Was this 1960, your first year there?

Admiral Davidson: I have a feeling it was maybe my--I don't recall whether it was '60 or '61. Probably 1960, because I remember the aide--Dodge McFall was my aide.* So Dodge was there with me when the commandant confessed all this. At that time it was Captain Mini, so that means it definitely was '60.** So I left football practice and went home and just sat there, just having a terrible time wrestling with this thing and what to do. All of a sudden, I came up with an idea, and I called Dodge McFall. I said, "Dodge, I want a meeting of the first class in Mahan Hall at 7:00 o'clock tonight, and I particularly want all of the football team there. I want to try out on you my proposal." I had great, great admiration and confidence in this particular aide's judgment. He was in the class of '50.

I said, "I propose to get up and disclose to this group, the first class and the football team, what we know. We know that a naval officer's daughter out in town is the go-between; she's the mailbox, and that there's a rather dubious character in Philadelphia who scalps tickets in the racket, and we have pretty good evidence that all the people there, many of the first class involved, and they could be guilty of two things--not only scalping, but undue pressure on plebes, and that the football

---
*Lieutenant Albert D. McFall, USN.
**Captain James H. Mini, USN, was Commandant of Midshipmen from 1960 to 1961.

team is guilty of being involved in scalping. Then I'm going to propose to them my solution, and my solution is that every one who has received any money will personally go to the Athletic Association and hand it over, no matter whether it came from a plebe ticket or a football player's ticket or whatever. It will all be taken in there. Then I'm going to tell them that if this breaks and gets in the newspapers, there will be no Army game. We couldn't do anything, but to cancel. Therefore, it has to be kept absolutely quiet, and that I will take full responsibility for the fact that it happened. My answer to any question about that is that I, as the head of the Naval Academy, have the Athletic Association under me, and I should have made certain that they didn't give out tickets to midshipmen, that the system in use ought to be, if a plebe wanted two tickets for his father and mother, he would turn in his father and mother's name at the Athletic Association and the tickets would be mailed direct, that if a football player was to get eight tickets, he turned in the names of the eight people whom he wanted to have them, and they would be mailed from the Athletic Association."

Then I told the director of athletics that hereafter during my time here, that's the way it would be done, with no possibility of scalping if the tickets were mailed, because if a number of people gave the same name in Philadelphia, then we'd begin to smell them out. Anyway, it never broke. I was very fortunate. It didn't break. I didn't feel dishonest about it; I felt that by agreeing to take the responsibility, I was just quashing something that never should have happened anyway. I don't know if I should have thought of it ahead of time, but I probably should have thought about it. I didn't know just what the procedure was for issuing tickets. I hadn't gotten into those details. But anyway, as far as I know, we never had any more problems with it. That was one of the real crisis times that I remember of my very first year.

Q: That sort of let the scalper off the hook that way, though, didn't it?

Admiral Davidson: Well, I guess so. I don't know what he got out of it. The Athletic Association did recover some money from it.

Q: They had a windfall, probably.

Admiral Davidson: Yes. That was one of the many things that happened.

Q: The Navy had one of the top football teams in the nation by that period. I'd be interested in your recollections of Coach

Hardin and the athletic director, and some of those games.*

Admiral Davidson: To begin with, let's start with when I first arrived. I took a look at the football schedule, and I saw that--I won't remember figures exactly--I saw that we were playing only about three games a year that the midshipmen could see. I thought, "This team is for the midshipmen. It's not for the nation; it's for the midshipmen. Therefore, we have to play more games here in Annapolis." So I sent for Red Coward, who was then the athletic director, and said, "Red, I want some changes made in the football schedule, because I think if we have ten games, the midshipmen should see five of them at least."**

He said, "Admiral, maybe sometime we can accomplish that, but you know how schedules are made out. They're made out eight, nine, ten years in advance." He said, "Your predecessors have already approved schedules up for at least eight years."

So I took a look at that schedule, and I saw that we were playing Penn State the first game every year at Penn State.*** So we had two things that I didn't like about it. One was Penn State was a power house, and for us to go up there for the first game every year just got us off to a bad start.

So I telephoned the president of Penn State, whose name

---
*Wayne Hardin was Naval Academy head football coach from 1959 to 1964.
**Captain Asbury Coward, USN.
***Pennsylvania State University at University Park, Pennsylvania.

was Eric Walker, and I said, "I think this is a terrible setup that we come up there five straight years for the first game of the year. Why don't you come down here and play us every other year?"

He said "I couldn't agree with you more, Admiral. Let me look into it." He called back and said, "My athletes tell me they can't afford to come down and play you because Navy will guarantee only about $20,000, and we have to have more of a guarantee for our budget."

So I talked to our people, and they said, "Well, we could go up a little bit, but not too much."

To make a long story short, Eric and I worked out a system whereby we alternated years. That helped with one game, anyway. We finally got around to the point where I think now the midshipmen can see pretty much half the schedule. The only games that they all went to in those days were the Army game and the games here in Annapolis, so we had to have four here in Annapolis in order to do it. I think they do have at least four now.

But the money angle was the big thing. At that time, I think our stadium held a maximum of about 30,000, and it was just a case of money, money, money. For instance, that year, 1960, our star was Joe Bellino, who won the Heisman Trophy.[*] We had a rule

---

[*]Midshipman Joseph M. Bellino, USN, class of '61, was awarded the Heisman Trophy as the nation's outstanding college football player for the 1960 season.

that the Navy Department sort of approved of that we wouldn't accept a bowl invitation unless we beat the Army. So that year we received a bowl invitation to play Missouri in the Orange Bowl.

Admiral Davidson: We had the invitation when we went to play Army, and we did squeeze out that victory, just barely. So Mr. Franke, the Secretary, and Arleigh Burke and I went to the dressing room.

Q: You squeezed that victory was over Army, not Missouri.*

Admiral Davidson: Over Army. Yes. We just squeezed it out, too, because we were leading, and Joe Bellino intercepted a pass in the end zone and ran it back to the middle of the field in the last minute of play. Otherwise, Army would have won.** But anyway, we went to the dressing room, Mr. Franke, Secretary of the Navy, and Arleigh Burke and I went down there. Here were all the kids, they'd just got their football suits off and most of them were stark naked, coming out of the shower. Mr. Franke said, "Would you all like to go to the Orange Bowl?"

"Yea! Yea!" They all wanted to go.

---

*Missouri defeated Navy 21-14 in the Orange Bowl, New Year's Day, 1961.
**The final score was Navy 17, Army 12.

Well, a month later, they were a very unhappy group. Coach Hardin had them practicing every day. They lost Christmas leave, and finally went down to the Orange Bowl in Miami. I was there, and the officer representative came to me and asked me if I would intercede with Wayne Hardin because the boys were being required to be in bed at 9:00 o'clock every night. The beach was covered with beautiful girls, and the Missouri boys were all out there courting girls around, and would I intercede. I said, no, I wouldn't intercede, but I couldn't help but agree that they had given up so much, really. It turned out that the only reason for going there was in those days it meant a half a million dollars to the Athletic Association, clear profit. That, I think, still holds. If you can get on TV or anything, you can pick up an extra half million.

The aftermath of that season was the Joe Bellino problem. After the season was over, of course, Joe Bellino was on the banquet circuit, and he went every place. He even went out to the Bob Hope show in Hollywood. It finally became sort of apparent that his grades were suffering badly, and that by mid-term, which would be about the first of February, he was going to be lucky if he was satisfactory. So the commandant and I agreed that we should put a stop to it. Even the director of athletics agreed. He'd already won the Heisman Trophy. So we put the kibosh on it and said he couldn't go anymore. Well, that's when Cardinal Cushing of Boston wrote and invited him to speak at a

Catholic father and sons' banquet in Boston, and Joe had to say no.* Whereupon, the cardinal called me and tried to persuade me, and I explained to him that we were concerned about Joe's academic progress, and so on and so forth. I thought it was all settled until the Speaker of the House, McCormack, called me and asked me why I had turned Cardinal Cushing down.** I explained it all to him, and he said, "All right. Let me ask you something now. If I get the cardinal to change the date of the banquet to after the mid-year exam, and if Joe has passed, may he go then?"

Well, of course, I was over a barrel. I had to say yes. The finale of that was that when the day came for Joe to go, we put him in an official car and sent him up to Washington to the airport to go to Boston. He called about 11:00 o'clock to say that the airport was snowed in and the planes couldn't take off. So I directed him to come on back to the Naval Academy. Then I called Mr. McCormack, and that's when I told him that I thought that the cardinal's boss had decided Joe shouldn't go. He said, "Touche."

Q: You didn't mention the outcome of the business about the 9:00 o'clock in bed for the football team.

---

  *Richard Cardinal Cushing was the archbishop of Boston from 1944 to 1970.
  **John W. McCormack (Democrat-Massachusetts) was Speaker of the House of Representatives from 1962 to 1971.

Admiral Davidson: Wayne relented a little bit and let them stay up, I think, til 11:00, or something like that.

Q: Was he more practical to deal with than other coaches had been?

Admiral Davidson: In the beginning. I remember this incident. I think it was one day down at practice, I was sitting in the stands with Rip Miller, who was the assistant director.* The plebes were scrimmaging the varsity, and Roger Staubach was a plebe.** He was making the varsity look just silly. So every time he'd cross the goal line, which he did frequently, the whole varsity team would pounce on him and pound on him until I couldn't take it any longer. I walked right out in the middle of the field and got ahold of Hardin and said, "Hey! Duden needs this kid for Saturday.*** Call off your dogs." And Hardin agreed with that.

Rip told me later that Hardin said to him, "My goodness, where did we get this new Superintendent? I heard he was a former head of the English department, that he was interested only in academics and Shakespeare. What's he doing coming around

---

*Edgar E. "Rip" Miller, assistant director of athletics.
**Midshipman Roger T. Staubach, USN, class of 1965, quarterback, was the Heisman Trophy winner in 1963.
***Henry R. Duden, department of athletics, was the plebe, or first year, football coach.

here telling me how to run football practice?"

Well, after that, Wayne and I became a little better acquainted, and he realized then that both Mrs. Davidson and I were very avid supporters of all the athletic events. I think he thought, when he heard who was coming as Superintendent, that he supposed there wouldn't be any interest.

But Wayne, over the years, then became a little bit impressed with his own success and importance, and so on, and eventually we clashed in this particular respect. There was a first class lecture series, and historically it had been held on Friday nights. We had very, very top speakers--the ambassador to Russia, the Chairman of the Joint Chiefs, the CNO. We had really top speakers. It soon became apparent to me that none of the first classmen on the football team were ever present. I felt that they were being deprived of part of their educational benefits. So I, with quite a bit of effort, telephoned the remaining list of speakers to see if they could change their dates to a Tuesday night, which seemed to be the best available night here for it. I arranged that. The very first lecture that came up on Tuesday night, none of the football players were there. So I called Red Coward and asked him what the hell had happened, and he said, "Well, Wayne decided that's the night to show them after-game movies from the previous week, and he needs them all there for that."

That's when I got Wayne Hardin and said, "Hey, I'm still

running the Naval Academy, and I've gone to a lot of trouble to do this. You can have your game movies any night in the week except Tuesday. That's my night." So we got along very well for a while.

When spring came, we had, of course, a championship lacrosse team. Dinty Moore was our coach, as he had been for years and years and years.* He stomped into my office one day and said, "I'm resigning."

I said, "Why?"

"Well," he said, "we went down to our lockers there in Macdonough Hall, and everybody's gear had been thrown out on the middle of the deck and the lockers were full of the spring practice football team gear. I inquired and found that Wayne had told the team that those lockers were for the football team and that the lacrosse team didn't rate them." He said, "Always in spring the lacrosse team has had the preference. I'm not going to compete with something like that."

Well, then I had to get Wayne. Really, I got the director of athletics, and I'm not sure it wasn't by that time Bill Busik, because he relieved Red Coward.** Anyway, we got that straightened out, and we put the lacrosse players back in, because they were having an undefeated season, too. That's the extent that I used to get involved in the athletic programs

---
*William H. Moore III.
**Captain William S. Busik, USN.

around there. Of course, Wayne eventually--I remember telling him one time in my office, "If you keep on trying very hard, you're going to be just as impossible as Eddie Erdelatz. If you get that impossible, then things have to happen." Because Charlie Melson had had to fire Erdelatz.*

Q: I'm interested in the social side that went with the athletics. That is, meeting people like Father Joyce of Notre Dame.**

Admiral Davidson: Oh, yes. One of the interesting nights I had, and this was really, really something, we had the board of visitors here, and number two on the board of visitors was Father Joyce from Notre Dame. He was number two at Notre Dame. Actually, the chairman of the board of vistors that year was Milton Eisenhower.*** We had the board here, and a message came through that Father Joyce's mother was very, very ill and not expected to live. We were able to muster up an airplane for him and send him down to Carolina to his mother.

The next day I went to New York to the big football Hall of

---
*Edward Erdelatz was fired as head football coach in early 1959. See the oral history of Captain Slade D. Cutter, USN(Ret.)
**Father Edmond P. Joyce, vice president of the University of Notre Dame, South Bend, Indiana.
***Youngest brother of the President, Milton Eisenhower was a career government officer and former president of Pennsylvania State University, who became a personal advisor during his brother's term of office.

Fame dinner, and as I walked into the dining room, a retired Army officer by the name of Garbisch, who was famous for having kicked four field goals against Navy in 1924, came over to me and said, "Admiral, will you do us a great favor tonight?"*

I said, "I'll try."

He said, "Will you make Father Joyce's speech?"

I said, "What's Father Joyce supposed to talk about?"

He said, "He's going to talk about the student athlete."

I said, "Fine. Let me have a copy of his speech and a chance to look it over." I was walking in to dinner at that time.

He said, "Well, we don't have a copy. We'd just like you to give a speech on the student athlete, and we'd like you to sit at the head table."

Well, at the head table on my right was Buzz Borries, who had been a star athlete back in the early Thirties here at the Naval Academy; but two of the principal speakers that night were Douglas MacArthur and Herbert Hoover.** And here I am sitting with a paper napkin, trying to make notes. I don't think I ate a bite. I tried to make notes. What in the world do you say about a student athlete? I don't remember to this day what I said, except I received some compliments--one because it was so brief.

---
*Colonel Edgar W. Garbisch, AUS, U.S. Military Academy class of 1925.
**Captain Fred Borries, Jr., USN, class of 1935; General of the Army Douglas MacArthur; Herbert C. Hoover, 31st President of the United States, from March 1929 to March 1933.

It was brief. Anyway, that was one of the experiences I had with Father Joyce. I never knew Father Hesburgh as well, because Joyce was always the one here on our board.*

Q: What about the hoopla of the Army-Navy games in Philadelphia?

Admiral Davidson: The most interesting one I remember--the night before the game, we always had a big combined dinner. It was an opportunity for speakers to make jabs of all kinds at the others. Of course, Westmoreland was the "Sup" at West Point, and I was down here.** And it so happened the host speaker spoke last, and it was Navy's year to be host. So during the cocktail hour, Westy said, "Oh, boy, I've got one on you tonight." I don't know what it was.

I said, "You'd better be careful, Westy, because I've got a honey on you. If you embarrass me too much, I'm going to tell one on you."

He said, "Oh, go ahead." So he gave me a hard time. I forget what it was, but rather eloquently done, too. He's a pretty good speaker.

So I got up and I told a story that had been told to me out at the University of Detroit. We were out there for the

---
*Reverend Theodore M. Hesburgh, president of Notre Dame University.
**Major General William C. Westmoreland, U.S. Army, later general, was Superintendent of the U.S. Military Academy from 1960 to 1963.

Detroit-Navy football game. They had a luncheon, and, of course, the president of the University of Detroit was a Catholic priest, whose name I can't remember now. But he said to me, "I'll have to tell you a story about your big opponent, General Westmoreland. This is one of the first years we've ever played both Army and Navy. On the occasion of the Detroit-Army game, I received a letter from General Westmoreland which said, 'Dear Father Callahan [or whatever it was], On the occasion of the Detroit-Army football game, it would give Mrs. Westmoreland and me a great deal of pleasure if you and Mrs. Callahan would be our house guests.'" Well, it brought down the house.

I went back to my seat, and in the second row behind there was a poor Army colonel. He tapped me on the shoulder and said, "I will probably be given a new job tomorrow."

I said, "Why?"

He said, "I wrote the damn letter. He signed it without looking at it."

We had great fun at those things. That's the only one I can really remember, because that's the one when I was one up on Westy. I had the last say. Westy used to get very upset, because in those days Army couldn't seem to win from us. We had a basketball game, and I had as my guest the Chairman of the Joint Chiefs, who was Lemnitzer.* At the halftime, Army led Navy

---
*General Lyman L. Lemnitzer, U.S. Army, Chairman of the Joint Chiefs of Staff from 1960 to 1962.

by almost 20 points. My guests were the chairman, Arleigh Burke, and I think Smeddy was there, quite a group. Westy was seated across the basketball floor with a large group of Army supporters, but because he was my guest, the Chairman of the Joint Chiefs was sitting with me. They led about 20 points at the halftime, and all of a sudden in the last five minutes, Navy just went bang, bang, bang, and we won by one or two or three points. When the game was over, I was standing there with the chairman and with Arleigh Burke and Smeddy and Westy came across the floor to congratulate me, I guess. The chairman said to him, "Westy, there was no goddamn excuse for that," and turned and walked away. Well, for an ambitious two-star general to be told that by the top four-star, Westy was just not fit to live with that night at all. At dinner he was so upset it was very apparent.

At a 150-pound game up at West Point, when we won in the last minute, because of a big mistake by Army, when they were leading and about to score again and increase their lead, they threw a little pass out in the flat and the captain of our 150-pound team, a fellow by the name of O'Brien, grabbed it and headed for the sidelines to go out of bounds.* The coach was yelling at him, "Go out of bounds! Stop the clock!" Instead, he cut back across the field and went all the way for a touchdown.

---

*Midshipman Edward J. O'Brien III, USN, class of '61.

Westy looked at me and said, "Tell me, what the hell do I have to do to beat you once?" So I enjoyed it.

Q: Staubach played for some of those basketball games, too.

Admiral Davidson: Oh, yes. But this year I'm thinking about, I'm not sure which Army basketball game that was, whether that was my first year or my second year. I can't remember. Staubach was a plebe when I was here. I didn't have Staubach on any of the varsity teams, because we didn't play plebes in those days.

Q: You mentioned the board of visitors. What was their role?

Admiral Davidson: The board of visitors were appointed by the Secretary of the Navy, and they consisted of sort of a combination of a senator or two, a representative or two, usually college presidents, and any other talent that the Secretary felt ought to look over the program here at the Naval Academy. They make recommendations for improvements, changes, and so on. The board that I remember particularly well was the year that Milton Eisenhower was on it, and a representative from Pennsylvania by the name of Dan Flood was on it.*

---

*Daniel J. Flood (Democrat-Pennsylvania) served in the House of Representatives from 1945 to 1947, 1949 to 1953, and from 1955 to 1980.

Q: The one with a little mustache.

Admiral Davidson: Yes, a black waxed mustache. And Father Joyce. But in any event, to give you an idea of what happened, we had it over in that hall adjacent to Dahlgren Hall. It was new, more or less, in those days, toward Porter Road from the armory. It was the ordnance department at one time, Ward Hall. Well, anyway, we had a big conference room there with all kinds of setups for putting slides and pictures up. Mr. Eisenhower called the meeting to order, and Dan Flood said, "Point of order, Mr. President, point of order." Mr. Eisenhower recognized him. He said, "I do not wish to go any further with this board until it has been satisfactorily explained to me why West Point and the Air Force Academy have three swimming pools and the Navy has only two."

Well, we sort of fumbled around to try to give reasons for this, that, and the other. I knew where it came from, because I was getting that same sort of thing from Admiral Rickover.* He wanted to do away with varsity football and all that, and have swimming and hiking in the country. That was all I needed.

Anyway, as you may know, Flood, was a Shakespearean actor in his day. After we got the pool business settled and were about to start the meeting again, "Point of order, Mr. President.

---

*Rear Admiral Hyman G. Rickover, USN, renowned as the father of the nuclear submarine.

Point of order." He wanted to know who designed the stage in the auditorium adjacent to the brigade library down there behind Bancroft Hall, on the seaward side of Bancroft Hall. In my day we had Smoke Park. There still is a little park there outside of the mess hall.

Q: Mitscher Hall?

Admiral Davidson: Is that Mitscher Hall? No, Mitscher Hall is up, I think, where the old tennis courts used to be.

Q: Mitscher Hall is that low building seaward of Bancroft Hall.

Admiral Davidson: All right. That's where it is. Anyway, we had a stage down there. He wanted to know who designed the stage. He said whoever did certainly didn't know anything about theatricals or this or that. He wanted absolute assurance on that before he would go any further. So he was an obstructionist from way back. In any event, the board of visitors usually made some very, very good observations. They were people who came from all over the country. I remember one year we had the president of the University of Nebraska on it. That was back in the days when I was head of department. I remember because I in those days was presenting the Naval Academy curriculum. That was my chore to do, and that's a dull subject. To present any curriculum is a dull subject.

Q: Do you have some examples of some constructive things that did come out of those meetings?

Admiral Davidson: I think that out of those meetings came the appointment of the Ben Moreell Commission, which was to study how to expand the Naval Academy.* I think they recommended that. Of course, they went into everything. They went into the curriculum, they went into all physical facilities, and decided what was adquate and what wasn't adequate, and what the future might hold and what we needed to be prepared for the future. I don't remember any specific things, except I wouldn't be surprised that the demolishing of Isherwood Hall was probably one that came out of those recommendations. I know that the Moreell Commission was the one that recommended that we take over three blocks of the city of Annapolis. I don't know whether you ever saw that or not.

Q: I heard that there was an attempt.

Admiral Davidson: That was sort of a sad period in my career

---

*The commission was headed by Admiral Ben Moreell, CEC (Civil Engineering Corps) USN (Ret.), the founder of the Construction Battalions (Seabees) of World War II, and the first Navy staff officer to attain four-star rank.

here. Admiral Smedberg was Chief of Naval Personnel, and he appointed a commission to make a study about expanding the Naval Academy. It was called the Moreell Commission. I was a member, and Admiral Ben Moreell was a four-star civil engineering type, retired.

Q: Former Chief of the Bureau of Yards and Docks.

Admiral Davidson: Right. The commission included various college presidents and it included some architects, some pretty prominent--some pretty knowledgeable people. We sat down here for about two weeks time, almost daily, and had presentations made by all departments and all the athletic people, everything, to show what was needed here for a Naval Academy that was expected to grow from 3,600 midshipmen to 4,600 or something like that, and so on and so forth, and what was needed with respect to the fact that we were expanding our educational opportunities for the midshipmen to allow them to major in all sorts of things and get all sorts of degrees.

Well, when we finished our deliberations, a booklet was prepared, and it was very elaborate; color photographs, everything. It was a very beautiful thing. That, with a cover letter, was sent to Smedberg, who sent it to CNO, who at that time, I think, was probably George Anderson, who then sent it to the Secretary of the Navy.* And there it sat. Among the things recommended in it was that we straighten the Naval Academy wall, which comes up from Gate 1, you know, and then dips in right behind the chapel, and there are a lot of houses along King George Street, and then comes out again by Gate 4 and the wall goes on. To straighten out that wall and take those three blocks. In those three blocks it was recognized that there were a certain number of houses that were of historic importance. For instance, the Peggy Stewart House on Hanover Street, and there was a house owned by Jack Stone across from the Alumni House, and several others that were considered historically very, very important.** So the proposal--and I think it was suggested more by the architect than by some of the college presidents--was that we retain those houses, that we completely overhaul them, put them in the best of shape, try to get as much of the old furniture that had been in them, and treat them pretty much like they do the Hammond-Harwood House, something like that, and make them museum pieces.*** It would be on Navy land, but they could be opened to the public as showplaces.

---

*Admiral George W. Anderson, Jr., USN, was Chief of Naval Operations from 1961 to 1963.
**Peggy Stewart House was built and owned by Anthony Stewart in the mid-1770s. A shipowner, Stewart ordered the burning of one of his vessels which was carrying English tea in what was called the "Annapolis Tea Party" in 1774.
***Hammond-Harwood House was designed by Architect William Buckland in the 1760s and is a classic example of early Georgian design.

The study called for tearing down everything else. As you go out of Gate 3 there on Maryland Avenue, there's a big apartment house on your right there. That was to be torn down completely, and some of the houses between there and the corner of King George were to be torn down on both sides of the street. With the exception of the Peggy Stewart House on Hanover, most of the rest were to be torn down. Well, to compensate the owners, we proposed that in addition to a fair price for their homes, we would pay $140,000 an acre for their land. This $140,000 was determined by a study of what it had cost to dredge and build the athletic field along the seawall. Those fields were water when I was a midshipman. It seemed like a very fair offer, and as it turned out later, I was told that about 99% of the people involved were in favor of it, because it was going to be quite a windfall for them.

In any event, this thing leaked to the Baltimore Sun before the Secretary took any action. The minute it leaked, all hell broke loose. I was down in Pinehurst playing golf; it was spring leave. Some of the midshipmen were gone. I had gone down there for ten days of golf. The phone rang and it was Smedberg, the Chief of Naval Personnel, who said, "Johnny, come on back. You're in trouble. We're going to have to have a town meeting."

So I came back. By this time Charlie Minter was my

commandant.* We made a mistake. We had the town meeting in Mahan Hall, with us sitting up on the stage and all the attackers down front; we had very little control over them. They could shout and do anything they wanted to. We probably should have had the thing chaired by somebody out in town, held it out in town, and then we could have been just called on to answer questions. The most vociferous objectors were a few Historic Annapolis types, plus the president of St. John's, who was a good friend of mine, Dick Weigle.** We were great friends, but he was very upset, because his thought was that if they allowed us to do that, it wouldn't be long before we'd want St. John's College, too, and take over everything.

Q: There had been some covetous eyes in that direction previously.

Admiral Davidson: In any event, somebody wrote to John Kennedy and demanded that I apologize to the city of Annapolis, which really wasn't my doing, but Smedberg took over that letter, and I don't know how he answered it, but I didn't have to.*** Of course, the whole plan was knocked into the scrap heap. Officially, we felt that 95% of people involved were in favor of

---
*Captain Charles S. Minter, Jr., USN, Commandant of Midshipmen, 1961-1964.
**Richard D. Weigle.
***President of the United States John F. Kennedy.

it, and the 5% were the vocal group who were not in favor. Actually, Admiral Harry Hill, former Superintendent, who was a resident and who was a charter member, as was I, of Historic Annapolis, was very, very much opposed to it. As it turned out, I was in error. I could have kept quiet. They asked the question why the commission did not have on it anyone from the city of Annapolis. The question was directed to me. My answer was, "I cannot answer for the appointing officer. However, if I were to make a guess, I would say probably the appointing officer did not know anybody in the city of Annapolis with the particular qualifications or talent that he was looking for to be a member of the commission."

The next day up the steps to the Superintendent's office bounds Harry Hill, former Superintendent, four star, everything under the sun.* I had worked for him when I was head of department and he was "Sup." He said, "Johnny, how in hell could you say such a thing? After all, you know, I live in Annapolis."

Well, the good Lord attended me again that time. I said, "Well, Admiral, you know, when they select the jury, they don't select somebody who's prejudiced. I'm sure that you had your mind already made up."

He looked at me and said the same thing that Mr. McCormack

---

*Admiral Harry W. Hill, USN (Ret.), had been Superintendent of the Naval Academy from 1950 to 1952 as a vice admiral.

once said to me. He said, "Touche." We remained friends.

Anyway, it was squashed. The only sad part of that--and I don't mind this being on the record--Dick Lankford was House of Representatives representative from this district.* Before we sent this to Washington, I suggested to Admiral Moreell it might be a real smart thing to get Congressman Lankford, and cut him in on it. So we did. We gave him a complete presentation with slides. When we finished, he said, "My golly, that's the most beautiful plan I ever saw. I commend all of you." Very complimentary. When it broke in the Baltimore Sun, they went to him right away and asked him for his comments, and according to the paper, he said, "I think it's unfortunate that Admirals Moreell and Davidson did not see fit to consult me."

I told Smeddy, "I'd like to play my tape to the press."

Smeddy, of course, said, "You can't do it." And I knew I couldn't, but it burned me. For a long time afterwards, I had a very, very cool feeling toward Dick Lankford.

I have since gotten over it, but I did a terrible thing to him one time. We were having a reception. I think there were 800 people coming to the "Sup's" house. Most of them were from out in town, civilians, and most of the faculty, I guess. It was about that time that Dick Lankford was quoted in the newspaper as coming out questioning the use of stewards in flag and general

---

*Richard E. Lankford (Democrat-Maryland) served in the House of Representatives from 1955 to 1965.

officers' quarters. He was coming out opposed to it, thought we were being given too much. So as he approached in the receiving line, I happened to look up and saw him coming with his wife, and said to my aide--and I said it loud enough so that he heard--"Maybe you'd better stop the line a minute." And I turned to my wife and said, "Would you like to go put on your apron?" I shouldn't have said it, but I did, and he heard it.

Q: You probably didn't have a very high opinion of politicians by that point.

Admiral Davidson: Well, some of them, yes, and some of them, no. I had already learned a lot about politicians. The father-in-law of my stepdaughter was a great politician. He used to come down to my house, and he would hold forth on all sorts of things that the Congress was voting on. I knew one item that he was absolutely opposed to. I picked up The New York Times one Sunday, and it had him voting for it. He came down to chapel that day, and I said to him, "Stub, how in the world could you tell me all that and then vote for this thing?"*

He said, "I wanted to be here to vote next time." That, to

---

*William S. "Stub" Cole (Republican-New York) served in the House of Representatives from 1935 to 1957 and was a member of the Joint Congressional Committee on Atomic Energy. He resigned from Congress in 1957 to become director general of the International Atomic Energy Agency, headquarters in Vienna, Austria.

Davidson #5 - 394

me, explained the politicians. To me, I don't think I could be dishonest enough to be a politician. I don't know if you call it dishonesty or just evading.

Q: What do you recall about your associations with the two Presidents during that tenure--Eisenhower and Kennedy?

Admiral Davidson: My main association with Mr. Eisenhower was when he came down here for a football game, and I believe that's the only time I ever had an association. He came down for a football game, and I have a lot of pictures of him with me, so on and so forth. I asked him to come to the Army game, and he said he would if I'd build him a heated setup up in Philadelphia like the one we had over here.

Now, Mr. Kennedy, there are two things that happened. Kennedy came to an Army-Navy game. Once again, I talked when I should have been listening, I guess, but this is what he did. He sat on the Army side with General Westmoreland for half the game, and at that point Navy was leading, I think, 13 to 0. He came across the field, and I went out with the midshipman six-striper, and we met him in the middle of the field and escorted him back. Of course, Mrs. Kennedy was not with him. She never was for things like that. In the middle of the row in the box there were three seats, one for the President, one for Mrs. Davidson, and one for me. Mrs. Davidson and I had been sitting in two of them, with an empty seat beside us. When he came up, he said to me, "I wonder if you and Mrs. Davidson would mind moving. I have two old friends from Philadelphia that I'd like to sit with." Now, what do you do? You do it. But I thought it was practically rude, because I was his host. It sort of burned me to think that he would do that. Well, I got over it. But Army scored right after he got over there, so I got up and walked down a little behind him and whispered to him, "I wonder if you'd mind going back over and sitting with General Westmoreland." He had the courtesy to laugh, but we came out of it. The final score was 13 to 7.

The next occasion I had with Kennedy is an interesting story, I think. He came down to make the graduation address. At the time we issued the invitation, and it's customary for each of the academies to invite him the President every year, so we invited him and he accepted, but I was told that I could not disclose it until the White House disclosed it. Meanwhile, I went out to Colorado Springs to the Air Force Academy to a conference, and Westmoreland was there, the Coast Guard Superintendent was there, Bill Stone, the Air Force Academy Superintendent was there. They all turned to me and said, "Is the President going to speak at the Naval Academy?"[*]

---

[*]Rear Admiral S. H. Evans, USCG, Superintendent of the Coast Guard Academy; Major General William S. Stone, USAF, Superintendent of the Air Force Academy.

I said, "I don't know."

Westy said, "Johnny Davidson, tell the truth now."

I said, "I can't tell you," which was true.

He said, "Well, he's already turned Bill Stone down. He turned me down, and he turned down everybody else. He must be going to go to you. Has he turned you down?"

I said, "No, he hasn't turned me down."

"Is he going to be there?"

"I don't know." So this went on and on.

Well, anyway, he was in Vienna on some sort of conference. I believe it was with the Soviets.*

Q: That's where he met Khrushchev.

Admiral Davidson: He did not return til two days before graduation. They had called from the White House beforehand and had given us a list of 40 people from Washington to be invited and to be included for staying for lunch in the Superintendent's garden. We invited all 40 of them, and all 40 of them regretted. Then two days before graduation, he announced that he was coming here, and all 40 of them called up and wanted to be re-invited. I told either Dodge McFall or Bill Greene, one of them, I said,

---
*The Vienna Summit Conference was 3-4 June 1961. Graduation that year was on 7 June.

"Tell them we don't have room."*

He said, "Well, you can't do that." I was always being told I couldn't do what I wanted to do.

But in any event, the afternoon before graduation, the White House called. It was a Navy captain who said he was preparing the President's graduation address for him. He said, "I need a little research on something to do with the Tripolitan wars that we were involved in, because he wants to talk about that a little bit."** So somebody from the history department went over to the library, I believe, and did the research and called back to the White House and gave them all the dope.

On the day of graduation, Kennedy arrived by chopper and landed down near the Severn River on those athletic fields there beyond the midshipmen's store. He landed down there and I met him, and we drove in an open Chevrolet Impala, white, to the field house for graduation. The temperature outdoors was about 90 degrees. It felt about 110. We drove down there and we went to the visiting teams' dressing room. All the ladies were in there, and they all had a chance to meet him. Then all the

---
*Lieutenant Albert Dodge McFall, USN; Commander William M.A. Greene, USN, who was then also secretary-treasurer of the Naval Institute.
**The Tripoli-U.S. war in the Mediterranean, 1801 to 1805, was fought over demands for tribute by the Barbery states. Although Tripoli lost this early war, the question of tribute demanded from American commercial ships wasn't ended until the successful campaigns of Commodore Stephen Decatur against Tripoli, Tunis, and Algeria in 1815.

ladies were ushered into the field house to be seated out in front. The President and I were left alone. All of a sudden he said to me, "You haven't got a Coca-Cola, have you?"

Well, we had everything under the sun. We had iced tea, iced coffee. We didn't have a Coca-Cola. So I put my head out the door and I saw an attendant out there. I said, "Here." I gave him some money. "See if you can find a Coca-Cola for the President." So he went on and he got two, brought them back. Fortunately, I didn't want one, because I watched President Kennedy down two Coca-Colas from the bottles.

Q: Chugalug.

Admiral Davidson: Chugalug, while he read his speech. Now, this nobody really wants to believe, but the aide told us that on the way down in the chopper, he was handed the speech for the first time. While on the chopper, he read it once or maybe twice. It was going to be about a ten- to 12-minute address, not much more than that. Then he read it again while he was having the two Cokes. At graduation when it came his turn to speak, he got up there, without his notes, and made the speech. We taped it, and we couldn't find where he left out a comma, even. The most amazing reproduction of what had been written for him. I have to believe everybody who said he hadn't seen it until that morning.

Q: Whether he had or not, it was still amazing.

Admiral Davidson: Yes. Then on top of that, he started giving out the diplomas to those who graduated with distinction. There were about 100 of those in the graduation class that year of probably 700, something like that.* That was all he was supposed to do, because in those days we were still using the system where, after those with distinction received their diplomas, then one person from each company came up and got the diplomas for the whole company. So he had not yet finished, when he turned to me and said, "Admiral, I wonder if somebody could finish handing out these diplomas." He was perspiring. His clothes were just soaking wet. He looked like he was in a lot of pain. I didn't realize at the time, but it was his back problem he was having trouble with.

So I said, "I will take over." I could have asked the Secretary or CNO or someone, but no one else was briefed, so I took it over and handed out the rest of the diplomas. Then we gave the diplomas to the companies, and finally we finished the ceremony there.

As he and I walked back toward the car, he said to me, "Admiral, would you please make my regrets and apologies to Mrs. Davidson? I think that I must return to Washington immediately."

---

*The total was 786.

So with that, he got in his Impala convertible. The driver had put the top up during the period of graduation to keep it cool, and it was a power-operated top, and it wouldn't work. So the Secret Service people said, "Maybe we should send out to the Chevrolet place and see if they've got somebody to fix it."

I said, "Well, it happens that I own a Chevrolet convertible with a top that can be put down by hand. It's right up at the corner."

They said, "We can't let him ride in that. He's got to ride in his own." So just about that time, somebody hit the right button and the top went down. We drove to the athletic fields, and he got in the chopper and returned to Washington.

I then went up to the Superintendent's house, and there stood Mrs. Davidson. "Where's the President?"

"Well, he had to go back to Washington."

There stood the 40 people who had said no and then said yes, and then he wasn't there.

Q: They got what they deserved.

Admiral Davidson: Oh, I thought that was the best story of my life.

This happened after I left here as Superintendent. The Navy came out to play the University of Southern California, and I was on the West Coast by then, and I went to the game. I went with a cousin of mine who was a Yale man, but who was a great supporter of Southern Cal. He said, "I've heard a lot of stuff about some kid by the name of Staubach, but this afternoon you're going to see him put in his place."

So I sat there with Herb. Time after time, Southern Cal would bottle Roger up in the backfield someplace, and he'd break away and make a nice big first down or something. After the game, Herb had to admit, "I never saw anything like that in my life." Even though Southern Cal did eke out a win, Roger performed beautifully.

So that night at a dinner party, I said to Wayne, "How did it happen that Roger had such a great year as a plebe and you didn't even use him for the first half of the year?"

Wayne said, "I always believe in going with experience, and he didn't have experience. But then luckily the regular quarterback was hurt, and I had to put him in." I believe he said it was in the Colgate game or the Cornell game or some game. From then on, he was the starting quarterback.

Q: And the year after that he won the Heisman Trophy.

Admiral Davidson: Yes.

Q: Briefly on that expansion business, had you already had a fall-back plan in mind if the Moreell plan wasn't approved?

Admiral Davidson: I don't think we did. As a matter of fact, what developed out of that might be what are now those two academic buildings which you see from the chapel steps. Those two buildings are where our tennis courts used to be. We had a very beautiful view of the river from the chapel steps. That was one of the things that disturbed me to see them building down there, but that's what was substituted. I don't recall that while I was here we had that plan at all, but that's what came out of it. Plus, I think whatever is going to be put up over where Isherwood Hall has gone down, that may be part of the long-range plan, too. I don't know what goes there. Do you?

Q: Supposedly it's an auditorium big enough to seat the whole brigade of midshipmen.

Admiral Davidson: Really?

Q: Had there been talk about the enlarged library yet when you were Superintendent?

Admiral Davidson: That, I think, had to have been part of the plan. Nimitz Library--I think that probably was in the wind, because it is on ground that was once part of the supply department. The laundry was down there, the dry cleaning plant was down there. The power plant was down there, and that was all moved out to an area off King George Street.

Q: They're building a new fire station down there now.

Admiral Davidson: They sure are, aren't they? I don't remember any more about Mr. Kennedy.

Q: Was there any residual ill will in the community after that plan died down?

Admiral Davidson: There didn't seem to be, because I never suffered from it that I know of. The only thing I can think about some of these things, it might have affected my future without my knowing it. Nobody offered me much in the way of a good job after I left there, at least nothing that I had thought was a good job, anyway.

Q: What about the social side of the job? How much entertaining was there?

Admiral Davidson: All the time. It has been said, and I know it's true, that when Washington didn't know what to do with a VIP, they sent him to the Naval Academy. I spent an inordinate amount of time getting up at luncheons saying, "Your country and my country just can't get along without each other, and you're the greatest, so on and so forth." Then somebody else got up and said the same thing back to me. It seemed to me I was doing that all the time.

The social side, as far as the midshipmen were concerned, we gave all kinds of gatherings over at the Superintendent's quarters. One of my favorites was to have quite a few in after chapel every Sunday. The Superintendent's garden party, which still goes on now, two days now, we did it all in one day. Mrs. Davidson and I once shook hands with 3,200 other people in one night. The lines went out the front door on what we called the pious entrance. You'd go out that door to the chapel. They went out that door, down the street, down past Dahlgren Hall, down to Porter Road, people in line to shake hands.

Q: Were there any midshipmen besides Bellino that you especially remember from that time?

Admiral Davidson: Not in particular. I suppose if names were furnished to me, I might recall something. But in general, you knew the star athletes, you got to know the people who were unsatisfactory in academics, because they were always coming before the board. We had a lot of little things happen that might not be of much interest to anybody. One of the problems that was a concern, it seemed to me that never a year or even six months went by that the son of a very good friend was in trouble of some sort, and that was difficult. I had to kick out Jack McCain's son and Jack Coye's son, all old friends of mine. That is a very difficult thing to have to do.*

A very cute story, just to fill in--one night the telephone operator at the Naval Academy received a call, and a female voice said that she'd like to have--and she gave an extension number like 233, something like that. The operator knew that that was in Ward Hall. She knew that that was a room in Ward Hall, a classroom, and she knew that at 2:00 a.m. there shouldn't be anybody in it. But she rang it anyway, and a male voice answered. So she promptly reported to the main office that somebody was answering the phone in Ward Hall. Of course, they called the head of department, who said, "Well, the only problem is that all the exams for next week are in there, and if somebody has broken in, they're compromising the exam." So they immediately sent somebody over there, and they got to Ward Hall and the room was dark, the door was locked, everything was secure, nobody in there.

So the next morning the commandant and his detectives started out, and this is what they found. They found a wire leading from that room attached to the telephone in that room which went out the door and ended up crossing through Dahlgren Hall, through the

---
*Midshipman Joseph P. McCain, USN, son of Admiral John S. McCain, Jr., USN; Midshipman John S. Coye, USN, son of Rear Admiral John S. Coye, Jr., USN.

tunnel under Bancroft Hall, all the way to an area adjacent to the midshipmen's store. Then it went up the outside of the building to the fourth deck and in a window. In the window they traced it, and in the closet they found what was described to me as a telephone lineman's instrument that he could use to tap into all sorts of lines, and it was in the room of a first classman. Then there were some other lines that led to another room of another first classman. They went in there, and these lines went to a hand-hole access door in the wall of the room. When they took it off and reached in there, they found several boxes of ladies' lace panties, stenciled very beautifully on the seat, "Go Navy. Beat Army." So they finally traced this all down to two first classmen, both of whom were unsat in electricity, probably because they spent their time doing what they were doing.

Anyway, they traced it down and here again, the girl out in town who had been calling was the daughter of a naval officer. They had a business. She secured the panties and delivered them to them, and they stenciled them and returned them to her. She was selling them for so much a pair.

So Charlie Minter and I decided, after much thought, we really didn't feel they deserved any great number of demerits, because we thought it was pretty darn funny. But, you know, here they were unsat in juice, and yet they could wire this whole damn thing at night and get away with it, and actually use it once in a while before they got caught.

Davidson #5 - 407

Q: Do you remember any other midshipmen pranks?

Admiral Davidson: No. They teased us a lot. We used to have a ceremony called burial of math. I don't know whether they still do or not. But you took math for two years until the middle of second class year, and then you buried math. Over in Dalhgren Hall they'd have a stage set up and a big show and put on skits.

It had happened in the spring of one year that we had some lovely warm weather in April, and they were still in blues. The midshipmen wanted to go into white works. I had never believed that that was very military for them to be around the yard all the time in white works. It was all right for gym class, but not for ordinary wear. Not only that, in the old days we wore a full blue service uniform--white shirt, tie, blue uniform, made out of 16 ounce serge. If we could take it in those days, we thought maybe they could still take it. And they now had the blue trousers and blue shirt they could wear without a coat. So we said no when they wanted to change out of blues to white works. We couldn't put them in khaki because the cleaning facility couldn't handle the khaki uniform that would be required, and we certainly couldn't put them in whites. We didn't have the white short sleeve shirts in those days at all. So anyway, we said no.

One morning, Tecumseh was completely dressed in white works, and there was a big sign there which said, "Please, Big Momma, White Works!" This was supposed to get Mrs. Davidson to talk me into letting them have white works.

Subsequently they had the burial of math skit. They had me sitting at a desk in my office, and I'm in a short sleeved white shirt, and everybody coming in to see me is dressed in the heavy winter overcoats, mufflers, everything, faces streaming wet. Oh, I sat there on the front row and laughed because they were having so much fun with me. Then the next skit after that, they had two boys dressed up as colored boys, their faces were blacked, and one of them had a lady's hat about this big around.

Q: About two feet.

Admiral Davidson: A tremendous, big sun hat. They were supposed to be yard workmen, working on the various--one of the skits had been what they called "The diggers and the fillers." There was always someplace in the yard being dug up, another place being filled in, and that was sort of a cute skit. In this one, all of a sudden there's this worker with the big hat, and one of them said to the other, "Where did you get that hat?"

He said, "Don't you know where to get that hat? You know Big Momma. She buys a new hat for chapel every Sunday, and if you peek around Monday morning, you'll find it in the garbage can." We always thought that these things showed they sort of loved us a little bit or they wouldn't pay that much attention to it.

Q: What are your recollections of religious services at the Naval Academy?

Admiral Davidson: Greatest disappointment of my life came--it didn't come when I was Superintendent--when they didn't have to go to church, because in my day they had to go to church. They didn't have to come to chapel, but they had to go someplace. All of that varied, you know. Some chaplains are excellent and some are not quite. If they could all be like Larry Ellis was when we had him, why, I think the midshipmen would have gone more and more, but they weren't always that way.* But I really believed in it and I always enjoyed my chapel. I was very proud to be sitting down in the front pew with tears in my eyes by the time they got through "Eternal Father." I think that was a terrible mistake on the part of the Supreme Court to rule that they didn't have to go, because I don't think that's really coercing anybody.**

In the first place, they're going to deal with men all their lives, some of whom are very, very religious, and they have to understand that. In order to understand people like that, they

---
*Commander Larry H. Ellis, CHC, USN, Naval Academy chaplain from July 1982 to August 1985.
**In a class action suit, Anderson v. Laird, 466 Fed 2d, 283, (1972) the District of Columbia Court of Appeals ruled in favor of the plaintiff that mandatory attendance at religious services violated first amendment rights. Upon appeal, the U.S. Supreme Court refused to review the case, affirming the lower court's decision.

ought to have a little bit of exposure themselves. I think that was a mistake. As I understand it, that movement started at West Point. One lone boy decided he shouldn't be made to go to church. The Civil Liberties Union got ahold of it, and it got to the Supreme Court. Has Willy Mack ever been interviewed?*

Q: Yes.

Admiral Davidson: I think he was here when it went into effect that they didn't have to go. He was practically told by the Secretary of Defense that he couldn't get them up in the morning and make them put on a dress uniform, that that would be coercion.

Q: What role did the chaplains have in calming the fears and concerns of people who find out that the Academy is a lot harder than they expected?

Admiral Davidson: The only evidence I've seen of that role--of course, they have conferences all the time--the only evidence I've seen is that sermon that Larry Ellis used to preach called, "You Can Do It." Did you ever hear that?

---

*Vice Admiral William P. Mack, USN(Ret.), Naval Academy Superintendent from June 1972 to August 1975. The Supreme Court decision abolishing compulsory chapel attendance was handed down in December 1972.

Q: I don't believe so.

Admiral Davidson: That's the best sermon you ever heard. He starts off by saying, after they've been here about a month, "I'm sure you're all saying, 'How did I make this terrible mistake? How did I ever get myself into this?'" Then he goes on to say they've been picked out of several thousands who wanted to come, been picked by people who realize they're picking somebody who can do it, and you can do it. It's a very, very effective sermon, I think, and he usually preaches it when the parents are here, too, so that's helpful.

Q: Did you have much contact with parents of midshipmen?

Admiral Davidson: Not too much. Not too much. Just once in a while, usually when a boy was going home. Then I had one very sad one when I was about to get in the car to go to graduation one time, I was informed that there was a lady in the carriage entrance in the waiting room there crying. I went down to find out what the trouble was. She had just learned that her son was not going to be graduated; he was going to be held over for the summer because he hadn't passed the physical requirement. She thought that I was being very unreasonable and that I should grant an exception. In looking into it, I discovered that there wasn't any reason he couldn't pass the physical, except he never tried. He wouldn't show up for it. So we made him stay a couple of months and he passed in short order. He stayed around a couple of months, and he didn't lose any numbers or anything. But those are trying things, because here's a mother crying her eyes out.

There are many things that happen there that people wouldn't ever guess would happen. We had a widow of a retired admiral show up at the Maryland Avenue gate one time in tears because she didn't think her husband's grave was being properly cared for. She demanded to see me. My chief of staff went right out to see her and found out that what she complained about was that the headstone was just the ordinary type, government issue. He went back to the records and found that she had been interviewed and told that the standard headstone was so and so, government furnished, and if she wanted more, she'd have to pay for it. She had said that she would accept what the government gave. Then she came back a year or two later. It was a very difficult sort of thing to have to get involved in.

Then one like this, this was a real honey. My senior chaplain called me one morning to say that he had been called about 1:00 a.m. by a young Marine officer who asked him to go to the officers' club with him because his wife was in bed with a Catholic chaplain over there. He said, "I went over and verified that he was telling the truth. I want to go to Washington and have that chaplain transferred as fast as I can."

I said, "Not only that, but we want to keep it quiet. I don't want this in the Annapolis newspaper. If the Chief of Chaplains raises any objection to transferring him right away, let me know and I'll talk to Smedberg, because we want him out of here by 3:00 o'clock this afternoon." And we accomplished that. The worst part of this turned out that the young lady in question was the daughter of a retired vice admiral who was a friend of mine, and he called up two or three days later and asked me why we were chastising his daughter. I said, "Now, wait a minute." I told him the story.

He said, "That isn't the story she told me." But I had to believe my chaplain, who was there as a witness.

Nobody would believe little things like this take up your time. You remember some of them.

Q: How much contact and concern did you have from alumni?

Admiral Davidson: Only when you made some change that they thought--like not marching to class. We had quite a protest on that. I always went out each year to the annual meeting of the board of the alumni at the Alumni House and had to speak to them as a rule. On homecoming weekend, the Superintendent always gives a little talk.

Q: How much were you involved with the operation of the naval station across the river?

Admiral Davidson: Practically none. At that time we had what was known as the Severn River Naval Command, but I think it's now the Potomac River Naval Command that it comes under, although I don't know what the Superintendent's responsibility now is for the naval station.

Q: You had a chief of staff to deal with that?

Admiral Davidson: I had a chief of staff to deal with the naval station. He had the cemetery, the housing, all of the quarters business, so on and so forth. The commandant was the military number two, and the chief of staff was sort of the administrative number two.

Q: Could you comment, please, on the role that the commandant played and how much relationship he had with the Superintendent?

Admiral Davidson: I considered the commandant as number two in command. I kept my commandant cut in all the time on absolutely everything, and he kept me cut in. I don't suppose we had a day that we didn't confer about something. He was in charge of Bancroft Hall and was responsible for the military performance of all the midshipmen.

Davidson #5 - 415

Q: BuPers usually makes a practice, I think, to send particularly good officers for that billet.

Admiral Davidson: You're drawing me out a little here. One of the things that bothered me a little bit was when I arrived here, they had just sent in a new commandant by the name of Jim Mini.* He was an aviator. His wife was the stepdaughter of an officer who had been on a battleship with me, and I had known his two girls from way, way back. As far as I could tell, Jim certainly should have been a capable officer, but it didn't take me long to lose confidence in him, for one reason or other. Everything he recommended to me was wrong. The other thing was, he'd go on the football trips and he'd come back on the bus with the team, and he'd obviously had too much to drink. He'd get up at smokers and not make the best impression. However, it hadn't gotten to the point where I was ready to ask for a detachment. What bothered me a little bit was in my career it had seemed that it was customary and usual to ask the head man before you sent somebody. I had not been even consulted on the thing. But I saw fit not to make any real complaint.

What happened, I've never known, but I was down on my annual vacation down in Pinehurst, the first spring I was here. I came here in the summer of '60, so this was spring of '61, when I had a call from Jim Mini at my hotel down there, and he said that he

_____
*Captain James H. Mini, USN.

had just received orders, and he was to go to the staff of an aviator admiral down in Norfolk, and wouldn't I intercede because he'd been here only a year. I didn't hesitate too long and said, "I don't know the occasion for your orders, but I don't think I'll intercede." Well, he became my bitter enemy from then on. He told me so in front of other people at times.

When I got back, I found that Smedberg just originated the orders, and then said to me, "How would you like to have Charlie Minter?" Well, Charlie Minter had been in the athletic department when I was the head of the English department, so I knew him well and I knew I'd like him. So I said, "Fine." That suited me, and that worked out beautifully. Jim Mini never really forgave me, and the funny part of it was the admiral to whom he reported down there didn't forgive me either. He was an aviator. He wasn't very happy about it. I think that was Frank O'Beirne.* Anyway, Jim Mini subsequently died very suddenly, of what I don't know.**

Q: What are your recollections of Captain Minter in that role?

Admiral Davidson: Just tops, just tops. I never found him lacking in anything. He worked hard, he played hard, he did everything. His personality was such, you couldn't help but like

---

*Rear Admiral Frank O'Beirne, USN.
**Mini, by then a rear admiral, died 7 December 1973.

him.

Q: In a way, he can deflect heat, too, so that you can still be this lovable father figure.

Admiral Davidson: Right. Of course, that's the job of any executive officer. I've always felt there is no job more difficult than being the exec. I really think that all down the line, even when you're a lieutenant and a skipper of a submarine, the exec is the one that has the more difficult job, because he has to somehow protect the old man.

Q: He catches it both ways.

Admiral Davidson: Yes, that's right. He catches it both ways. But I don't think Charlie Minter ever caught much from anybody, because I'm sure everybody else thought highly of him and so did I. I can tell you, there were two people in my life that I gave fitness reports to that I found very difficult to write. One of them was the chaplain while I was here, Jim Kelly, and after sitting at my desk for, I'm sure, an hour, trying to figure out what to say, I said simply, "This chaplain should be promoted to rear admiral and become chief of chaplains."* That's all I said, and he was. That gave me an idea later when I was writing Charlie Minter's. I said, "This officer should be promoted to rear admiral and become Superintendent of the Naval Academy." And he was.

Q: You had the right touch there.

Admiral Davidson: It was pretty easy to write, too. It takes one line, and you don't go through a lot of gobbledygook that somebody has to interpret. Because I read fitness reports from the time I was a young lieutenant in the detail office. And let me tell you that learning to interpret what the writer says is almost as important as what he says, because some people can write a few words that really are not too bad, but are really damning. A lot of people can't express themselves at all, so you have to know your marking officer as well as the recipient of the mark to be able to evaluate these things at all. Damn with faint praise.

The worst one I can remember is, "This is a fine young officer who will improve with experience." That's the old favorite, "who will improve with experience."

---

*Captain James W. Kelly, CHC, USN, was chaplain at the Naval Academy during Davidson's duty as Superintendent. He later was promoted to rear admiral and served as Chief of Chaplains, the highest ranking chaplain in the Navy, from 1966 to 1970.

Q: How much did you get involved with the admissions process?

Admiral Davidson: Let me see if I remember. It seems to me the academic board used to meet. We didn't have an admissions officer as such, not like we do now. I'll have to go way back. When I was in the Naval Academy, all you had to do was have an appointment and pass the substantiating exam. John Kennedy was one of the first to introduce the system of nominating more than one boy for the same vacancy and then let the Academy pick from those. I'm trying to remember how we went about picking them. I don't think the academic board did it. We must have. There wasn't any higher authority than the academic board. The academic board in those days consisted of every head of department, plus the commandant.

Q: Were there pressures from congressmen or parents to get their sons in?

Admiral Davidson: I never had that kind of pressure on me that I know of at all. If there were any pressure, it probably was on BuPers up the line. I don't recall pressure on anybody here at the Academy.

Q: Was there at that time a ground swell to get more blacks in, or was that still in the future?

Admiral Davidson: That was still in the future. We didn't have too many. That was in the future. I don't think quotas had really come into being in 1960-61. I don't know when that started.

Q: I think it was when President Johnson was in office.

Admiral Davidson: Probably. Johnson was Vice President under Kennedy, so he was around, but he wasn't President at that time.*

Q: What do you remember about your service on the Naval Institute board as vice president?

Admiral Davidson: Very little different than it was as a member of the board where you voted on all the articles submitted and picked the essay contest winners, and so on and so forth. You had a tremendous amount of reading to do, some of it very good and some of it rather dull to read. In general, I think everything about the Institute was pretty good.

Q: Any matters about June Weeks that stand out in your memory?

---

*Lyndon B. Johnson served as vice president to John F. Kennedy from January 1961 to 22 November 1963, when Kennedy was assassinated and Johnson became President. He left office in January 1969.

Admiral Davidson: Not while I was Superintendent. Of course, I was here on the terrible June Week when the class of '52 all took off their shoes and marched in the color parade. Did you ever hear about that?

Q: No.

Admiral Davidson: Harry Hill was the Superintendent, and Bob Pirie had been the commandant, and he had just been relieved by Charlie Buchanan in about April or May.* Charlie had just come. At the color parade for the graduating class of '52, when the word came to pass in review, every midshipman out there in the field stepped out of his shoes and they came parading by in their stocking feet. Many of the file-closers, instead of having rifles, had parking signs. There was a certain amount of work going on, particularly outside the officers' club, and they had a base with a wooden stick that went up like that which said "No Parking." Some of them had red lanterns hanging from them. These midshipmen went by carrying those as guns with red lanterns hanging out, in their stocking feet. As soon as the midshipmen left the field, there was a mad scramble from the stands to recover all these shoes. It was just a madhouse out there, all

---

*Captain Robert B. Pirie, USN, was commandant from 1949 to 1952; Captain Charles A. Buchanan, USN, held the billet from 1952 to 1954.

these kids. Well, Admiral Hill probably made the smartest decision anybody ever made, because many of the staff were just incensed. I can remember Taylor Keith, who later became a vice admiral. Taylor Keith wanted to confine all the first class for the remainder of June Week.* That was his recommendation. Poor Charlie Buchanan was so new, he wasn't sure what to say.

Admiral Hill finally told all of us, "You know, if we want to be in every newspaper in the country, that's what we should do--confine the first class, not let them see their parents, not let them see their girls, anything. We can make every newspaper in the country. But if we want this thing to sort of hush up and go away, all we do is get the first class together in a meeting and tell them how completely uncalled for was this action, and that they, as leaders, haven't made a very good demonstration of leadership to allow this to happen, because they had to set the pace and let the other classes follow suit. And that's what happened. They called them in, and Charlie had to give them a good talking to, not just the first class. Then they didn't restrict them in any way, and the thing passed away. I met a lot of people who have never heard of it. But that's the only big June Week thing I ever had, and it didn't happen during my watch, thank goodness.

---
*Captain Robert Taylor Scott Keith, USN, secretary of the academic board, later Commandant of Midshipmen from 1954 to 1956.

Davidson #5 - 423

Q: Did you enjoy the ceremonial part of being Superintendent?

Admiral Davidson: Yes. Yes, I enjoyed going to those parades and having a guest take the parade each time, entertaining at a reception right afterwards. I met a lot of very wonderful people that way.

As I say, when I left, I wanted to sell the Superintendent's quarters, but they wouldn't let me. I offered to rent it to somebody, and they wouldn't let me do that. As I think I might have mentioned before, I told Secretary Korth, "I'm perfectly willing to stay here the rest of my life." He thought maybe they ought to get somebody else in there.

I do agree now with President Eisenhower's decision, which happened when I was there, that the Superintendents should lean toward youth. He decreed that no Superintendent of any of the academies should be more than a two-star officer, because he thought that the older people were just maybe getting a little too old to keep up with the pace or something like that. Maybe he knew more than I did about it. But I can assure you it would be very difficult for a person 65 years old--most people 65 years old, I don't mean all of them, but some of them are pretty active. It would be very difficult to keep up that pace.

Q: On the other hand, with somebody like Admiral Hill, age didn't seem to be a factor.

Davidson #5 - 424

Admiral Davidson: No, that's right. He was a rather amazing youth, always. I can't imagine some of the others. Yet, I was down at the football game the other day and saw Freddy Boone, and he went to all the trouble to go all the way down there to Virginia to go to the football game, so he must have still maintained some of his youth.* I agreed in general with Eisenhower's decision. He was trying to get people in their 50s, at least, and he didn't want somebody that was all ready to retire. It used to be we had to retire at 62.

Q: You said you were disappointed by the choices you had for billets after that. What were they offering?

Admiral Davidson: The first one I was offered, I can't remember what it was, except that it was a staff job in Paris. At the time, they wouldn't permit wives to go. I think it was a temporary one-year restriction, but they wouldn't. So when I was asked why I turned it down, I just said, no, I didn't want it. When I was asked that, I told the CNO that when my wife was with me, she was half the team, and when she wasn't with me, she was three-quarters of the team, and I didn't think he wanted a quarter of the team over there. That didn't do me any good either. As I say, every now and then I said things I probably

---
*Admiral Walter F. Boone, USN, class of 1921, Superintendent of the Naval Academy from 1954 to 1956.

shouldn't have said, but I felt that way and I still do.

In any event, the next job I was offered was Yokosuka. Somehow or other, I didn't feel like going all the way to Japan to start over again after having had this wonderful job here.

After that, I wasn't given any choice, because what happened was that Mr. Korth, who had been down here that year for graduation and spent the first 15 minutes of his graduation address praising Ann and me as being the greatest thing that ever happened down here, then turned around and eased me out of here without much consideration whatsoever. The first I knew where I was going was when Admiral Kirkpatrick, who was ComTraPac, called me and said, "Congratulations."*

I said, "For what?"

He said, "You're going to relieve me. You're coming to TraPac."

I said, "What are you going to do?"

He said, "I'm going to relieve you." He tried to tell me, "You're getting one of the best jobs in the Navy."

I said, "You _are_ getting the best job." So that's the way I left. Of course, my time theoretically was up. Any time after two years, I was supposed to go. I lasted two years and four months, something like that.

---
*Rear Admiral Charles C. Kirkpatrick, USN, Commander Training Command Pacific, relieved Davidson and was Superintendent of the Naval Academy from 1962 to 1964.

Davidson #5 - 426

Q: What do you recall about that job out in San Diego?

Admiral Davidson: Just a pleasant place to spend a year. I had a nice set of quarters; I had a nine-hole golf course in the backyard; I had another competent staff. The training command consisted of at least a half a dozen other commands, like the sonar school, all these other things that were involved in training.

Q: Fleet training group.

Admiral Davidson: Fleet training group and all. All of them were, as far as I was concerned, very competent. I went out and rode ships just for the pleasure of going to sea and watching the performance, so on and so forth. I had what I would call a very pleasant year without overdoing in any way, and I don't think I was particularly contributing anything, either. We had very well-established training programs. Ships which reported to he training command here were given advice if they needed it, but I didn't have to give advice. There were captains and commanders on the staff who could do that. I went around to all the various commands and visited them and watched their performance, but I don't remember that I contributed anything. I was just there. I think, in a way, I felt like more of a figurehead than anything else.

Davidson #5 - 427

Q: Was there a place for innovation and updating of training, training on new weapons and equipment, and so forth?

Admiral Davidson: There may have been, but, of course, you know, I told you before, I never had much knowledge about weapons. That wasn't my field.

One of the experiences I had out there, another one that had to do with Kennedy, was that I was riding one of the carriers one time during training, and Mr. Kennedy came to town, and he wanted to take a ride on a carrier. We all flew out there. I believe we went out on a chopper and landed on a carrier. I don't remember which one it was.

Q: I think he visited <u>Kitty Hawk</u> about that time.

Admiral Davidson: It could be. I can't remember which one. What I remember is along the same line as his speech here at the Naval Academy. We all gathered in the admiral's cabin, and the first thing that surprised me was he said, "Let's all have a cocktail." By golly, his staff had arranged to have booze and everything on there, and we weren't used to that, but we all had a cocktail.* Secondly, he asked somebody to get him some information about something in history, Navy history, because he

---

*Drinking alcoholic beverages is prohibited on board U.S. Navy ships.

wanted to talk to the crew. They got him the information, and that son of a gun got up and made a speech of about 15 minutes to the crew and it was just the most beautiful thing you ever heard, just extemporaneous. It was about the glories of the old Navy, the battles of the past, how they could contribute to the future, and so on. He just had it when it came to making speeches.

Q: Any specific episodes you recall from your time in the training command?

Admiral Davidson: I recall one real well, and to this day we are very, very good friends, and I wonder if he even remembers it. We had a submarine tender under training, and it was alongside a tanker fueling as part of the training exercise. The two ships came together. Then they were separated with minor damage, a couple of boat davits were scratched off, a little paint here and there, and so on. But I had to order an investigation, and I assigned a captain from my command to investigate the accident and give me a report. He found that the tanker had lost steering for less than a minute. It was just enough with these two ships proceeding at about 15 knots to slide them together. He found that the real cause was the tanker had lost steering and once the steering was regained, that the two captains did quite a good job of getting the ships separated and continuing their fueling exercises with very little damage. So I approved it with one paragraph--wrote my approval. It went to P.D. Stroop.* P.D. Stroop was the fleet commander out there at the time. The next thing I know, I have a copy of his endorsement on my endorsement, and it was a page and a half long. It said, in effect, that the cause of the accident was unavoidable, all right, but that the captains did not show much expertise in seamanship in separating the ships, or there might not have been any damage whatsoever.

Shortly thereafter, I was at a cocktail party at P.D.'s quarters on North Island. People were standing around. I don't know what teed off the conversation, but I finally said to P.D. Stroop, whom I'd known ever since I was a young ensign, I said, "You know, I have to bow to your judgment in the case of that collision between the tanker and the submarine tender." I said, "In my 25 years, I've never had a collision. I understand you've had three." And he had. He made vice admiral after three collisions.

Q: How to endear yourself to your boss.

Admiral Davidson: That's what I say. Every now and then I say the wrong thing.

---
*Vice Admiral Paul D. Stroop, USN, Commander First Fleet from 1963 to 1964.

Q: And what was his reaction?

Admiral Davidson: He let me get away with it at the time. I might have said it just to him privately, but I shouldn't have said it in front of a couple of his friends.

Q: Would it be fair to say that that was pretty much an anticlimactic tour, then, after the Naval Academy?

Admiral Davidson: Yes. Right. And that's the reason I retired at that point. Smedberg wrote to my wife and said that he was sorry to see me retire, that he thought I was acting a little in haste, that if I'd held on, he thought that the following year might produce something real worthwhile. He was retiring, too.

Meanwhile, I had this offer, with a certain amount of pressure, to take over this private school. I thought I could be Mr. Chips and do it until I was 99 years of age.* Also there was no money problem.

Q: Did you have a big, formal retirement ceremony with all the bands playing and so forth?

---

*Mr. Chips--the British schoolmaster hero of James Hilton's novel Goodbye, Mr. Chips.

Admiral Davidson: It wasn't that big, but I did it the way I wanted to, on the deck of a submarine. There's a little submarine base there in Point Loma, and one of the submarines was in. The Commander Submarine Force very graciously offered me a platform for a retirement ceremony, and I retired there, made my retirement speech, turned it over to the younger people and drove off happily.

Q: How about a quick recap on the years since you retired from active duty?

Admiral Davidson: We went to Wilmington, Delaware, where I became the headmaster of a private school. The school's name is Tatnall. It had been founded in a lady's kitchen back about 1930, and Mrs. Tatnall had a small class of young girls. From that point on, it had grown. By the year 1964, it was about to graduate the first high school class with any boys in it, because some place along the line the angel, who was a member of the Du Pont family, had said that he would be willing to pay the tuition of any of the boys in kindergarten who would stay on and finish all the way through high school. This was the first year that any boys had lasted long enough to graduate. They had a headmistress up until that time, and she was my sister's very closest friend at home. They went to high school together and she went to Mount Holyoke and so on. She became interested in looking for a headmaster. She wrote to me, because I had had her down here at the Naval Academy when Kennedy was here. She said, "You ought to take this job because you don't have to worry about money; the angel supplies all the money. It's just a wonderful opportunity to have a nice home and a nice retirement."

So I finally accepted that, and I went ahead with my retirement plans and went up there. I arrived up there about May of 1964 and took over after the graduation ceremony that year. The first thing I discovered was that they didn't have a budget. I asked the business manager how it was run. He said, "Oh, the faculty goes downtown and buys anything they want for the classroom and charges it to the school. Each month I get all the bills together and call up the angel's office and tell him how much we need, and he deposits it in the Wilmington Trust Company, and we pay the bills. It usually doesn't run over about $80,000 a month, and he never complains."

So I said, "$80,000 a month? That's $1 million a year." I called up the angel and said, "Hey, I'm in the wrong job. All my life I've had to work on a budget. Suddenly I find you don't even have one here."

He said, "You're just the man I want. I'm tired of not knowing from one year to the next how much they're going to ask me for." So we had lunch together, and I said I'd set up a budget, but it would probably take about four years to make it work, and it did, because most of the faculty didn't know how to spell budget. They certainly never expected this.

The other thing was--and you might find this of interest--when I got there, the teacher to student ratio was one teacher for every four and a half students. The salaries were considerably above public school. I didn't have much to go on except the public school salary list. So I set out to put the school on a somewhat paying basis. At that time the angel had a philosophy that the children of the butcher, the baker, and candlestick maker should be able to go there just as well as the wealthy, so that he didn't think that tuition should be over about $450 a year even for high school. Well, the average throughout the nation at that time for a school of that type was closer to $1,500. So we set out. He said, "Well, I'll settle for maybe a tuition of $650." That gave me one step up. The other step up was I made a survey and found that the average private school had a teacher to student ratio of about one teacher per 12 students, something like that, or maybe as much as one to 15. So I proposed that, and the angel said, "I'll go along with one per ten, because I don't want you to fire anybody." Just normal attrition. He said, "Of course, if you have an attrition of a teacher that's the only one in the school then you have to replace that teacher. But you have to figure out some way to get them to teach more." Well, I had people who were teaching a total of four or five hours a week. That's how silly it was. So then I became a little bit unpopular when I had to put these new things in, but not enough to bother them. They were all very good about it.

I think the big thing there was that the majority of the faculty, I think, were in their thirties. I got there in '64 just as the youth started the pot-smoking, long hair episodes and all. The faculty weren't very interested in trying to hold down on that. I remember the Wilmington paper came out one time after something I had said about general appearance and hair and so on and so forth, "Admiral Orders Bangs Away." Finally, the mothers and fathers were about the age of my children, so you see what I was dealing with. Most of them had lots and lots of money, and one of them asked me after church one Sunday, at the parish house, "What's your biggest problem here, Admiral?"

I said, "Well, the biggest problem is that it seems to me that if Johnny's unhappy, you buy him a new car." That made the papers, too.

See, most of my trouble is talking. I'll get in trouble here, probably.

Anyway, I spent four years there, and then I decided that I didn't have to work. Meanwhile, they had a piece of property out in the woods with a stream running through it, and it had to be connected by a road to one of the streets. The angel wanted to build a headmaster's home there, and spent $175,000 building a beautiful home back in the Sixties. I enjoyed being there, but I didn't teach. Some of the members of the board felt I should try to teach a course in something, but I had so much to do with administrative work and that nobody there had ever heard of a budget. They had great difficulty figuring out how to figure out what they were going to need and how to estimate. So I wasn't any expert on budgeting either, but at least I knew how to spell it.

Q: Who is this wonderfully generous angel?

Admiral Davidson: His name was W.W. Laird, Jr. This is his background. His mother was a Du Pont, and she was the sister of the three principal Du Ponts of the early 1900s--Irenee, Pierre, and Eleuthere. E.I. Du Pont stands for Eleuthere Irenee Du Pont. His mother was their sister. He had one or two sisters. When his mother died, she left all these many, many millions for him to administer. He had to say what his sister could have, so on and so forth. His principal job was to give away a couple of hundred million dollars every year, just a plain, everyday philanthropist. He maintained a whole floor of offices in a building downtown in Wilmington, had all his accounting people there. He just gave it away, but he insisted on getting something for it.

He did some wonderful things. He took over the Wilmington Country Club and they built a new one, but he took it over and gave the golf course to the city as a public course, then converted the clubhouse into a cultural headquarters of some kind with all kinds of cultural activities. He owned most of the old stone houses along the Brandywine, where the Du Pont Company had been developed, and he renovated all of them, and he used to rent them to newly embarked employees and give them two years to get themselves on their feet, and then he'd take them away from them. They could have them for free for two years until they could get on their feet. He was just so busy doing good things--a great individual to know and be associated with. I've just heard that he's not very well, and he's younger than I am.

Q: Was that a job that you enjoyed?

Admiral Davidson: Yes, I did. I enjoyed it. I was trying to be the old schoolmaster. One of the things, I was making every effort not to be military, because that was what was bothering some of the people. They were afraid that a military man might try to make a military school of it. So I bent over backwards not to make a military school out of it. But there were certain standards that I felt could be enforced even in a civilian school. One of them was proper appearance, because, oh, boy, they were going downhill fast.

Q: Tattnall is a famous old Navy name. Was there any connection at all?*

Admiral Davidson: I don't really think that this particular Tatnall had any connection to the Navy. Of course, we had a Du Pont in the Navy, too--Admiral Du Pont.** Wilmington is a lovely place to live. I don't know how they did it, but I was number 82 on the waiting list to get into the Wilmington Country Club, and the next day I was number one, which was nice.

Q: Did you move back to Annapolis afterwards?

Admiral Davidson: Yes, moved back here. The only thing I did after I got back here was that I commuted to Washington for almost a year as the sort of executive director of NAUS--National Association for Uniformed Services, which was just trying to get off the ground at that time. They came and asked me if I would work at it, and I worked at it for a year, but I was commuting to Washington every day. That grew old in a big way. Once we started there, they didn't need anybody full time anyway. The staff was pretty good. I turned it over to an Army brigadier.

---

*Flag Officer Josiah Tattnall, USN, resigned his commission in 1861 to assume appointment as Senior Flag Officer in the Navy of Georgia, Confederate Navy, during the Civil War. There is no connection to the Tatnall School.
**Rear Admiral Samuel F. Du Pont, USN, earned his commission in 1815 and served through the Civil War to 1865.

Davidson #5 - 438

Q: I've been struck by the last few weeks, even now you're still a busy person, so what occupies your time? We might add that you were married earlier this year.

Admiral Davidson: I was married the tenth of April this year. I married the widow of a classmate of mine, who was a submariner. His name was Stovall.* He died in '65, and she married an Army major general by the name of Willems, and then he died.** Both of my previous wives are dead. So we decided to try to take care of each other for our remaining few years.

Q: Do you have any summing up, any overall thoughts about your Navy career, which included nearly 40 years in uniform?

Admiral Davidson: I wouldn't trade it for anything, really. There were many, many times when I would have, but now that it's over with, I wouldn't trade it for anything. It was a privilege. I was lucky, because my brother was too old, and I got the job. I'm happy that I was able to do as well as I did. I suppose if I were to go back and review it in detail, I might think of some things that I should have done and some things I should not have done, but I did enjoy it. I have a great deal to be thankful for. I still think the Navy is a great opportunity for anybody

---
  *Rear Admiral William S. Stovall, Jr., USN (Ret.)
 **Major General J.M. Willems, U.S. Army (Ret.)

coming along today. It's a far greater opportunity than some other things I can think of.

Q: It's been a privilege for me to have this opportunity to share it with you, Admiral, and on behalf of the Institute and the people who will be using this material, I'm very grateful to you for the contribution.

Admiral Davidson: Thank you, Paul. It's been a pleasure to know you. You've been very helpful in prompting me here. As I say, so many of the things that I've talked about are just plain everyday memory. It could be faulty. It's not as bad as a program I saw this morning on Alzheimer's disease. My goodness, I saw some people--oh, what a pitiful thing. But this ought to wind it up now, I suppose, because I've got a lot of things to do about this house.

Q: You'll be able to get on with it, then.

Admiral Davidson: And then some day I'm going to get back on the golf course. I haven't been near the golf course.

Q: I hope that's pretty soon.

Index

to

Reminiscences of

Rear Admiral John F. Davidson

U.S. Navy (Retired)

U.S. Naval Institute

Annapolis, Maryland

1986

Academic Board, U.S. Naval Academy
  Discussion of Academic Board in early 1950s, pages 281-282; role in admissions in the early 1960s, page 419

Air Conditioning
  Benefits for submarines, page 91

Air Force-Navy Rivalry
  Navy's reluctance to accept strategic bombing as a catchall solution causes problems in the mid-1950s, pages 327-328

Albany, USS (CA-123)
  Favorable assessment of executive officer Richard Colbert in the mid-1950s, pages 76-77, 298; Davidson allowed to leave U.S. Naval Academy department head duty early in 1954 to assume command, pages 276-277; overhaul at the Norfolk Navy Yard in mid-1954, page 296; Davidson's fitness report from division commander Arleigh Burke, page 297; exercises in mid-1950s, pages 298-300, 304; handling and power, pages 300, 305; chaplain promoted good behavior ashore and cleaned up language during Mediterranean cruise, pages 300-303; liberty ports in the Mediterranean, page 303; Marine detachment, page 307; rode out hurricane at mooring in Portsmouth, Virginia, pages 315-316; helicopters on board, page 316; crew pitched in to help small Greek town destroyed by an earthquake, pages 317-319

Alcohol
  See Liquor

Andrews, Rear Admiral Adolphus, USN (USNA, 1901)
  As Chief of the Bureau of Navigation in the mid-1930s, forced to crack down on married junior officers after pressure from the media, pages 120-123

Annapolis, Maryland
  Proposed U.S. Naval Academy expansion into Annapolis in the early 1960s caused hard feelings, pages 386-392

Argentia, Newfoundland
  U.S. submarines used Argentia as a base for patrols in 1941, pages 165-166; water deep right up to shore, page 225

Arizona, USS (BB-39)
  Officers aboard in early 1930s, pages 53-54, 58; Davidson's run-in with executive officer Thaddeus Thomson, pages 54-56; Davidson's duties as aide to executive officer Commander Baughman in the early 1930s, pages 59-60; mast case, pages 59-60; duties as turret officer, pages 60-61, 63; junior officers'

mess, pages 61-62; ship quarantined in early 1930s, page 67; junior officer liberties in the Long Beach area, pages 68-70; took on crews' dependents after March 1933 earthquake in Long Beach, California, pages 70-73

Army-Navy Football Game
Ticket scalping scandal in 1960, pages 365-369; President Kennedy attended in 1961, pages 394-395

Ashford, Lieutenant (junior grade) George W., USN (USNA, 1929)
Davidson's friend at U.S. Naval Academy in late 1920s, page 39; incident with Davidson during parade, page 41; at Davidson's home during March 1933 earthquake in Long Beach, California, pages 70-71; introduces Davidson to his future wife, page 73

Astor, Lady Nancy
Befriended Blackfish (SS-221) crew during World War II, page 174

Ballinger, Midshipman Richard R., USN (USNA, 1929)
As U.S. Naval Academy boxer and Davidson's friend in late 1920s, page 39

Baltimore Sun
Brought pressure on Bureau of Navigation chief, Adolphus Andrews, to crack down on married junior officers in the mid-1930s, pages 121-123; leaked story of U.S. Naval Academy's planned expansion into the city of Annapolis in the early 1960s, pages 389, 392

Basketball
Military Academy William Westmoreland was upset when the Naval Academy won an Army-Navy basketball game in the early 1960s, pages 381-383

Baskett, Lieutenant (junior grade) Thomas S., USN (USNA, 1935)
Experience as officer of the deck of the USS S-44 (SS-155) in the late 1930s, page 147

Battle, Lieutenant Commander Charlton E., Jr., USN (USNA, 1910)
Battalion officer at U.S. Naval Academy in late 1920s attempted to get Davidson's punishment for neglect of duty lessened, page 28; helped Davidson change an incorrect grease mark and raise class standing in 1929, page 37

Baughman, Commander Cortlandt C., USN (USNA, 1907)
Assessed as executive officer of Arizona (BB-39) in early 1930s, pages 58-59; handling of mast case involving relations with a minor, pages 59-60

Beach, Commander Edward L., USN (USNA, 1939)
  Chosen as President Dwight Eisenhower's naval aide in the early 1950s despite the President's idea that the billet should be menial, pages 126-127

Becker, Lieutenant Albert L., USN (USNA, 1934)
  Blackfish (SS-221) executive officer got last look at German merchant ship before it was torpedoed in 1942, page 175

Bellino, Midshipman Joseph M., USN (USNA, 1961)
  Instrumental in win in 1960 Army-Navy game, page 372; numerous public appearances after winning the Heisman Trophy in 1960 adversely affected his grades, page 373-374

Benefits for Servicemen
  Few perks for naval officers in Washington, D.C., at end of World War II, page 223

Benson, Rear Admiral Roy S., USN (USNA, 1929)
  Davidson's classmate and head of NA 10 band at U.S. Naval Academy in the late 1920s, page 40; as a bachelor in Washington, D.C., right after World War II, pages 223-224; filled in for Davidson as Commander Cruiser Division Five in 1958, page 338

Berry, Ensign Howard B., Jr., USN (USNA, 1938)
  Mackerel (SS-204) deck officer's unorthodox approach to New London pier in early 1940s, pages 160-161

Blackfish, USS (SS-221)
  Problems with torpedoes, pages 109, 175, 197, 205-206; competent chief petty officer had personal problems that forced his disqualification from submarine duty during World War II, page 153; originally given secret orders to transport French general to North Africa in 1942, then redirected to Dakar, pages 169-171; poor quality of radar, pages 169-171-172; torpedoed alleged French ship off Dakar that may have been a merchant vessel, pages 172-173; while patroling from Roseneath, Scotland, attacked only one ship and then was severely depth charged, pages 173-175; trials in 1942, pages 176-178; discussion of World War II crew, pages 172, 178-181, 184, 200, 204-205; difficulty with gyro compass, pages 184-185; patrols in the Denmark Strait, pages 180-181, 184-188; unsuccessful in attempts to get evaporator coils through normal channels in 1942, Davidson wrote to CominCh Ernest King and they are sent, pages 190-191; transpacific trip to Australia with low fuel, pages 191-193; patrols off Australia, pages 194-206; attacked by zero, page 195; ultra-supplied lead on a convoy proved useless, pages 197-198; morale, pages 200-201, 206

Black Market
   In Turkey in the late 1950s, pages 343, 346-347

Blakely, Lieutenant (junior grade) Robert T.C., USNR
   World War II <u>Blackfish</u> (SS-221) reservist an example of equal treatment afforded regular and reserve officers, pages 204-205

Boone, Admiral Walter F., U.S. Navy (Retired)   (USNA, 1921)
   Former U.S. Naval Academy Superintendent from the mid-1950s still active in the mid-1980s, page 424

Brindupke, Lieutenant Commander Charles F., USN   (USNA, 1932)
   Put in for duty on Asiatic station following graduation from submarine school in the mid-1930s, page 86

Brown, Rear Admiral John H., Jr., USN   (USNA, 1914)
   As training officer for Commander Submarines Pacific Fleet in World War II, page 209

Bruton, Rear Admiral Henry C., USN   (USNA, 1926)
   Recalled situation between Chief of Naval Operations Nimitz and OP-05, Vice Admiral Radford, concerning aviator detailing in the late 1940s, pages 331-333

Buchanan, Captain Charles A., USN   (USNA, 1926)
   New U.S. Naval Academy Commandant faced with handling brigade-wide prank during 1952 color parade, pages 421-422

Buerkle, Lieutenant (junior grade) Elmer C., USN   (USNA, 1925)
   Engineering officer in <u>Cachalot</u> (SS-170) in the mid-1930s tried to warn Lieutenant Max Stormes that the submarine was approaching a tender too rapidly, but the skipper quieted him, pages 95-96, 104

Bureau of Naval Personnel (BuPers)
   At the end of World War II, Davidson was assessing submarine personnel needs for the following year, pages 213-217; efficient machinery available to BuPers in the mid-1940s, page 218; detailing of submarine officers following war's end, pages 219-222; OP-05, Vice Admiral Radford, insisted on making all aviator assignments in the mid-1940s, pages 332-333

Bureau of Navigation (BuNav)
   Method of keeping track of personnel in the mid-1930s, before advent of computers, pages 112-114; anecdote about parents trying to get their son transferred closer to home, pages 114-115; officers assigned to BuNav in mid-1930s, pages 111-112, 124; detail of submarine officers in mid-1930s, pages 127-128;

assignment of junior officers, pages 130-137; exclusion of Green Bowl Society members from detailing duty, pages 138-140

Burke, Admiral Arleigh A., USN (USNA, 1923)
Chief of Naval Operations Burke unhappy with one of Davidson's assistants in late 1950s, asked that he be removed but Davidson handled it in his own way, pages 98-99; as commanding officer of Albany (CA-123) in the mid-1950s, Davidson had infrequent dealings with his division commander Burke, pages 296-297; chastised Davidson for reluctance to reprimand crew, pages 306-307; allowed Davidson to handle situation with Prime Minister of Malta in 1957, pages 320-322; stands up for Davidson when he was being yelled at by Rear Admiral Don Felt, pages 321-322; dealings with OP-61, pages 322-323; demanded quick service from Davidson before a presidential briefing in mid-1950s, page 328; set trap for State Department official who had been intercepting Navy messages, page 337; message from Burke congratulating Davidson on his selection as U.S. Naval Academy Superintendent in 1960, page 355; expectations of Davidson as Superintendent, pages 364-365; congratulated U.S. Naval Academy football team after 1960 win over Army, page 372

Cachalot, USS (SS-170)
Built in Portsmouth in the early 1930s, pages 93, 99; discussion of engines, pages 94, 107-108; automatic pilot malfunctioned while Davidson was officer of the deck and caused submarine to go in circles, pages 94-95; officers in mid-1930s, pages 95-97; skipper Merrill Comstock's method of handling unsatisfactory inspection of the submarine, page 97; frigid cold during sea trials in January 1934, pages 99-100; tendency to roll causes seasickness, page 100; habitability, page 101; Filipino stewards accidentally sent hair flying throughout the submarine, pages 105-106; Davidson's submarine qualifications aboard, pages 102-104; hit whale while approaching San Diego, page 106; best suited for scouting, pages 108-109; torpedo practice and Pacific operations in the mid-1930s, pages 109-110

Canada
U.S. submarines used Argentia, Newfoundland, as a base in 1941, pages 165-166; Canadian position regarding the Korean War, pages 257-258, 260; favorable assessment of Canada's military system in the early 1950s, pages 259-260

Canadian National Defence College (CNDC)
State Department directed that the Canadian request for a U.S. naval officer at their Defence College be filled in 1950, even though there was no space for reciprocating at U.S. National War College, page 250; Davidson's living arrangements on Lake

Ontario, pages 250-251; format of studies, pages 252-253; anecdotes from defense course, pages 254-256; potential of exchange program to bring United States and Canada closer, pages 257-258; religion versus Communism studied, pages 252-253, 258-259

Carde, Lieutenant (junior grade) Freeland H., USN
USS Blackfish (SS-221) officer of the deck who almost caused collision by losing sight of the escort ship in a convoy, pages 244-246

Carver, Midshipman Lamar P., USN (USNA, 1929)
Midshipman Davidson ate dinner at classmate Carver's table in the late 1920s and was eventually punished for neglect of duty, page 27

Challenger, Lieutenant Harold L., USN (USNA, 1919)
Company officer at U.S. Naval Academy in late 1920s gave Davidson a break when he caught the latter smoking, pages 11-12

Chapel Services
See Religion

Chew, Captain John L., USN (USNA, 1931)
As commanding officer of the Roanoke (CL-145) in the late 1950s, given orders to remain undetected in the South China Sea, page 339

Chief of the Boat
Importance to quality of enlisted submarine crew, pages 153-154; ex-chiefs used as trials crew at Electric Boat in 1940s, page 177

Christie, Captain Ralph W., USN (USNA, 1915)
Davidson remembers his submarine division commander in 1941 as a poor sport, pages 166-168; Davidson feels Christie should have been held more responsible for difficulties with torpedoes during World War II, pages 167, 175-176; Davidson refused to gamble with Christie during visit to his mess in Perth in the late 1940s, pages 242-243

Clagget, Lieutenant (junior grade) Bladen D., USN (USNA, 1935)
Role as engineer officer in S-45 (SS-156) in the late 1930s often usurped by engineering-minded commanding officer, pages 143-144

Coal-burning Ships
   Difficulties of shoveling coal for Midshipman Davidson in 1926, pages 13, 15-17, 51

Coe, Commander James W., USN (USNA, 1930)
   As student at submarine school in 1933, Coe had interesting explanation for a traffic accident, pages 84-85

Colbert, Vice Admiral Richard G., USN (USNA, 1937)
   Naval War College professor requested information from Davidson about his former executive officer Colbert, pages 76-77; assessed by Davidson as Albany (CA-123) executive officer in mid-1950s, page 298; Davidson turned down on request for Colbert as his assistant in OP-61 in 1957, page 331

Colclough, Lieutenant Commander Oswald S., USN (USNA, 1921A)
   Selected as aide to the Naval War College president in the late 1930s over detailer Sunshine Murray's objections, pages 137-138

Cole, William S. (Republican-New York)
   Congressman's philosophy on voting for things he didn't agree with sums up Davidson's thoughts on politicians, pages 393-394

Command
   Satisfaction of cruiser command for Davidson in mid-1950s, page 306

Commissions
   Revocable commissions used in the early 1930s allowed the Navy to strongly discourage junior officers from marrying, pages 120-123; only half of U.S. Naval Academy class of 1933 commissioned initially as an austerity measure, pages 123-124

Communism
   Officers at Canadian National Defence College studied religion versus Communism in the early 1950s, pages 252-253, 258-259; communistic leanings within the State Department in the mid-1950s, page 329

Comstock, Lieutenant Commander Merrill, USN (USNA, 1917)
   Praised for laissez-faire method of command in the Cachalot (SS-170) in the mid-1930s, pages 95-98, 103-105; stood bridge watch in cold weather, page 100; ordered Filipino stewards to cut their hair before going ashore in Panama, pages 105-106; convinced Davidson to go to the Bureau of Navigation as assistant submarine detail officer in 1936, page 111; Comstock and Davidson visited Ralph Christie in Washington in mid-1930s, page 168

Connally, John B., Jr.
   Secretary of the Navy who misled Davidson on political aspirations in 1961, page 359

Cook, Dr. Allen Blow (USNA, 1921)
   U. S. Naval Academy English professor who was demoted in the early 1950s, pages 269-270

Coward, Captain Asbury, USN (USNA, 1938)
   Superintendent Davidson contacted U.S. Naval Academy athletic director, Coward, about arranging for more home football games in the early 1960s, page 370; contacted by Davidson when football players don't show up at professional lectures, page 376

Cruiser Division Five
   Duties of division commander in the late 1950s, pages 339-340

Cuba
   Battleship target practice at Guantanamo in late 1920s, page 17; Utah (BB-31) officers smuggled liquor aboard at Cuba during Prohibition, page 19; submarine detailer finessed a captain into an undesirable billet at Guantanamo Bay in the mid-1930s, pages 127-128; precarious approach of Albany (CA-123) to Guantanamo in the mid-1950s with Assistant Secretary of the Navy Franke on board, pages 310-311

Cushing, Richard Cardinal
   Tried to finagle an appearance by Heisman Trophy winner Joe Bellino at a banquet in 1961 but was thwarted by bad weather, pages 373-374

Dakar
   Blackfish (SS-221) sent to patrol off African coast in 1942 to make sure French ships couldn't leave Dakar, pages 170-171; Blackfish attacked alleged French ship off Dakar that may have been a merchant vessel, pages 172-173

Davidson, Rear Admiral John F., USN (USNA, 1929)
   Birth and early years, pages 1-6; parents and siblings, pages 1-6, 231-232; midshipman at Naval Academy (1925-1929), pages 5-18, 21-47; wife and children, pages 70-71, 73-75, 79, 86, 120, 145, 148, 150, 223, 250-251, 261, 314-315, 336, 353, 355, 393-395, 399-400, 407-408, 424-425, 430, 438; engineering department, USS Utah (BB-31) (1929-1930), pages 15, 18-21, 49-53; communications and gunnery officer in Arizona (BB-39) (1930-1933), pages 17, 49-50, 53-74; temporary duty in New York (BB-34), summer of 1929, pages 18, 49, 52; submarine school at

New London (1933), pages 70, 74-93; duty in Cachalot (SS-170) (1934-1936), pages 93-111; assistant submarine detail officer in Bureau of Navigation (1936-1938), pages 111-140; executive officer, USS S-45 (SS-156) (1938-1939), pages 130, 143-144; commanding officer, USS S-44 (SS-155) (1939-1940), pages 90, 154-168; commanding officer, USS Mackerel (SS-204) (1940-1942), pages 90, 154-168; commanding officer, USS Blackfish (SS-221) (1942-1944), pages 169-206, 244; training officer, Submarine Training Command Pacific (1944), pages 207-213; detail officer, Bureau of Naval Personnel (1945-1947), pages 119, 129, 213-223, 246; Commander Submarine Division 62, (1947-1948), pages 224-229; commanding officer, USS Orion (AS-18) (1948-1949), pages 229-238; Commander Submarine Squadron Two (1949-1950), pages 239-248; student, Canadian National Defence College (1950-1951), pages 249-261; chairman of English, History, and Government Department, U.S. Naval Academy (1951-1954), pages 23, 25-26, 125-126, 149, 251, 264-296, 385-386; commanding officer, USS Albany (CA-123) (1954-1955), pages 76-77, 270, 276-277, 296-319; Assistant Director, Politico-Military Division, Office of the Chief of Naval Operations (1955-1957), pages 98-99, 258, 297, 319-336; Director, Politico-Military Division (OP-61) (1957), pages 320-322, 336-337; Commander Cruiser Division Five (1957-1958), pages 333, 337-340; Chief of the Navy Group, Joint U.S. Military Mission for Aid to Turkey (1958-1960), pages 340-353; Superintendent, U.S. Naval Academy (1960-1962), pages 283-285, 354-425; Commander Training Command, Pacific Fleet (1962-1964), pages 400-401, 425-430; retires in 1964, pages 430-431; headmaster of Tatnall School, Wilmington, Delaware (1964-1968), pages 431-437; Executive Director, National Association for Uniformed Services (NAUS) (1968-1969), page 437; health, pages 9-10, 37-38, 138, 145-146, 338;

Davidson, Dr. Bruce M.
Assessed as U.S. Naval Academy dean in the 1970s and 1980s, pages 358, 364

De Rivera, Lieutenant Horace L., USN (USNA, 1921B)
Davidson relieved De Rivera as turret officer in Arizona (BB-39) in early 1930s, page 61; anecdote about showering De Rivera's child in Arizona after March 1933 earthquake, pages 71-72

De Tar, Lieutenant Commander John L., USN (USNA, 1927)
World War II submarine skipper chastised by his division commander for not being aggressive enough, page 216

Dealey, Commander Samuel D., USN (USNA, 1930)
Audacious submariner as skipper of the USS Harder (SS-257) in World War II, pages 81-82; Dealey's daring tactics discouraged by submarine trainers at Pearl Harbor in 1944, page 210

Denmark Strait
Difficulty on U.S. submarine patrols in 1942 caused by 24-hour light and extreme cold, pages 181, 186, 201

Dennison, Captain Robert L., USN (USNA, 1923)
As first OP-61 director in the mid-1940s, not only saved career, but wound up with command of the Missouri (BB-63) and flag rank, pages 323-325

Depth Charges
Helpless feeling during attack, pages 194-196; on board the submarine Blackfish (SS-221) during World War II, fear of caused submarine skippers to operate cautiously, pages 203-204

Deputy Chief of Naval Operations (Air)
OP-05, Vice Admiral Arthur Radford, butted heads with Chief of Naval Operations Chester Nimitz in the mid-1940s regarding detailing of aviators, pages 332-333

Detailing Duty
Clerical handling of personnel in mid-1930s before the advent of computers, pages 112-114; outside influences on the handling of personnel, pages 114-115, 120-123; anecdote showing submarine detailer's finesse in assigning a captain to an undesirable billet, and being thanked for it, pages 127-128; anecdote about a submariner who protested an overseas transfer for his wife's sake while secretly accepting it and thanking his detailer, page 128; selection board for submarine school billets set up because of overflow of requests, incited resentment among aviators, pages 130-131; rationale behind assignments, pages 131-132; small number of detail officers in the mid-1930s, page 135; known Green Bowl members barred from detail duty in 1930s, pages 139-140; Davidson in Pearl Harbor assessing personnel needs for the Bureau of Naval Personnel when the war ends, pages 213-214; benefit to Davidson's career from detailing duty, page 217; difficulty for detailers at end of World War II when reservists were released from command billets, pages 219-220; OP-05, Vice Admiral Radford, insisted on making all aviator assignments in the mid-1940s, pages 332-333
See also Bureau of Navigation, Bureau of Personnel

Deyo, Lieutenant Commander Morton L., USN (USNA, 1911)
   U.S. Naval Academy duty officer caught Midshipman Davidson on class offense in late 1920s, pages 27-28

Diesel Engines
   Engines in the new submarine Cachalot (SS-170) in the 1930s had to run at critical speeds, page 94, 107-108; NELSECO engines in the new Mackerel (SS-204) in the early 1940s, page 155

Diplomatic Restrictions
   Restraints put on U.S. subs patroling the North Atlantic during World War II, page 173

Donaho, Lieutenant Glynn R., USN (USNA, 1927)
   Submarine commanding officer with a reputation for not delegating duties, pages 160-161

Drought, Dr. A. Bernard
   Circumstances surrounding Drought's appointment as first U.S. Naval Academy academic dean in 1962, pages 356-358

Earthquake
   Earthquake in Long Beach on 10 March 1933, pages 70-73; Albany (CA-123) crew helped small Greek town destroyed by a quake in the mid-1950s, pages 317-319

Eddy, Lieutenant Ian C., USN (USNA, 1930)
   S-44 (SS-155) commanding officer Davidson wrote to proposed executive officer Eddy to welcome him in 1939, page 142; interceded with Davidson on a young ensign's behalf, page 148; anecdotes about Eddy from long friendship with Davidson, pages 148-149, 151

Education
   Pennsylvania high school as preparation for U.S. Naval Academy in early 1920s, pages 6-8; teaching methods at U.S. Naval Academy in 1920s versus 1950s, pages 22-26

Edwards, Admiral Richard S., USN (USNA, 1907)
   Vice Chief of Naval Operations Edwards's colorful way of explaining to Davidson in 1945 why an exception wouldn't be made in regard to personnel assignment, page 215

Eisenhower, President Dwight D. (USMA, 1915)
   Grew up in Kansas with Davidson's boss, Edward Hazlett, pages 124-125; as President, asked for Hazlett's recommendation for his naval aide, pages 124-125; Davidson's guest at U.S. Naval

Academy football game in 1960, page 394; directed that service academy superintendents be no more than two stars, pages 423-424

Electric Boat Company, Groton, Connecticut
Company trial crew handled the Blackfish (SS-221) in 1942, pages 176-178

Elliott, Lieutenant (junior grade) James F., USNR
Blackfish (SS-221) first lieutenant during World War II heard story by merchant seaman that could explain torpedo attack off Dakar, pages 172-173

Ellis, Commander Larry H., CHC, USN
U.S. Naval Academy chaplain who preached inspirational sermons for midshipmen in the mid-1980s, pages 409-411

Engineering Plants
Diesels in the new submarine Cachalot (SS-170) in the early 1930s had to run at certain critical speeds, pages 94, 107-108; NELSECO diesels in the new submarine Mackerel (SS-204) in the early 1940s, page 155; submarine Blackfish (SS-221) inadvertently made a transpacific voyage in 1942 with a fuel tank of water instead of oil, pages 190-193

English, History, Government Department, U.S. Naval Academy
Division of civilian versus military among professors in early 1950s, page 264; difficulty grading English in all subjects, page 265; various department heads since 1922, page 268; professors in the early 1950s, pages 269-271; experiments with spelling and speed reading, pages 272-273; fought for importance with technical subjects, pages 274-275; individual cases of deficiency in English, pages 279-281

Enlisted Personnel
Crew members of the USS Arizona (BB-39) sent to captain's mast in the early 1930s for having sex with a minor, pages 59-60; quality of enlisteds in submarine duty in the late 1930s, page 152

Erdelatz, Edward J.
U.S. Naval Academy football coach in the 1950s allowed his players to put football before academics, page 283

Erdelhun, General Rustu
Turkish officer irons out housing and customs difficulties for Davidson in the late 1950s, pages 344-345

Evaporators
    New coils needed for the evaporators in the submarine Blackfish (SS-221) in 1942 to enable her to cross the Pacific, pages 190-191

Fenno, Captain Frank W., USN (USNA, 1925)
    Wartime submarine skipper sent from U.S. at end of World War II to bring ship home, page 220; directed by Admiral Fife to get slot machines off the USS Orion (AS-18) in the late 1940s, page 237; took Davidson's intended place at the National War College in 1950, pages 248-249

Fernandez, Arturo
    Spanish professor at U.S. Naval Academy in late 1920s had been in the Spanish-American War, pages 24-25

Ferrara, Commander Maurice, USN (USNA, 1937)
    At the end of World War II, turned down submarine command for a shore billet to spend more time with his family, page 246; shiphandling ability questioned, pages 246-247

Fife, Rear Admiral J.M., Jr., USN (USNA, 1918)
    As Commander Task Force 72 during World War II, complimented Davidson's ingenuity in requesting evaporator coils from Admiral E.J. King, page 191; chastised Davidson for bringing Blackfish (SS-221) into Australian harbor at excessive speed in 1924, pages 192-193; assessed by Davidson, pages 202-204, 241-242; chided Davidson for trivial offense immediately upon return from a tiring cruise in the late 1940s, pages 235-236; ordered removal of Orion's slot machines, pages 237-238

Fisher, Lieutenant Commander Robert, USN
    USS Orion (AS-18) first lieutenant facilitated dependent cruise in the late 1940s, pages 233-234

Fitness Reports
    As a detailer in the mid-1930s, Davidson used fitness reports to select from many candidates for a choice billet, page 136; Davidson received a weak evaluation from his cruiser division commander Arleigh Burke, who had little dealing with him, but made flag anyway, page 297; Davidson wrote short but highly favorable reports on head chaplain and commandant at U.S. Naval Academy in the early 1960s, pages 417-418, need to interpret what writer said, page 418

Flenniken, Ensign Clifton W., Jr., USN (USNA, 1937)
    Newlywed Flenniken missed the boat as S-44 (SS-155) left on time for a day patrol in late 1930s, and then sweated out

feared punishment from commanding officer Davidson, pages 147-148

Flood, Daniel J. (Democrat-Pennsylvania)
Obstructionist congressman on U.S. Naval Academy Board of Visitors in the early 1960s delays board meeting by nit-picking, pages 383-385

Fluckey, Commander Eugene B., USN (USNA, 1935)
Davidson sought to detach this successful World War II submarine skipper for his own safety, page 83; anecdote about the Nimitzes's catastrophic visit to the Fluckey home in the mid-1940s, pages 117-120; Fluckey's daring tactics discouraged by submarine trainers at Pearl Harbor in 1944, page 210

Football
Davidson's Naval Academy football experience ended soon after it began in 1925 because he was too slender, pages 8-9; in the early 1960s, Naval Academy coach Wayne Hardin tried to keep his players from attending evening lectures, pages 283-284; ticket-scalping scandal before Army-Navy game in 1960, pages 365-369; the Naval Academy had one of the top college teams in the nation in the early 1960s, pages 370-378

Franke, William B.
As Assistant Secretary of the Navy in the mid-1950s, riding in Davidson's ship, _Albany_ (CA-123), witnessed young officer of the deck's skilled but precarious approach to anchorage at Guantanamo, pages 310-311; explains Davidson's assignment to Turkey in 1958, pages 341-342

Freeman, Rear Admiral Charles S., USN (USNA, 1900)
Stern commanding officer of _Arizona_ (BB-39) in early 1930s, pages 53-54, 58-59; put Davidson as an ensign in a more senior billet and directed him to dine in the wardroom instead of the junior officer mess, page 61; served as Commander Submarine Force in 1930s with no submarine experience, pages 53, 94; insisted that submarines steam in formation without knowing the difficulty it caused, page 94; cast in eye gave Freeman a stern appearance, page 97; asked Davidson to be his flag lieutenant in late 1930s, pages 129-130

French Navy
British submarine with U.S. naval officer aboard transported French general to North Africa in 1942, page 170; _Blackfish_ (SS-221) sent to Dakar to keep French ships in place, page 170; distrust of the British, pages 170-171

Frocking
   Davidson frocked to rear admiral for trip to London in the mid-1950s and then had to go back to rank of captain until his promotion came through, page 336

Gambling
   Slot machines that had been funding the crew's welfare and recreation were ordered removed from the submarine tender Orion (AS-18) in the late 1940s, pages 237-238; high stakes poker game played by Admiral James Fife in the late 1940s, page 241; officers' mess gambles for cigarettes at Perth in late 1940s, pages 242-243

Gannon, Captain Sinclair, USN (USNA, 1900)
   U.S. Naval Academy Commandant in the late 1920s talked to midshipmen about conduct, pages 35-36

Gates, Thomas S.
   Secretary of the Navy Gates sent Davidson to Turkey in 1958 with understanding that he would have a shot at U.S. Naval Academy Superintendent when he returned, pages 341-342

German Navy
   The submarine Mackerel (SS-204) had an encounter in 1941 with something which might have been a German submarine, pages 163-164; German warship attacked the submarine Blackfish (SS-221) during a patrol in 1942, pages 173-175; U.S. patrols in Denmark Strait in 1942 to search for U-boats, pages 186-188

Giraud, General Henri Honore
   French general transported to North Africa in British submarine in 1942, pages 169-170

Greece
   Albany (CA-123) crew pitched in to help when Volos was destroyed by an earthquake in the mid-1950s, pages 317-319

Green Bowl Society
   Bureau of Navigation became aware of the existence of this secret group after a plane crash in the 1930s, and excluded known members from detail duty, pages 138-140

Grenfell, Captain Elton W., USN (USNA, 1926)
   Joke played on Grenfell by other Commander Submarine Force Pacific Fleet officers in 1944, page 209

Guns - 14-inch
   On USS Arizona (BB-39) in the early 1930s, page 63

Gyro Compass
  Caused difficulty in the submarine Blackfish (SS-221) in the Arctic in 1942, pages 184-185

Halsey, Captain William F., Jr., USN (USNA, 1904)
  While commanding officer of Reina Mercedes (IX-25) in late 1920s, gave Davidson 40 demerits for improper performance of duty, pages 30-31

Hannegan, Captain Edward A., USN (USNA, 1928)
  Lake Champlain (CVA-39) commanding officer "crosses paths" with Davidson in Albany (CA-123) during Mediterranean operations in mid-1950s, pages 299-300

Hardin, Wayne
  U.S. Naval Academy football coach in the early 1960s allowed his players to put football before academics, pages 283-284, 376; strict with players before 1961 Orange Bowl appearance, pages 373, 375; remarks about Davidson, pages 375-376; angered U.S. Naval Academy lacrosse coach by removing gear from players' lockers for spring football practice, page 377

Hart, Rear Admiral Thomas C., USN (USNA, 1897)
  As chairman of the general board in the late 1930s, opposed the development of large submarines, pages 155-156, 159-160

Hattendorf, John
  Requested information from Davidson about his former executive officer, Richard Colbert, page 76-77

Hazing
  At the Naval Academy in the late 1920s, hazing often had a playful aspect, pages 27-30, 42-43

Hazlett, Commander Edward E., Jr., USN (USNA, 1915)
  Very influential on Davidson as submarine detail officer in mid-1930s, pages 111-112, 127; grew up in Kansas with Dwight Eisenhower, pages 124-125; recommended Davidson as naval aide to President Eisenhower, pages 125-126; health, pages 125, 127; anecdotes showing skill as detail officer, pages 127-128

Helicopters
  Precarious on cruiser Albany (CA-123) in mid-1950s, pages 316-317

Hill, Vice Admiral Harry W., USN (USNA, 1911)
  U.S. Naval Academy Superintendent in the early 1950s started concept of honor code, page 43; impressed by Davidson's use of

senior midshipmen to introduce guest speakers, pages 277-279; defended a midshipman deficient in English, pages 279-280; big supporter of U.S. Naval Academy athletics, page 284; supported Davidson's selection as Superintendent in 1960, page 285; former U.S. Naval Academy Superintendent retired in Annapolis, concerned when the Academy studies acquiring land from the city in the early 1960s, pages 391-392; skillful handling of midshipmen's prank during 1952 color parade, pages 421-422; vigorous as Superintendent in the early 1950s, despite his age, pages 423-424

Hobby, Lieutenant William M., Jr., USN (USNA, 1923)
As executive officer of Cachalot in the early 1930s, followed skipper Merrill Comstock's lead in allowing Davidson no supervision when participating in a synchronized drill, pages 97, 104

Holloway, Vice Admiral James L., Jr., USN (USNA, 1919)
On the value of traditions at U.S. Naval Academy, page 48; on the importance of picking the right person for a job, page 77; convinced by Rear Admiral Smedberg to allow Davidson to be his deputy in the politico-military division in the mid-1950s, pages 319, 334; frocked Davidson to rear admiral for overseas trip in mid-1950s, page 336

Hooven-Owens-Rentschler (HOR)
HOR engine in Cachalot (SS-170) built in the early 1930s, was modified from eight to nine cylinders, page 107

House, Lieutenant (junior grade) Arthur C., Jr., USN (USNA, 1934)
Stern engineer officer in S-44 (SS-155) in the late 1930s, page 146

Humphrey, Midshipman Pat L., USN (USNA, 1929)
Classmate inadvertently caused Davidson trouble while they were serving punishment in late 1920s, page 30

Hurricanes
Mackerel (SS-204) survived Atlantic hurricane in 1941, pages 156-159; Albany (CA-123) rode out hurricane at mooring in Portsmouth, Virginia, in the mid-1950s, pages 315-316

Inspections
On S-boats at Coco Solo in the late 1930s, page 151

Intelligence
British provided information about torpedoed enemy ships in World War II, page 174

Intraservice Politics
  Davidson irked by steps taken to keep any one community from getting too much power in a division, pages 330-333

Ireland
  U.S. naval officers forced to land in Limerick by engine trouble during World War II had to scrounge civilian clothes to respect Ireland's neutrality, pages 188-189

Irvin, Captain William D., USN (USNA, 1927)
  Issued an order in the late 1940s decreeing that only commanding officers be allowed to dock submarines at New London, page 247

Italian Naval Academy
  Dinner party during visit of Albany (CA-123) in mid-1950s interrupted when the cruiser was sent to bring aid to a Greek town ravaged by an earthquake, pages 317-319

Ives, Commander Norman S., USN (USNA, 1920)
  Submarine division commander during World War II concerned when Blackfish (SS-221) engineer was relieved for emotional problems, page 180

Jackson, Captain Edward S., USN (USNA, 1900)
  Commanding officer of Utah (BB-31) in the late 1920s was a dapper dresser, page 52

Jackson, Lieutenant (junior grade) Roy, USN (USNA, 1929)
  Fought for a more senior position in the Arizona (BB-39) wardroom in the early 1930s, pages 61-62

Japan
  Zero attacked Blackfish (SS-221) off Australia during World War II, page 195

Johnson, Captain Alfred W., USN (USNA, 1899)
  As assistant to the Chief of the Bureau of Navigation in the early 1930s, responded with doubt to an inquiry about Davidson's chances of attending submarine school, page 138

Johnstone, Harold H.
  Electric Boat employee supervised building of Blackfish (SS-221) in 1942, page 176

Joint U.S. Mission for Aid to Turkey (JUSMAT)
  Davidson disappointed with assignment to this group in 1958, pages 340-342; country team dealt with black market case

involving a U.S. Navy chaplain and a high Turkish official, pages 346-347; country team used double standard in relaxing customs rules, pages 347-349; objectives of mission in late 1950s, page 349

Joy, Vice Admiral C. Turner, USN (USNA, 1916)
As U.S. Naval Academy Superintendent in the early 1950s, flexible about possibility of losing department head Davidson to President Eisenhower to be naval aide, pages 125-126; strong supporter of humanities from Korean War negotiations duty, pages 26, 274, 276; assessed by Davidson as Superintendent, page 276; allowed Davidson to leave early to take command of Albany (CA-123) in 1954, pages 276-277

Joyce, Father Edmund P.
Davidson filled in for Joyce, Notre Dame vice president and U.S. Naval Academy Board of Visitors member, as a banquet speaker in the early 1960s, pages 378-380

JUSMAT
See Joint U.S. Mission for Aid to Turkey

Kefauver, Lieutenant (junior grade) Russell, USN (USNA, 1933)
Advanced through crew of Tambor (SS-198) between 1940 and 1943 to become skipper, page 219

Keith, Captain Robert Taylor Scott, USN (USNA, 1928)
Fellow Arizona junior officer borrowed Davidson's car to buy government alcohol during Prohibition and almost got caught, pages 69-70; stationed at U.S. Naval Academy, recommended strict punishment after brigade-wide prank at the 1952 color parade, page 422

Kelly, Captain James W., CHC, USN
Davidson wrote short but highly complimentary fitness report for this U.S. Naval Academy chaplain in the early 1960s, pages 417-418

Kempff, Rear Admiral Clarence S., USN
Characteristics of and circumstances of his promotion to flag rank in the 1930s, pages 65-66

Kennedy, President John F.
Rude to his host, Davidson, at 1961 Army-Navy football game, pages 394-395; gave U.S. Naval Academy graduation address in 1961, pages 395-400; during visit to a carrier off San Diego, had cocktails served and demonstrated gift for extemporaneous public speaking, pages 427-428

Kerrick, Captain Charles S., USN   (USNA, 1902)
  As commanding officer of Arizona (BB-39) in early 1930s, pages 58-59

King, Admiral Ernest J., USN   (USNA, 1901)
  Blackfish (SS-221) commanding officer Davidson wrote to CominCh King in desperation in 1942 to get evaporator coils and is successful, pages 190-191; decreed in 1945 that senior submariners who had not made a combat patrol could not command a division or squadron, pages 214-217

Kinsella, Lieutenant William T., USN   (USNA, 1934)
  Davidson's assessment of his Blackfish (SS-221) executive officer, page 204

Kirkpatrick, Rear Admiral Charles C., USN   (USNA, 1931)
  Swapped assignments with Davidson in 1962 when latter left the Naval Academy, page 425

Korean War
  Canada's true position on the war not made public at the time, pages 257-258, 260; U.S. negotiator appreciated value of strong background in English and humanities, pages 274, 276; boys entered U.S. Naval Academy to avoid draft until Congress passed law requiring them to finish enlistment if they dropped out, page 282

Korth, Fred
  Misled Davidson and other naval leaders in discussion of necessity of an academic dean at U.S. Naval Academy in the early 1960s, pages 357-358; praised Davidson for his good work as Superintendent in June 1962 and then had him relieved in September, page 425

Koruturk, Admiral Fahri, Turkish Navy
  As Turkish Chief of Naval Operations in the late 1950s, page 342; dissatisfied with use of personnel in Turkish armed forces, page 350; impressed by Davidson's effort to converse in Turkish, page 351

Krulak, Colonel Victor H., USMC   (USNA, 1934)
  Opinionated as U.S. Naval Institute board member in the early 1950s, page 289

Laing, Captain Frederick W., USN   (USNA, 1930)
  Davidson relieved Laing as commanding officer of the Orion (AS-18) in 1948 and the next day Laing reverted to commander, page 230

Laird, W.W., Jr.
   DuPont heir provided incredibly generous funding to private school in Wilmington, Delaware, and the surrounding area in the mid-1960s, pages 431-436

Lake Champlain, USS (CVA-39)
   Crossed paths with the cruiser Albany (CA-123) during fleet exercise in the Mediterranean in mid-1950s, pages 299-300

Lankford, Richard E. (Democrat-Maryland)
   Congressman disappointed Davidson in the early 1960s by dishonesty concerning U.S. Naval Academy's proposed land acquisition, page 392; against use of stewards for flag officers, pages 392-393

Leadership
   Davidson's philosophy of letting inexperienced officers make mistakes, pages 312-313

Lemnitzer, General Lyman L., USA   (USMA, 1920)
   Complained to West Point Superintendent William Westmoreland after he attended an Army-Navy basketball game as Davidson's guest and Army lost, pages 381-382

Libby, Rear Admiral Ruthven R., USN   (USNA, 1922)
   As Commander Battleship Cruiser Force Atlantic Fleet in the mid-1950s, conducted precarious close-order exercise at high speed and without lights, pages 299-300, 308-309, 313; advice on bringing one ship alongside another for refueling, page 308; agreed with Davidson's decision to keep Albany (CA-123) at Portsmouth, Virginia, mooring to ride out hurricane in the mid-1950s, but placed full responsibility for ship on Davidson, page 316

Liberty
   In the Los Angeles-Long Beach area in the early 1930s, page 68

Lidstone, Midshipman Nicholas A., USN   (USNA, 1930)
   Accused of hazing plebes at the Naval Academy in 1928, pages 27-28

Liquor
   Utah (BB-31) officers smuggle liquor aboard in Cuba in the late 1920s, pages 19-21; Arizona junior officers joke about executive officer's plan to arrest them for drinking, page 56; Arizona officers able to buy government brandy in California in the early 1930s, pages 68-70; Davidson and friends make homemade liquor, pages 68, 70; served to officers aboard a

carrier off San Diego in the early 1960s at President Kennedy's request, page 427

Lloyd, Midshipman Russell, USN (USNA, 1930)
Davidson's football hopes ended in 1925 when the plebe coach saw him try to tackle Lloyd, who was almost twice his weight, pages 8-9

Lockwood, Vice Admiral Charles A., Jr., USN (USNA, 1912)
As Commander Submarines Pacific Fleet during World War II, kept successful skipper Eugene Fluckey from overextending his luck by preventing further patrols, page 83; as Commander Submarine Division 13 in the mid-1930s, scolded Cachalot (SS-170) skipper Merrill Comstock for relying too heavily on newly-qualified Davidson, pages 103-104; sent Davidson to Bureau of Personnel in 1945, despite his protests, because of his previous experience there, page 129; unhappy with Davidson about personnel detachments in 1945, page 214; comments on submariners versus sub-mariners at Washington dinner, page 243

Long Beach, California
As liberty port in early 1930s, page 68; March 1933 earthquake led to Navymen's families moving aboard ship, page 70

Lynch, Commander Frank C., Jr., USN (USNA, 1938)
Recounts reaction of World War II submarine skipper Sam Dealey to his own risky tactics, page 82; submarine division commander Davidson rode in Lynch's submarine on a cruise around Cape Horn in 1947, pages 224-225; favorable assessment by Davidson, page 228; accident caused Lynch's retirement in 1954, pages 228-229

Mackerel, USS (SS-204)
Low tonnage made it impractical for wartime use, page 90; specifications, page 155; survived Atlantic hurricane in 1941, pages 156-159; used to train prospective commanding officers in the early 1940s, pages 160-162; fired at what lookout perceived to be a German submarine in 1941, pages 163-164; patrols for U-boats in the Atlantic prior to U.S. entry into war, pages 165, 168-169

Magruder, Lieutenant Commander Cary W., USN (USNA, 1908)
Anecdotes as duty officer from his tour at U.S. Naval Academy in the late 1920s, pages 12-13

Malta
Chief of Naval Operations Burke allowed Davidson to handle the situation when Malta's prime minister tried to levy huge tax on cars at U.S. naval base in 1957, pages 320-323

Marlin, USS (SS-205)
   Had difficulty with Atlantic hurricane in 1941, pages 156-157, 159; used to train prospective commanding officers in the early 1940s, page 161

Married Officers
   Revocable commissions offered in the early 1930s made it possible for the Navy to get rid of junior officers who married within two years of being commissioned, pages 120-123

Mast Cases
   In Arizona (BB-39) in early 1930s, pages 59-60

McCain, Ensign John S., Jr., USN (USNA, 1931)
   Assessed by Davidson, pages 78-79; family, pages 79-81

McCain, Midshipman Joseph Pinckney, USN
   Admiral's son kicked out of U.S. Naval Academy in 1961 for having too many demerits, pages 80-81, 405

McCormack, John W. (Democrat-Massachusetts)
   Pressured Davidson to allow Heisman Trophy winner Joe Bellino to accept a speaking invitation in 1961 from Cardinal Cushing, page 374

McDougal, Midshipman David S., USN (USNA, 1933)
   Often in trouble at U.S. Naval Academy in the late 1920s, page 29

McFall, Lieutenant Albert D., USN (USNA, 1950)
   Davidson relied on aide McFall during football ticket scalping scandal at U.S. Naval Academy in 1960, page 367

McKinney, Commander Eugene B., USN (USNA, 1927)
   Anecdotes about McKinney from World War II duty as submarine training officer at Pearl Harbor, pages 209, 211-212

McMillen, Lieutenant Commander Gervase C., CHC, USNR
   Anecdotes involving Albany (CA-123) chaplain during Mediterranean cruise in mid-1950s, pages 300-303

McNamee, Rear Admiral Luke, USN (USNA, 1892)
   Inquired to Bureau of Navigation Davidson's chances of getting into submarine school in the early 1930s, page 138

Melson, Rear Admiral Charles L., USN (USNA, 1927)
   Circumstances of assignment as U.S. Naval Academy Superintendent in 1958, page 341

Mini, Captain James H., USN (USNA, 1935)
As U.S. Naval Academy Commandant in 1960, broke news of Army-Navy ticket scalping scandal to Davidson, page 367; made a poor impression on Davidson as commandant, pages 415-416

Minter, Captain Charles S., Jr., USN (USNA, 1937)
As U.S. Naval Academy Commandant in the early 1960s, unsuccessfully attempted to keep Admiral John S. McCain's son at the Academy, pages 80-81; traced unauthorized phone line into first classman's room, page 406; assessed as commandant, pages 416-417

Mitscher, Commander Marc A., USN (USNA, 1910)
As officer in charge of flight division at Bureau of Aeronautics in the mid-1930s, resented submariners have selection board for selecting candidates when naval aviation did not, pages 130-131

Momsen, Lieutenant Charles B., USN (USNA, 1920)
Davidson recalls submariner credited with developing escape lung, pages 87-88

Momsen Lung
Question about who developed this rescue breathing device for submariners, page 87

Moore, Midshipman Clarence J., USN (USNA, 1929)
Davidson's friend at U.S. Naval Academy in late 1920s, page 39

Moore, William H. III
U.S. Naval Academy lacrosse coach in the early 1960s angered when the football coach had Moore's players' gear removed from lockers, page 377

Moreell Commission
Studied expansion possibilities for the Naval Academy in the early 1960s, pages 386-392, 401-403

Morton, Ensign Dudley W., USN (USNA, 1930)
Submarine school classmate of Davidson in 1933, pages 81-82, 84

Mumma, Lieutenant Commander Morton C., Jr., USN (USNA, 1925)
Excelled as peacetime submarine skipper, but cracked under wartime pressure, pages 141-142; success as PT skipper, pages 218-219

Murphy, Robert D.
Davidson briefed Deputy Under Secretary of State Murphy in the mid-1950s, page 329; angry when shown by the Navy that a State Department officer was withholding messages, page 337

Murray, Commander Stuart S., USN (USNA, 1919)
As submarine detail officer in late 1930s, helped Davidson dodge undesirable assignment, page 129; defended Davidson's decision to set up a selection board for submarine school candidates over the protests of aviators, pages 130-131; won bet with Davidson when an officer, given leeway to choose travel arrangements, asked to change his orders, page 133; tried to discourage an officer's selection as an aide so he could take a command tour instead, page 137; issued Davidson orders as commanding officer of Mackerel (SS-204) in 1940, page 155

National Association for Uniformed Services (NAUS)
Davidson served as executive director of NAUS for a year in the late 1960s, page 437

National War College
Officers prevented from attending National War College during World War II rushed to head of list in the late 1940s, page 248

Naval Academy, U.S.
Background to Davidson's entrance in 1925, pages 5-8; sports in late 1920s, pages 8-9, 31, 39-40; smoking regulation, page 11; duty officers in late 1920s-early 1930s, pages 11-13, 51; summer cruises in late 1920s, pages 13-17, 21-22, 38; academics in late 1920s, pages 22-24; history professor's teaching method in 1950s, pages 23-24; instructors and officers in the late 1920s, pages 24-26, 35; former Spanish ship Reina Mercedes (IX-25) used as a brig for midshipmen in the late 1920s, pages 25-30; plebe hazing in late 1920s, pages 27-28, 29-30, 42; social activities in late 1920s, page 34; importance of grease mark, pages 36-37; sailing program, pages 38-39; parades in late 1920s, pages 41-42; honor code, pages 43-46; graduation in 1929, page 47; value of tradition, pages 47-48; only half of class of 1933 commissioned initially as an austerity measure, pages 123-124; commandant in early 1950s concerned about military conduct, pages 265-267; turn-backs, pages 281-282; guest speakers, pages 278-279, 283-284, 286, 376; Athletic Association and Preble Hall, pages 287-288; board of visitors, pages 292, 378, 383-386; faculty promotions, pages 292-295; civilian faculty committee, page 293; competition among service communities for commandant's billet, page 330; Davidson's satisfaction as Superintendent, pages 354, 423, 425;

circumstances of institution of academic dean in early 1960s, pages 356-358, 363-364; granting of bachelor's degree started in 1939, pages 359-360; validation program, page 360; faculty involved in curriculum changes in the early 1960s, pages 360-361; balance of military versus academic in early 1960s, pages 361-362; marching to classes stopped in the early 1960s, pages 362-363, 413; facilities discussed by board of visitors in early 1960s, pages 384-385; graduation in 1961, pages 395-400; graduation in 1962, page 425; Nimitz Library, pages 402-403; social activities in the early 1960s, pages 403-404, 423; first classmen wired phone into their room to conduct business in the early 1960s, pages 405-406; "burial of math" ceremony, pages 407-408; religious services, pages 409-411; uniforms, pages 407-408; Davidson's dealings with parents, pages 411-412; cemetery, page 412; Catholic chaplain involved in adultery in early 1960s, pages 412-413; relationship between commandant and Superintendent, pages 414, 417; admissions, page 419; minorities, pages 419-420; during 1952 color parade, midshipmen marched without their shoes, pages 421-422
See also English, History, Government Department; Academic Board; Moreell Commission

Naval Academy - Athletics
Sports in the late 1920s, pages 8-9, 31, 39-40; sailing program, pages 38-39; football coaches in the 1950s and 1960s, pages 283-284; as Superintendent in early 1960s, Davidson a big sports supporter, pages 365, 376; Davidson arranged for more home football games, pages 370-371; Navy played in Orange Bowl game, 1961, pages 372-373; swimming facilities studied by board of visitors in early 1960s, page 384
See also Army-Navy Football Game; Wayne Hardin; Midshipman Joseph M. Bellino, USN: Midshipman Roger Staubach, USN; Edward J. Erdelatz; William H. Moore III

Naval Aviation
Creation of selection board to narrow down submarine school applicants in the late 1930s angers officers in the Bureau of Aeronautics, because no screening was done before flight school, pages 130-131

Naval Institute, U.S.
Binding of Proceedings changed in the early 1950s, page 287; excellent financial picture resulted in the Institute hiring a brokerage outfit in the 1950s, page 287; Institute role in Preble Hall, pages 287-288; essay contests, pages 288, 420; personnel in the 1950s, pages 289-291; discussion of open forum, page 291; Davidson's recollections of being vice president in the early 1960s, page 420

Naval Reserve, U.S.
Problems for detailers caused by rapid release of reservists at the end of World War II, pages 219-220; incident concerning a reserve doctor, released as a hardship case after pressure from a Minnesota congressman, who ran off to a lucrative practice in Florida, pages 221-222

Navigation, Bureau of
See Bureau of Navigation

Nevada, USS (BB-36)
Midshipman cruise in 1927 through Panama Canal to West Coast, page 17

New London, Connecticut
Pier landings difficult for submarines in the early 1940s because of tricky river current, pages 160-161; submarines with skegs removed during World War II had difficulty docking at New London without damaging propellers, page 247

New London Ship and Engine Company (NELSECO)
Discussion of NELSECO engines in the submarine Mackerel (SS-204) in 1940, page 155

New York, USS (BB-34)
Davidson is temporarily attached to this battleship in the summer of 1929, pages 18, 49; officers aboard in mid-1929, page 52

Newport, Rhode Island
U.S. Naval Academy midshipmen entertained at the Breakers during summer cruise in 1926, pages 16-17

Nichols, Commander Stanley G., USN (USNA, 1926)
As Submarines Atlantic engineering officer, angered when Davidson went over his head for evaporator coils, page 191

Nimitz, Fleet Admiral Chester W., USN (USNA, 1905)
In the early 1960s, recounted an anecdote from his time as midshipman in 1905 concerning illegal beer and a benevolent officer, pages 31-33; anecdote about the difference between a lady and a diplomat, page 115; walked to work with Davidson every morning in the mid-1930s in Washington, D.C., pages 116-117; anecdote about the Nimitzes's visit to aide Gene Fluckey's house in the mid-1940s, pages 117-120; handles newly-uncovered Green Bowl Society in the 1930s, pages 138-140; as Chief of Naval Operations in the late 1940s, backs down to Vice Admiral Radford on aviator personnel assignments being made by OP-05,

page 332; gave U.S. Naval Academy Superintendent Davidson support when Davidson stopped the tradition of midshipmen marching to classes in the early 1960s, page 363

Nulton, Rear Admiral Louis M., USN (USNA, 1889)
As U.S. Naval Academy Superintendent in mid-1920s, gave impression of being dominated by Mrs. Nulton, page 35

O'Kane, Commander Richard H., USN (USNA, 1934)
On World War II submarine skipper "Mush" Morton, page 82

O'Leary, Commander Forrest Marmaduke, USN (USNA, 1920)
Submarine division commander who had never made a combat patrol chastised a skipper for not being aggressive enough, page 216

Officer of the Deck (OOD)
Desirable qualities for battleship OODs in the early 1930s, page 64

OP-05
See Deputy Chief of Naval Operations (Air)

OP-61
See Politico-Military Division

Orion, USS (AS-18)
Participation in fleet problem off Panama in the late 1940s, pages 230-231; Davidson brought his parents from Norfolk to Panama in Orion, pages 231-232; transported dependents from canal zone in the late 1940s, pages 233-234; picked up wounded man from freighter off Norfolk, pages 234-235; Davidson assesses ship during his command, page 236; Davidson ordered to remove slot machines, pages 237-238

Panama
Idiosyncrasies of S-boats going through Panama Canal in 1930s, pages 144-145; living conditions for officers at Coco Solo in the late 1930s, pages 145-146, 151; golf a big pastime, pages 146, 150, 228; cheap domestic labor available, pages 150-151; attitude toward Americans in late 1930s, pages 151-152; Americans stationed at Panama didn't have to pay income tax in the late 1940s, pages 224, 227; living conditions in the late 1940s, pages 227-228; submarine personnel in Panama in the late 1940s, page 230

Parish, Midshipman Elliott W., Jr., USN (USNA, 1929)
Captain of U.S. Naval Academy lacrosse team and Davidson's closest friend as a midshipman in late 1920s, pages 39, 41

Patrol Reports
　A skipper's literary prowess often enhanced details of World War II submarine patrols, page 199

Pearl Harbor, Hawaiian Islands
　Davidson's reaction to news of 7 December 1941 attack, page 168; conditions for officers in 1944, pages 211-213

Pearson, Lester B.
　Canada's Secretary of State in the early 1950s gave a secret briefing at the Canadian Defence College where he revealed sympathy for U.S. position in Korean War, pages 257-258

Pease, Dr. Royal S.
　Senior U.S. Naval Academy English professor in the early 1950s attacked by fellow professor and defended by department head Davidson, page 269

Personnel Administration
　Assignment of submariners and junior officers by the Bureau of Navigation in the mid-1930s, pages 111-115, 127-128, 130-137

Philippines
　Filipino stewards caught selling illegal liquor aboard Utah (BB-31) during Prohibition were eventually sent back to the Philippines, page 20; stewards in Cachalot (SS-170) in the mid-1930s accidentally sent hair blowing throughout the submarine and were grounded, pages 105-106

Pirie, Captain Robert B., USN (USNA, 1926)
　Anecdote about U.S. Naval Academy Commandant in the early 1950s misspellings in a memo critical of midshipman's spelling ability, pages 265-267; assessed by Davidson, page 267

Politico-Military Division
　Davidson handled situation when Malta prime minister tries to levy a huge tax on U.S. cars on naval base in 1957, pages 320-323; background of division, page 323; function in mid-1950s, page 325; relationship with other divisions, pages 325-326; handling of 1956 Suez Crisis, pages 326-327; selection as OP-61 an indicator of future promotion, pages 334-335

Portsmouth, New Hampshire, Navy Yard
　Frigid cold in January 1934 hampered sea trials for submarine Cachalot (SS-170), pages 99-100

Potter, Dr. E.B.
   Davidson's favorable recollections of this U.S. Naval Academy English professor's teaching skills from the early 1950s, pages 23-24, 271

Prisoners of War
   Navy promoted personnel held prisoner during World War II to the rank they would have obtained, and one case where that policy caused problems, pages 225-226

Prohibition
   Utah (BB-31) officers smuggled liquor aboard in Cuba in the late 1920s, pages 19-21; Arizona (BB-39) junior officers joked about executive officer's plan to arrest them for drinking, page 56; Arizona officers able to buy government brandy in California in the early 1930s, pages 68-70; Davidson and friends made homemade liquor, pages 68, 70

Propulsion Plants
   See Engineering Plants

Punishment
   Midshipman Davidson spent a week in the Reina Mercedes (IX-25) as punishment for neglect of duty and accumulated a threatening number of demerits, pages 26-30

R-Boats
   Used in submarine training in the early 1930s, pages 75, 88-89

Radar
   Poor quality of radar on submarine Blackfish (SS-221) during World War II, pages 169, 171-172

Radford, Admiral Arthur W., USN (USNA, 1916)
   As Deputy Chief of Naval Operations (Air) in the late 1940s, stood up to Chief of Naval Operations Nimitz on issue of personnel assignments not necessarily being made by the Bureau of Personnel, pages 332-333; reliance on Lieutenant Stansfield Turner for briefs in the mid-1950s, pages 335

Raguet, Commander Edward C., USN (USNA, 1909)
   Insisted on a proper wedding after Davidson eloped with his daughter to Mexico, pages 73-74

Randolph, Lieutenant (junior grade) Alfred P., SC, USN (USNA, 1924)
   Hampton Roads-based supply officer warned Utah (BB-31) officers of planned customs inspection while illegal Cuban liquor was aboard during Prohibition, pages 20-21

Reina Mercedes, USS (IX-25)
   Brought to U.S. Naval Academy after capture in Spanish-American War in 1898, page 25; Midshipman Davidson spent week in this station ship in the late 1920s as punishment for neglect of duty, pages 26-30

Religion
   Officers at Canadian National Defence College studied religion versus Communism in the early 1950s, pages 252-253, 258-259; Albany (CA-123) chaplain promoted good behavior during mid-1950s Mediterranean cruise, pages 300-303; religious services at U.S. Naval Academy, pages 409-411; discussion of U.S. Naval Academy chaplains, pages 409-413, 417-418

Replenishment at Sea
   Unnerving to Davidson as new skipper of Albany (CA-123) in mid-1950s, pages 307-308; Davidson ordered investigation after tanker and submarine tender suffered mild collision in early 1960s, pages 428-429

Rice, Vice Admiral Robert H., USN (Ret.)   (USNA, 1927)
   Favorable opinion of his Albany (CA-123) executive officer, Richard Colbert, page 77; replaced as submarine detail officer by Davidson in early 1945, page 129; as U.S. Naval Academy English department head in 1940s, difficulties with Academy-graduated professor, pages 268-269; recommended Davidson to replace him as department head, page 273

Rickover, Rear Admiral Hyman G., USN   (USNA, 1922)
   Proponent of eliminating varsity football at U.S. Naval Academy in the early 1960s in favor of swimming and hiking, page 384

Riley, Rear Admiral Herbert D., USN   (USNA, 1927)
   Sent back to OP-61 in mid-1950s when a suitable replacement couldn't be agreed upon for division head Smedberg, page 331

Roanoke, USS (CL-145)
   Temporary flagship of Commander Cruiser Division Five in the late 1950s ordered to remain undetected in the South China Sea, pages 338-339

Roseneath, Scotland
   Used as a base for U.S. submarines early in World War II, page 173

Royal Navy
   French Navy distrust of the Royal Navy during World War II, pages 170-171; amused by American confusion about torpedoes,

pages 141, 175; circuitous method of selling British submarines before U.S. entry into World War I, page 177

S-Boats
Living conditions, pages 90-91; quality of engines, page 107; effective for harbor protection and close inshore work, page 109; many S-boats based at Pearl Harbor in the mid-1930s, pages 110-111; officer allowance in the mid-1930s, page 135; idiosyncrasy when approaching pier, pages 144-145; impractical inspections in white uniforms at Coco Solo in late 1930s, page 151
See also S-44 (SS-155); S-45 (SS-156)

S-44, USS (SS-155)
Davidson's pride at first command in 1939, page 144; operations in late 1930s, pages 144, 151; officers in late 1930s, pages 142, 146-148

S-45, USS (SS-156)
Engineering-minded commanding officer, Lieutenant John Waterman, often took over engineer officer's job in the late 1930s, page 143

Sailfish, USS (SS-192)
When wartime commanding officer cracked under pressure during a Japanese depth charge attack, he turned command over to his exec, pages 141-142

Sallada, Commander Harold B., USN (USNA, 1917)
During Bureau of Aeronautics duty in the mid-1930s, voiced resentment that submariners had a selection board for candidates when aviators did not, pages 130-131

Sellars, Lieutenant Commander Robert F., USN (USNA, 1934)
Davidson's successor as Blackfish (SS-221) commanding officer was unsuccessful in hunting Japanese ships, pages 200-201, 206

Severn River Naval Command
U.S. Naval Academy Superintendent's chief of staff handled administrative details of the Annapolis naval station in the early 1960s, page 414

Shiphandling
Idiosyncrasies of handling S-boat submarines alongside a pier in the 1930s, pages 144-145; experiences in maneuvering the heavy cruiser Albany (CA-123) in tight situations in the mid-1950s, pages 307-313, 317-318

Skegs
   Removal of skegs from submarines during World War II caused some propeller damage when docking, page 247

Slot Machines
   Davidson was ordered to remove slot machines that had been funding crew's recreation fund from Orion (AS-18) in late 1940s, pages 237-238

Smedberg, Rear Admiral William R. III, USN (USNA, 1926)
   Wrested Davidson from Chief of Bureau of Naval Personnel, Vice Admiral Holloway, in 1955 to be his deputy in the Politico-Military Division, page 319; recommended Davidson to be OP-61 in 1957, pages 331, 334; assessed by Davidson, page 334; Bureau of Naval Personnel chief, Smedberg, sent Davidson to Turkey in 1958 with regrets, page 340; congratulated Davidson on selection as Superintendent in 1960, pages 355-356; angered by Secretary of the Navy Korth's sudden institution of civilian academic dean at U.S. Naval Academy in 1962, page 358; appoints the Moreell Commission to study possible U.S. Naval Academy expansion in the early 1960s and takes responsibility when the commission stirs up bad feelings, pages 387, 389-390, 392; disappointed by Davidson's retirement in 1964, page 430

Smoking
   As a Naval Academy midshipman in the 1920s, Davidson sometimes smoked before breakfast, despite official prohibition, page 11

Smoot, Captain Roland N., USN (USNA, 1923)
   Senior detailer in late 1940s planted seed in Davidson's mind that he might be ordered as skipper of Truman's presidential yacht, page 261-262

Social Customs
   Benefits of old custom of exchanging social calls, pages 57-58; Davidson joined Arizona (BB-39) wardroom as ensign because he filled a more senior billet, page 61

Squalus, USS (SS-192)
   Human error involved in the sinking of this submarine in May 1939, pages 142-143

St. John's College, Annapolis, Maryland
   College president concerned that U.S. Naval Academy might have designs on campus land in the early 1960s, page 390

Staubach, Midshipman Roger T., USN (USNA, 1965)
   Superintendent Davidson interceded when he thought plebe

Staubach was being roughed up by Navy's varsity football team in 1961, page 375; impressive in Southern California University game in 1962, page 401

Stewards
Sold illegal liquor on board the USS Utah (BB-31) around 1930, page 20; stewards on board the submarine Cachalot (SS-170) in the mid-1930s filled the boat with flying hair, pages 105-106; anecdote involving Davidson and Maryland congressman opposed to use of stewards in flag officers' quarters, pages 392-393

Stormes, Lieutenant Max C., USN (USNA, 1925)
First lieutenant in Cachalot (SS-170) in the mid-1930s allowed by the captain to approach a tender at too great a speed, and then put in charge of repairing resulting damage, pages 95-96, 104

Strategic Bombing
A divisive issue between Navy and Air Force in the mid-1950s, pages 327-328

Stroh, Captain Robert J., USN (USNA, 1930)
Chief of Naval Operations Arleigh Burke, unhappy with advice from Davidson's assistant Stroh, asked that he be transferred in the late 1950s, pages 98-99; Davidson not given first choice for OP-61 assistant when Stroh assigned in 1957, page 331

Stroop, Vice Admiral Paul D., USN (USNA, 1926)
Took Ensign Davidson up for his first flight in the early 1930s, page 18; First Fleet commander in the early 1960s ribbed by Davidson when he chastised two skippers who suffered a minor collision while refueling, pages 429-430

Stump, Admiral Felix B., USN (USNA, 1917)
As Commander in Chief Pacific/Pacific Fleet in the mid-1950s, frustrated to find messages to State Department Under Secretary were being intercepted and ignored, page 337

Submarine Design
Fleet type submarines' conning tower doors welded shut after flooding experience of Blackfish (SS-221) during World War II, page 174

Submarine Division 12
Components in 1934, page 93; Submarine Force Commander Freeman insisted submarines steam in formation, which was extremely difficult, page 94

Submarine Division 62
  Commanded by Davidson in 1947-1948, this division operated in both the Atlantic and Pacific from its base in Panama, pages 224-229

Submarine Duty
  Appeal of submarine duty, pages 89, 154, 226-227; living conditions in S-boats, pages 90-91; qualification procedures for submarine officers in 1930s, pages 101-103; detailers were able to deal more personally with submariners than some other specialties, page 132; criterion for excellence as a submarine skipper in the 1930s versus World War II, pages 140-141; inspections in white uniforms at Coco Solo in late 1930s, page 151; quality of enlisted personnel in the late 1930s, page 152; personal problems caused chief petty officer of Blackfish (SS-221) disqualification from submarine duty during World War II, page 153; officers in charge of training prospective commanding officers in the early 1940s, pages 162-163; patrol reports during World War II, page 199; difficulties with cold weather duty, page 186; at end of World War II, many submarine officers tapped for ship commands when reservists released because of their early command experience, pages 219-220

Submarine Force Pacific
  Mission in the mid-1930s, page 108

Submarine School
  Course of study in 1933, pages 75, 88, 91-92; Davidson's classmates in 1933, pages 78, 81, 84; instructors and competition among students, page 86; selection board necessary in the late 1930s because there were more applicants for submarine school than spaces, pages 130-131

Submarine Squadron Two
  Operated out of New London, Connecticut, while under Davidson's command in 1949-1950, pages 239-240

Submarine Tactics
  Commanding officers given greater freedom in lining up attacks as World War II progressed, page 205; daring tactics discouraged by submarine trainers at Pearl Harbor, page 210

Submarine Training
  See Submarine School; Submarine Training Commander Pacific

Submarine Training Command Pacific
  Short practical course for new commanding officers at Pearl Harbor in 1944, pages 207-208; duty as a training officer

served as relief between combat patrols, page 208; training officers in 1944, page 208

Suez Crisis
Handling of this 1956 incident by OP-61, pages 326-327

Taliaferro, Ensign Philip B., USN (USNA, 1943)
Blackfish (SS-221) broke the tension during depth charge attack, page 196

Tatnall School, Wilmington, Delaware
Background of school where Davidson was headmaster from 1964 to 1968, pages 431-437

Thomson, Earle W., ("Slipstick Willie")
As department head at U.S. Naval Academy in early 1950s, Davidson addressed Thomson's request that more emphasis be placed on electrical engineering, pages 25-26

Thomson, Commander Thaddeus A., Jr., USN (USNA, 1907)
U.S. Naval Academy executive officer refused to lessen Midshipman Davidson's punishment after he is accused of neglect of duty in 1928, page 28; got Davidson's class standing changed when shown his grease grade was wrong, page 37; after incident in September 1926, Thomson tough on Davidson during encounter in September 1928, pages 37-39; stern and unpopular as executive officer of Arizona (BB-39) in early 1930s, pages 54-56, 59; unpopular as commanding officer of cruiser Wichita (CA-45) in late 1930s, page 56

Tobacco
See Smoking

Tolson, Ensign David W., USN (USNA, 1927)
As junior officer in Utah in early 1930s, affected a deep voice when on duty, page 50

Torpedo Data Computer
Value to submariners during World War II, page 200

Torpedoes
Unreliability caused problems in the early days of submarines, page 109; accuracy firing torpedoes used as criterion for excellence among submarine skippers in the 1930s, pages 140-141; U.S. Navy weak in torpedo skills at outbreak of World War II, page 141; difficulties with magnetic exploders, page 175; difficulties with premature explosions, page 197; greater latitude given submariners when attacking improved successes, page 205

Training Command Pacific Fleet
   Davidson spent an enjoyable but undemanding one and a half years as head of this command from 1962 to 1964, page 426; Davidson ordered an investigation after a tanker and a submarine tender suffered a minor collision during refueling, pages 428-429

Travel Orders
   Navy travel arrangements in the 1930s versus today, pages 133-134

Trescott, Midshipman Charles E., USN   (USNA, 1929)
   Five-stripe midshipman in late 1920s sent by duty officer to investigate potential hazing at dinner table, page 27

Tucker, Lieutenant Houston C., Jr., USN   (USNA, 1939)
   Blackfish (SS-221) engineer was transferred early in World War II for emotional problems, pages 179-180

Tullibee, USS (SS-284)
   Crew member taken prisoner by the Japanese when this submarine sank caused problems after the war, having been given automatic promotions, pages 225-226

Turkey
   Difficulties with black market in late 1950s, pages 343, 346-347; housing difficulties, pages 343-344; inefficient organization of military in late-1950s, page 350; living conditions, pages 352-353
   See also Joint U.S. Mission for Aid to Turkey (JUSMAT)

Turner, Lieutenant Stansfield, USN   (USNA, 1947)
   Assessed as topnotch from duty in Politico-Military Division in mid-1950s, page 335

Twohy, Midshipman Henry B., USN   (USNA, 1929)
   Davidson beat classmate Twohy in golf finals in 1929, page 41

Ultra
   Blackfish (SS-221) got information on a Japanese convoy's rendezvous location, but navigation problems caused the Japanese ships to change course, pages 197-198

Uniforms
   Though impractical, white uniforms worn for submarine inspections at Coco Solo in the late 1930s, page 151; naval officers forced to scrounge for civilian clothes when they are grounded in Limerick, Ireland, during World War II to maintain

Irish neutrality, pages 188-189; appearance of Albany (CA-123) crew in mid-1950s, pages 304-305; at U.S. Naval Academy in early 1960s, pages 407-408

Utah, USS (BB-31)
Midshipman Davidson's discomfort during summer cruise in 1926, page 13; living conditions and status of sailors in 1920s, pages 14-15; made European cruise in mid-1929, but left Ensign Davidson behind, page 18; officers smuggle liquor from Cuba aboard ship, pages 19-20; officers aboard in 1929-1930, pages 48-50; Davidson's duties in engineering department, pages 49-52; converted from coal to oil-burning in late 1920s, page 51; demilitarized and converted to target ship in 1930, page 53

Voge, Commander Richard, USN (USNA, 1925)
As submarine operations officer during World War II, sent Blackfish (SS-221) off on back-to-back patrols without a break, page 206

Warren, Pennsylvania
Davidson's memory of boyhood town, page 3

Waterman, Lieutenant John R., USN (USNA, 1927)
As commanding officer of S-45 (SS-156) in the late 1930s, turned the submarine bridge over to executive officer, Davidson, whenever there was engine trouble, page 143; tendency to second-guess his officers, pages 143, 160

Watkins, Captain Frank T., USN (USNA, 1922)
Davidson's captain detail officer changed Davidson's orders twice within a short span in 1950, pages 248-250

Weather
Mackerel (SS-204) survived Atlantic hurricane in 1941, pages 156-159; difficulties in North Atlantic in December 1941, page 166; Albany (CA-123) rode out hurricane at mooring in Portsmouth, Virginia, in the mid-1950s, pages 315-316

Westmoreland, Major General William C., USA (USMA, 1936)
Davidson "roasted" West Point Superintendent at banquet before Army-Navy football game in 1960, pages 380-381; chastised by the Army Chairman of the Joint Chiefs of Staff when Army blew a big lead in an Army-Navy basketball game, pages 381-383

Wilkinson, Ensign Eugene P., USNR
Wilkinson excelled at first duty aboard the Blackfish (SS-221) during World War II, pages 178-184, 200, 205

Williamsburg, USS (AGC-369)
　Davidson displeased when he almost received orders to command Truman's presidential yacht in the late 1940s, pages 261-263

Wright, Captain Jerauld, USN (USNA, 1918)
　Given temporary command of a British submarine transporting a French general to North Africa in 1942, page 170

Yeomans, Commander Elmer E., USN (USNA, 1924)
　Commander Submarines Pacific Fleet Charles Lockwood unsuccessfully requested a submarine squadron in 1945 for his staff officer Yeomans even though he had never made a combat patrol, pages 214-215, 217

Zero
　Attacked submarine Blackfish (SS-221) off Australia during World War II, page 195

duct-compliance